Forty-Four Months in the Alps

The Resistance of the Piedmontese Army Against Revolutionary France, 1792–1796

Enrico Ricchiardi

Helion & Company

Helion & Company Limited
Unit 8 Amherst Business Centre
Budbrooke Road
Warwick
CV34 5WE
England
Tel. 01926 499619
Email: info@helion.co.uk
Website: www.helion.co.uk
X (formerly Twitter): @Helionbooks
Facebook: @HelionBooks
Visit our blog at http://blog.helion.co.uk/

Published by Helion & Company 2025
Designed and typeset by Mach 3 Solutions (www.mach3solutions.co.uk)
Cover designed by Paul Hewitt, Battlefield Design (www.battlefield-design.co.uk)

Text © Enrico Ricchiardi 2025
Illustrations © as individually credited
Cover: Piedmontese troops, by Emanuele Manfredi © Helion & Co. 2025

Every reasonable effort has been made to trace copyright holders and to obtain their permission for the use of copyright material. The author and publisher apologise for any errors or omissions in this work, and would be grateful if notified of any corrections that should be incorporated in future reprints or editions of this book.

ISBN 978-1-804516-77-5

British Library Cataloguing-in-Publication Data.
A catalogue record for this book is available from the British Library.

All rights reserved. No part of this publication may be reproduced, stored in a retrieval system, or transmitted, in any form, or by any means, electronic, mechanical, photocopying, recording or otherwise, without the express written consent of Helion & Company Limited.

For details of other military history titles published by Helion & Company Limited, contact the above address, or visit our website: http://www.helion.co.uk

We always welcome receiving book proposals from prospective authors.

Contents

Preface		iv
Acknowledgements		vi
Chronology of the War in the Alps (1792–1796)		vii
Glossary of Piedmontese Military Terms		ix
1	The Kingdom of Sardinia Between 1789 and 1792	11
2	Vittorio Amedeo III's Army	22
3	The Piedmontese Army in Action	34
4	Infantry Uniforms, Flags and Equipment	46
5	The Militia	76
6	The Elite Units: Forge of Heroes	79
7	Infantry Weaponry	87
8	Volunteer Light Troops	90
9	Other Corps	118
10	The Loyalty and Vicissitudes of a Small Navy	134
11	The War (1792-1793): Recovery from Setback and the Start of the Fighting	139
12	1794: Resistance at All Costs!	152
13	1795–1796: Last Hopes	165
Bibliography		176
Further Reading		179

Preface

Nunc pugnandum est!
(Now we must fight!)

When, on 19 February 1773, Vittorio Amedeo III of Savoy (1726–1796) ascended the throne of the Kingdom of Sardinia, he was 47 years old. His wife, Maria Antonia of Spain (1729–1780), had already borne him nine children, five of them boys. The well-organized state, the peace that had lasted for 25 years, the love of his people, the respect of the other reigning houses, the army (small but which the enemy had to consider), and the ensured continuity of the crown, all seemed to indicate a safe and peaceful future.

And so it was until the French Revolution when new ferments and new ideas led to storm clouds on the horizon for the Savoyard monarchy.

Kinship with the Bourbons of France (two daughters of Vittorio Amedeo III had married two brothers of Louis XVI, and a sister of Louis XVI had married one of his sons), which was an advantage during the previous years, was from 1789 a source of embarrassment and ultimately one of the causes of the animosity of Republican France towards the King of Sardinia.

In 1792, the French attacked both Savoy and Nice, trying to penetrate Piedmont. They succeeded only in the spring of 1796.

Like all lost wars, even the bitter one fought by Piedmont against the French revolutionaries has been substantially neglected. Forgotten also because those soldiers who fought to defend their homeland and their king were, without knowing it, called upon by history to use their weapons and their courage to block the overwhelming advance of new political ideas and a new way of life. The French Revolution was changing the world, but the revolutionary armies were trying to change it by force. It was, therefore, necessary to fight to defend Piedmont from the enemy.

The faithful Savoyard soldiers, the nobles, many bourgeois, and the commoners left for the Alps, marching in the ancient regiments of the Piedmontese army. They had to face the French again. They had been doing it for centuries, and it was nothing new. Sometimes, they had won, sometimes, they had lost. This time, however, the enemy was not dynastic, but an army made up of greedy, sometimes exalted, revolutionaries who fought with unknown impetus. They attempted to cross the Alps in waves, between pauses and offensives, but they had to wait 44 months and for the genius of Napoleon Bonaparte to succeed.

The Piedmontese army, almost without help from the allies, scattered on a frontier that went from Mont Blanc to the Apennines (immense for the means of transport of the time), managed to hold back the French in all the clashes. Bonaparte, who introduced a new style of warfare, won the war by taking Piedmont from the rear after crossing the Apennines near Savona and defeating the allied Austrian army at Dego. For the few Piedmontese regiments present from Ceva to Mondovì, on the southern slopes of Apennines, it was impossible to resist the tactical capacity and numerical superiority of the army led by the young general and, after a few days of bloody resistance, they had to surrender.

With the Armistice of Cherasco, the Piedmontese army became a satellite of the French one and was shortly after disbanded, released from their oath to the King, and absorbed into the French army.

With the battle won by Bonaparte at Magenta (14 June 1800) and the inclusion of Piedmont into France (1802), Carlo Emanuele IV (1796–1802) lost all hope of returning to Turin and, discouraged, decided to abdicate in favour of his brother Vittorio Emanuele I (1802–1821), retiring to a convent. The new monarch wandered around Italy to finally land in Sardinia in 1806, where he remained until the first fall of Napoleon, reorganising, with British help, a small army in defence of the last possession of the House.

It is not among the purposes of this book to narrate in detail the fights of the War of the Alps. They are very complex due to the numerous more or less important events that took place during the campaigning season and, sometimes even in the middle of winter, for almost four years. Their narration is nearly exclusively carried out in French and Italian-language publications. This book, on the background of the history of the period, illustrates with documents and iconography of the time the organisation, uniforms, flags and individual armament of the Piedmontese army of the period and, finally, whenever possible, the hard life of ordinary soldiers and officers in the Alps.

In the surviving examples of Piedmontese uniforms, the colours that distinguished the regiments have been altered by time and their state of preservation, and sometimes more plausible colours are included in the colour charts accompanying the figures.

The army of Vittorio Amedeo III was formally known as the Sardinian army, but this way of describing it could mislead those who were not familiar with the history of the Kingdom of Sardinia when the island was under the rule of the Savoy. So, to avoid misinterpretation, it is referred to as the Piedmontese army.

A large part of the reconstruction of the role of the Piedmontese army in the War in the Alps comes from the series of documents preserved in the State Archives of Turin (see the archival sources in the bibliography).

Finally, for a detailed reconstruction of the events and battles of this war as seen from the Savoyan side, see: F. Pinelli. *Storia militare del Piemonte dalla pace di Acquisgrana al 1850* (Torino: De Giorgis, 1854). I. Thaon di Revel de St. André. *Mémoires sur la guerre des Alpes et les événement en Piémont pendant la Révolution Française* (Torino: Bocca, 1871). G. Merla. *O bravi guerrieri! L'arrivo di Napoleone in Italia e la guerra delle Alpi* (Pisa: Del Cerro, 1988). V. Ilari, P. Crociani, C. Paoletti. *La Guerra delle Alpi (1792-1796)* (Roma: Stato Maggiore dell'Esercito, Ufficio Storico, 2000). A. Lo Faso di Serradifalco. *La difesa di un regno. Il sacrificio dell'esercito del Regno di Sardegna nella guerra contro la Francia (1792-1796)* (Udine: Gaspari, 2009).

Acknowledgements

I would like to thank Ian Sumner, a British expert in military history, who spent a great deal of time and effort on correcting my English and for his help in compiling the glossary of Piedmontese-British military terminology. I would also like to thank my editor at Helion, Robert Griffith, for his clarity, patience, and availability during the long process of preparing and editing the book. I would also like to thank Emanuele Manfredi for the beautiful illustrations and the cover, and Roberto Vela for the drawings of the flags in colour plates 10 and 11.

Chronology of the War in the Alps (1792–1796)

1792
22 September   The French invasion begins. Savoy and Nice are occupied, but the Piedmontese stop the French in the mountain passes.

1793
Winter/Spring   Piedmontese army is reorganised and a small Austrian contingent arrives.
June   The French attack the Piedmontese defences in the Val Roia.
8–12 June   The Battle of Aution: Stubborn Piedmontese resistance repelled the furious French attacks, keeping their positions almost intact.
27 August   British Royal Navy ships enter Toulon harbour to support local Royalists. Vice Admiral Hood requests support from Spanish, Sardinian/Piedmontese and Neapolitan forces.
27 September   Piedmontese troops disembark at Toulon.
Autumn   Duca d'Aosta advances into Savoy, but the ill-planned and hesitant operation is unsuccessful and abandoned when the first snow falls.
17 December   Allies evacuate Toulon.

1794
April–May   Overwhelming French attacks on the Austro-Piedmontese army corps defending the Val Roia force a retreat. Other passes are also taken but the French attack peters out due to political turmoil in Paris.
21 September   First Battle of Dego: An Austrian army advancing into Liguria is repulsed by Massena's corps and retreats towards Acqui.

1795
June   The Austrians advance from Acqui along the Bormida valley, while the Piedmontese recapture part of the Tanaro valley.
Summer   The Piedmontese make unsuccessful attempts to retake the main Alpine passes. The Austrians advance through the Bormida valley as far as Loano, in Liguria.
22 November   Massena manages to push the Austrians out of Liguria.

1796
27 March   Napoleon Bonaparte takes over command from Massena.
10 April   Bonaparte attacks Austro-Piedmontese forces.

13-14 April	The French overcome the heroic resistance of the Austro-Piedmontese troops at the Castle of Cosseria.
14-15 April	Second Battle of Dego: The Austrians are defeated and retreat towards Acqui.
17 April	Ceva occupied by French.
21 April	The French arrive at Mondovì, forcing Vittorio Amedeo III to surrender.
10–11 May	Bonaparte defeats the Austrians at Lodi and conquers Milan on the 26th.

Glossary of Piedmontese Military Terms

Aiutante maggiore	aide major
Arciere	battalion or company provost
Armaiolo	armourer
Bandiera	infantry colours
Brigadiere	corporal in cavalry
Brigadiere generale	brigadier general
Cannoniere	gunner
Cannoniere ausiliario	auxiliary gunner
Cacciatore	light infantryman
Cacciatore carabiniere	light infantryman armed with a rifled carbine
Cacciatore volontario	volunteer light infantryman
Capitano	captain
Capitano generale	captain general
Capobanda	music leader
Caporale	corporal
Caporale maggiore	somewhere between corporal and platoon sergeant
Caporale tamburino	corporal drummer
Cappellano	almoner, chaplain
Casalina	cloth for carrying cartridges
Centuria	two infantry companies
Chirurgo maggiore	surgeon major
Colonnello	colonel
Cornetta	guidons, with two points at the fly
Dragoni	dragoons
Falegname	carpenter
Fiamma	cornet (flag), with one point at the fly
Frater	private trained in first aid
Fucile	infantry flintlock musket
Fucile da dragone	dragoon flintlock musket
Fucile a canna rigata	rifled carbine
Fuciliere	infantry soldier of centre companies armed with a flintlock musket
Furiere	fourrier or quartermaster sergeant
Garzone chirurgo	assistant surgeon
Giberna	infantry cartridge box

Granatiere	grenadier
Granatiere delle fregate	marines. Lit. frigate grenadier
Guastatore	pioneer
Ingeniere militare	military engineer (an official)
Insegna	ensign. An NCO promoted to standard bearer
Luogotenente	lieutenant
Luogotenente capitano	lieutenant captain
Luogotenente colonnello	lieutenant colonel
Luogotenente generale	lieutenant general
Maestranze d'artiglieria	artillery workers
Maggiore	major
Maggior generale	major general
Maggiore di reggimento	regimental major or regimental adjutant
Maggiore di battaglione	battalion major or battalion assistant
Maniscalco	harness maker
Maresciallo d'alloggio	squadron sergeant major
Minatore	miner
Musicista	bandsman
Palafreniere	groom
Patrona	small cartridge box
Piffero	fifer
Pioniere	pioneer
Prevosto	regimental provost
Quartiermastro	quartermaster
Quartiermastro generale	quartermaster general, equivalent to chief of staff
Sellaio	saddler
Sergente	sergeant
Sergente di compagnia	company sergeant
Sergente di plotone	platoon sergeant
Sergente maggiore	sergeant major
Sergente sovrannumerario	supernumerary sergeant
Serpentou	grenadiers' or light troops' serpentine (waved) chevron
Sotto brigadiere	lance corporal in cavalry
Sotto cappellano	sub chaplain
Sotto luogotenente	second lieutenant
Sotto maresciallo d'alloggio	squadron sergeant
Stendardo	cavalry standard
Tamburo maggiore	drum major
Tamburino	drummer
Timballiere	kettle drums player
Trombettiere	trumpeter, bugler
Ufficiale del soldo	pay officer
Vivandiere	sutler
Zappatore	sapper

1

The Kingdom of Sardinia Between 1789 and 1792

The King and the Royal Family

On 13 February 1773, at the age of 47, Vittorio Amedeo III (1773–1796) became the third King of Sardinia. He inherited a well-established and organised kingdom, a respected army, a favourable economic situation, and a kingdom that had been at peace since 1748. One of his first decisions was to replace the capable heads of the secretariats appointed by his father Carlo Emanuele III (1730–1773) with men he liked but who were, unfortunately, less capable. He replaced the competent minister Giovanni Battista Lorenzo Bogino (1701–1784), who had headed the Secretariat of War since 1742, with Giovanni Andrea Chiavarina, *conte* (count) of Rubiana, a loyal follower of his who had worked for his entire career in the Secretariats of War and the Navy, who proved to be a good implementer of royal orders but did not take initiatives being unable to deal with the responsibilities of the post. The new monarch had not forgotten that Bogino had often kept him on the sidelines when he was still *principe* (prince) di Piemonte, the title given to the heir to the throne, but he should have chosen his successor more wisely. Vittorio Amedeo III must have realised his mistake because, in 1778, he replaced Chiavarina with the *conte* Giuseppe Ruffinotto Coconito di Montiglio. The latter, appointed *gran mastro della Real Casa* (grand master of the Royal Court) on 16 January 1789, the highest position in the Savoy court, was replaced as secretary by the *marchese* (marquis) Giovan Battista Luigi Fontana di Cravanzana, who held the post for the duration of the War of the Alps, although in a purely executive role. In this succession of high-ranking but militarily and organisationally inexperienced personalities, the new king may have wished to exercise personal command of the army, willing to take care of the smallest details of armaments, uniforms, and everything to do with the outward appearance of the army. In fact, during the weekly meetings with the war and naval secretariat the most varied and minute proposals were presented to him, to which he often replied by instructing the proposer to submit a report, a drawing, or a figure the following week in order to continue. However, there were few decisions to improve the quality of the civil service and military training. During the War of the Alps, Vittorio Amedeo III ceased to examine in his reports the army's uniforms, flags, and equipment. The minutes of the weekly meetings from 1792–1796 refer mainly to royal interventions in the supply of grain and fodder.[1]

---

1   Archivio di Stato di Torino (AST), Ufficio Generale del Soldo, Relazioni a Sua Maestà, mazzi 19–23.

A major problem was the slow progression of officers through the ranks and the fact that only older members of the nobility were allowed to command regiments. All this led directly to the disasters of 1792, when the incompetent and aged high commanders of the army corps of Savoy and Nice hastily abandoned those two possessions on the other side of the Alps without defending them, leaving behind numerous prisoners, supplies and weapons.

Vittorio Amedeo III was an absolute ruler, but one devoted to the welfare of his people. Domenico Carutti wrote of him: 'If Vittorio Amedeo III believed that kings should be constituted for the good of the people, he also believed that they should be accountable for their deeds to God alone, so that any resistance on the part of his subjects was a crime for him.'[2] Fortunately, the limits of power were established by a complex set of relationships that, in practice, mitigated the King's power over his ministers.

Queen Maria Antonia di Borbone-Spagna, daughter of Philip V, married Vittorio Amedeo on 31 May 1750. She was a close and discreet wife but died in 1785 after giving birth to 12 children, three of whom died young. Of the five surviving males, Carlo Emanuele (1751–1819) married Maria Clotilde Adelaide di Borbone-Francia (1759–1802) on 6 September 1775, but had no children by her. He was King of Sardinia as Carlo Emanuele IV from 1796 to 1802. In the latter year, he abdicated in favour of his brother Vittorio Emanuele (1759–1824), *duca* (duke) d'Aosta, who was King of Sardinia from 1802 to 1821 as Vittorio Emanuele I. He also lacked male heirs, and abdicated in 1821 in favour of his brother Carlo Felice, *duca* del Genevois (1765–1831), who reigned until his death in 1831, also without heirs. In that year, the crown of Sardinia passed to Carlo Alberto di Savoia-Carignano, a collateral branch of the family.

The other two males died in Sardinia when the dynasty was confined to the island in December 1798. Maurizio, *duca* del Monferrato (born 1762) in 1799 and Giuseppe Benedetto Placido, *conte* di Maurienne (born 1766) in 1802.

Vittorio Amedeo III's daughters were Maria Giuseppina (1753–1810), who in 1771 married the *comte* de Provence, Louis Stanislas de Bourbon, future King of France as Louis XVIII (1815–1824). Maria-Teresa (1756–1805) married in 1773 to Charles Philippe de Bourbon, *comte* d'Artois, who succeeded his brother and took the crown of France as Charles X (1825–1830). Maria Anna (1757–1824), who in 1775 married her uncle, Benedict Maurice, *duca* del Chablais (1741–1808), then *marchese* (marquis) di Ivrea, half-brother of Victor Amadeus III, and finally Maria Carolina (1764–1782), who in 1781 married Anthony of Saxony, who in 1827 became king with the title of Anthony I. Thus, with few exceptions, both the King and his sons and daughters married members of the Bourbon dynasty, which, as we shall see, had important consequences for the outcome of the War of the Alps.

The States of the King of Sardinia

The favourable political and economic situation could have allowed the King to continue the reforms initiated by his father. Instead, although he maintained the tradition of an absolute

---

2   D. Carutti, *Storia della Corte dei Savoia durante la rivoluzione e l'Impero Francese* (Torino-Roma: Roux, 1892), vol.I, p.121.

and enlightened sovereign, he gave too much space to the more conservative nobility, blocking in practice those indispensable reforms of the state order that were quite freely theorised in numerous writings of the time, including from Piedmont.[3]

Even the birth of a new nation, such as the United States of America, with its republican and constitutional system, did not make it clear that the new ideas on the horizon could affect the worldview of Vittorio Amedeo III and his entourage. However, in Europe, the American novelty was clearly interpreted. But America was far away, and no one thought that these distant events would endanger European stability. The social tranquillity that prevailed in the States of the King of Sardinia between 1773 and 1789 allowed the monarch to complete the decentralisation and strengthening of the state structure and to keep under control the changing power relations between the nobility, the bourgeoisie, and the people, unlike in neighbouring France.

Although a devout Catholic, the King did not allow the Church to interfere in state affairs and limited the power of the clergy.

The court and the household troops underwent no major changes: the organisation established by Vittorio Amedeo II in 1685 was essentially maintained.

While the bourgeoisie, magistrates and lawyers began to occupy most of the offices in the secretariats, court and high army positions were entrusted to the nobility. Those of the nobility who pursued military careers were, with a few exceptions, often among the most conservative and not very dedicated to study – an activity they considered unworthy of their status. However, as the war would prove, their loyalty to the Crown was unquestionable, and most of these nobles were able to give their subordinates undeniable proof of their courage and led by example.

Important court appointments and proximity to the King were the prerogatives of a few families, so the highest aspiration of the upper middle class was to become a noble. These new nobles rarely pursued military careers, preferring activities related to government or diplomacy. However, the old nobility, who identified themselves with the army and were partly dependent on it during the long years of peace, participated widely in the command of the troops during the war against France, paying a heavy toll in blood. The cohesion of the Piedmontese regiments, as we shall see, often in very difficult times, was fully demonstrated, as many peasants recognised their officers as cadets of the local nobility. This was particularly true of the provincial regiments, which had strong territorial ties but was also true of the national ordnance regiments.

In Piedmont, although with less upheaval than in Britain and France, the second half of the eighteenth century saw a slow evolution of the traditional relations between the social classes. While in France, the clear opposition of the nobility to the new visions of society led the bourgeoisie to lead the Revolution of 1789, in the Piedmont of Vittorio Amedeo III, this social class sought to be ennobled and thus co-opted into the system of power. As a result, the desire to undermine the state's power relations was present but had little effect.

The people, deeply religious, still poor and illiterate, but now freed from most feudal obligations, lived quietly, attending to their own duties. Peasants could achieve a higher

---

3 G. Ricuperati, *Lo stato sabaudo nel settecento. Dal trionfo delle burocrazie alla crisi d'antico regime* (Torino: UTET, 2001), Cap. IV-5.

standard of living by raising silkworms or producing silk organzine thread. The entire family participated in this widespread industry, using equipment provided by entrepreneur traders, who supplied the raw materials to obtain the finished product at an agreed price. In the most favourable cases, it was possible to take out a loan to buy the machinery, taking the plunge into small-scale entrepreneurship, still widespread in the area. Those able to pay their debts entered a new category of citizens with growing economic opportunities and became future members of the lower middle class. Those who could not, became heavily dependent on loans.

It was not until the 1780s that the growing popularity of large, landed estates drove more and more peasants into poverty. The nobility, mostly employed at court and in the army, tended to move to the cities and entrust the management of their land to tenant farmers. These, generally more interested in profit than in the welfare of the peasants, were naturally inclined to exploit the workers. The increasingly poor peasants began to express their discontent, but still in a non-violent way. Nevertheless, the great peasant uprisings of the last years of the century were rarely anti-monarchical, suggesting that Piedmont would probably have been able to cope with the phenomenon if the French Revolution, the war, and the defeat had not interrupted any rational analysis of the situation and any proposal for reform. Proof of this can be found in the numerous series of studies and reports, which attest to the authorities' awareness of the problem and the first proposals to remedy the most glaring injustices. The French attack of 1792 and the long war that followed, however, led to all attention and financial resources being concentrated on defence, and the search for a solution to the serious and progressive impoverishment of the peasants took a back seat.[4]

The power of the guilds, which had never been abolished in Piedmont as elsewhere, was limited by the merchants, who were able to ignore their statutes through their control of financial resources and trade. On the other hand, despite the fact that the masters of the professions constantly created obstacles to the admission of new craftsmen, thus protecting their own earnings, these restrictions were almost completely ignored in Piedmont and Savoy. In fact, anyone who had the will and the ability could practise any kind of craft.

The bourgeoisie was mainly found in towns of more than 5,000 inhabitants and included the salaried civil servants of the state. There was still a rural bourgeoisie, made up mainly of large tenant farmers. Although the contours of the eighteenth-century bourgeoisie are not well defined, it is possible to estimate the size of this class at around 10 percent of the Piedmontese population. Although it had no military tradition, the bourgeoisie tended to seek nobility and produced relatively few army officers, not least because of the difficulties imposed by the old nobility. This limitation disappeared with the War of the Alps, when the demand for officers became urgent, partly due to the necessary replacement of many who had been found too elderly and unsuited to the hardships of Alpine warfare.

Alongside the organzine factories, there were a number of others under state concession. They mainly produced the textiles and equipment needed by the army and objects of particular value necessary for the court: for example, the Royal Porcelain Factory in Vinovo, near Turin, active from 1775 to 1780.

---

4   Ricuperati, *Lo stato sabaudo nel settecento*, Cap. IV-5.

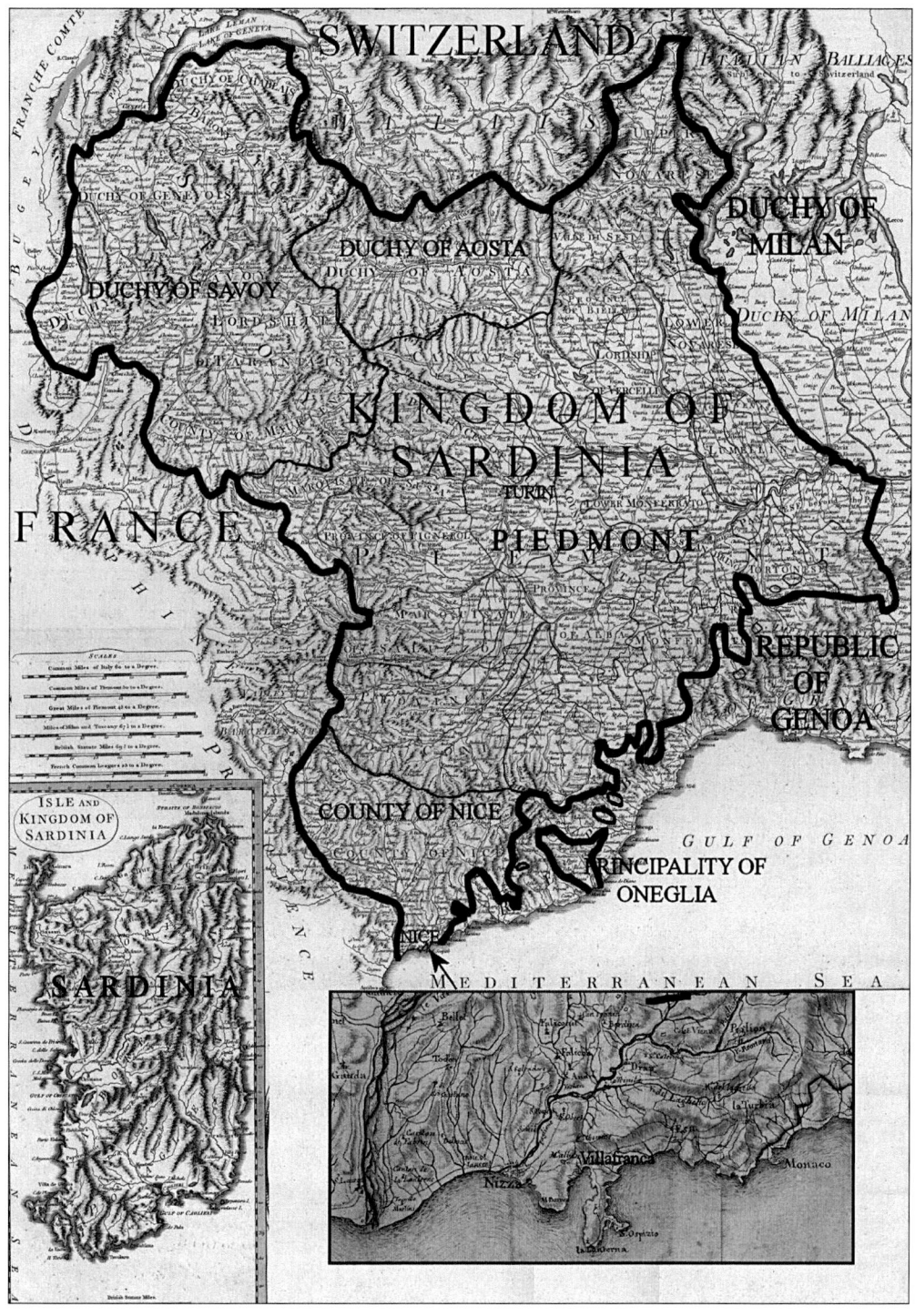

The Kingdom of Sardinia in 1791. (A. Antonicelli (2016, Fig. 1), with permission)

Vittorio Amedeo III also favoured improvements in the cultural climate, especially in the capital, allowing the establishment of the Academy of Sciences, the Agricultural Society and the Academy of Painting and Sculpture.

The King's openness to culture encouraged a new love of learning. This had a beneficial effect on the circulation of ideas, even under the restrictive umbrella of monarchical absolutism. Vittorio Amedeo III, a man of his time, was far-sighted in this respect: here too, Piedmont might have experienced the transition between the old and the new ideas without deep trauma if it had not been overwhelmed by the violence of revolutionary France.

The State: Boundaries and Possessions

The Kingdom of Sardinia was a minor state, but its geographical position meant that its importance far outweighed its size. In the second half of the eighteenth century, it dominated the main passes of the western Alps and acted as a barrier between the Bourbons and the Habsburgs. It was made up of five major areas: Piedmont, from the Alps to the river Ticino and beyond to Vigevano; the Duchy of Aosta, wedged between the Graian and Pennine Alps; the Duchy of Savoy, on the other side of the Alps; the County of Nice, also on the other side of the Alps; and finally, the island of Sardinia, which gave the kingdom its name.

The population of the kingdom was around 3.2 million, 500,000 of whom inhabited Sardinia. In addition to those mentioned above, in 1792, some enclaves in Liguria were among the territories of the Italian peninsula that belonged to Savoy. These territories came to Savoy from a small branch of the noble Genoese family of Doria (also known as d'Oria). Gian Gerolamo Doria (1523–1592) gave the Principality of Oneglia to Duke Emanuele Filiberto of Savoy (1528–1580). Also, in the Doria family, the small marquisate of Dolceacqua became a Savoy enclave and was later incorporated into the County of Nice. In exchange for the cession of Oneglia to Savoy, Gian Gerolamo was invested with the Piedmontese fief of Cirié, close to Torino (Turin). Increasingly powerful and well-connected at court, the Doria family acquired numerous other Piedmontese fiefs over the centuries, the title of which was often held by one of the family. During the War of the Alps, three members of the family served in the Piedmontese army: the *marchese* Alessandro Doria in the *Reggimento Aosta*, the *conte* Filippo Doria in the *Reggimento Guardie* and finally, the *marchese* Anselmo Doria del Maro fought with the provincial infantry *Reggimento Vercelli*.

Another small Savoy possession in Liguria was the territory of Loano, which was ceded to the Savoy family in 1737 by Charles VI of Hapsburg (1711–1740).

Mastering the Mountain Passes of the Western Alps

The territories of the Kingdom of Sardinia straddled the western Alps and dominated all the passes. From north to south: the Gran San Bernardo Pass (2,473m) towards Switzerland; the Piccolo San Bernardo Pass (2,188m) and the Moncenisio Pass (2,083m) towards Savoy; the Monginevro Pass (1,860m), Colle dell'Agnello Pass (2,748m), and Colle della Maddalena Pass (1,996m) towards France; and, finally, the Colle di Tenda pass (1,871m) towards the County of Nice.

For centuries, the French armies had ruled over the Piedmontese passes, but only until Vittorio Amedeo II of Savoy (1685–1730) was able to take possession of them, become king, and rule over a state strong enough to create an army and build imposing fortresses. Earlier, when the French had opened the passes, they still had to conquer the many strong fortresses on the plains. The most imposing of these was the Citadel of Turin, where the French had suffered a bitter defeat in 1706. On that occasion, the alliance with Austria was essential to Piedmont's salvation, unlike what happened during the War of the Alps, as we shall see.

A period had begun in which the Piedmontese army, although important, could not stand alone against its more powerful neighbours, France to the west and first Spain, then Austria to the east. It allied itself with one and then with the other to remain independent, even managing, as a reward, to extend its borders towards Lombardy each time. Thus, in the War of the Polish Succession (1734–1736), Charles Emmanuel III (1730–1773), at the head of his army, allied himself with the French and, victorious, was able to retain his independence and some new territory. His alliance with the Austrians during the War of the Austrian Succession (1742–1748) granted Charles Emmanuel III more territories in the east in the Peace of Aachen (18 October 1748).

French soldiers often found themselves marching towards the Alpine passes to invade Piedmont. The western side of the Alps was easy to climb, but the ease of the march did not deceive them. Soldiers had to listen to the tales of suffering of their former comrades who, having arrived near the border, found themselves among high peaks, snow and cold, with the certainty that on the other side were the Piedmontese soldiers, who were naturally used to mountain warfare.

Decades of peace followed: Charles Emmanuel III decided not to take part in the Seven Years' War (1756–1763). The long period of peace favoured the economic development of the Kingdom but brought with it an army whose commanders and soldiers were no longer very experienced and who were bored with garrison duty. The attack of the French Revolutionary army woke them up and after the first bitter setbacks, the Piedmontese war machine was set in motion.

The Long Border to Cover

It is difficult to measure the exact length of the Alpine border that separated Piedmont from France. It was very approximatively 400 kilometres, and a good part of it was impassable at a time when mountaineering was still in its infancy: The summit of Mont Blanc, both sides of which were then Savoy territory, was first conquered by two young men from Chamonix, Savoy, then part of domains of the King of Sardinia (8 August 1786). However, the mountain pastures had been frequented for centuries, as it was common practice to take cows and goats to the higher altitudes to spend the summer. In addition, local populations, such as those of the Valle d'Aosta, used to hunt chamois and ibex for their own food, climbing high up to flush them out. Despite this, legends flourished about the unknown world higher up, covered by eternal glaciers, where even mountaineers did not dare to go.

However, there were many ways to get to Turin, the capital of the Kingdom of Sardinia, and most of them had been tried and tested by the French over the centuries. The Republican army, much more numerous than the Sardinians', could easily choose where to attack, plan false attacks to mislead the Piedmontese, and force the Savoy regiments to march from one valley to another. Fortunately, the Piedmontese army was aided by good intelligence and the warnings of the mountain people loyal to the King, who organised efficient militia companies. The winter break, which made mass operations practically impossible from the end of October to the end of March, also helped. In winter, the Piedmontese army, with only a few regiments left in the Alps to support the militia, was able to leave the front and retire to the winter garrisons to rest, train new recruits and replenish uniforms and equipment. It was also possible to wait for the return of deserters and prisoners from the previous campaign to bring the regiments up to strength. This was true for the first two years of the War of the Alps, but after autumn 1795, the regiments became weaker, reducing the human resources available.

The defence of the Alps was aided by a system of fortresses, not located on the Alpine passes but in the valleys on the eastern side, where enemy advance routes could be effectively blocked.

The fortress of Bard, in the centre of the Valle d'Aosta, was strong but avoidable, as Bonaparte's manoeuvres of 14–21 May 1800 proved. It is surprising that Bonaparte decided on this occasion to direct the 40,000 men of his *Armée de Réserve* not to cross the Piccolo San Bernardo Pass but to choose the longer route through Switzerland and the Gran San Bernardo Pass. Perhaps he took this route around the bottleneck of the Pierre Taillé because he did not want a repeat of what had happened between 1793 and 1796, when the Piedmontese army had succeeded in blocking the French advance by defending that narrow passage through the Valle d'Aosta. As we shall see, the French attempts in 1793 to bypass the Piedmontese defences via the Col du Mont (2,635m) in the Val Grisanche were unsuccessful due to the lack of a road through the area and the presence of snow for many months of the year. However, from the Gran San Bernardo Pass, undefended on both sides, Bonaparte was able to attack Aosta and march quickly to surprise the few defenders of Bard.

The Moncenisio and Monginevro passes were easily crossed by the French, but once they were down in the valleys, they would have found their way blocked by the imposing fortress of Fenestrelle in the Chisone valley, the fortress of Exilles in the higher Susa valley, and the impregnable fortress of Brunetta near Susa. When Bonaparte succeeded in taking Turin, he hastened to have the heavily fortified Brunetta fortress razed to the ground, eliminating a possible obstacle to his future movements.

Proceeding southwards, they had to reach Val Varaita, where the Colle dell'Agnello was crossed by a road suitable, but only just, for artillery pieces but, due to its height, impassable for many months of the year. But the French experiences of 1743 and 1744, when their army had crashed into the Piedmontese defences after passing the frontier, had taught them prudence. Having overcome the Piedmontese mountain defence, in 1744, the French and Spanish regiments were pitted against the fort of Demonte and the stronghold of Cuneo, which they were unable to take. Then, they were confronted by the entire Piedmontese army in the Battle of Madonna dell'Olmo, near Cuneo, but were unable to prevail. The battle had neither winners nor losers, but the French siege of Cuneo had to be interrupted, and the advanced season induced the French to return to France. This was a constant in Piedmont's defensive strategy: the Alpine passes were blocked by snow from October to April, and being able to block the enemy for the few months of good weather ensured success.

The Colle di Tenda road led from Cuneo to Nice, then one of the domains of Savoy. On the side of the County of Nice, first came the fort of Saorgio, not particularly imposing but with its cannons able to effectively sweep the only all-weather impervious road through the narrows of the Val Roia, then the stronghold of Cuneo blocked it towards the plain. The French rarely chose this route to attempt an invasion of Piedmont. They tried in 1792 and 1793 but only managed to occupy the whole of the County of Nice, lying on the other side of the Alps in 1794, by bypassing the Piedmontese defences through the territory of the Republic of Genoa, theoretically neutral but historically hostile to the Kingdom of Sardinia, and which in any case had an army too weak to resist passage. And it was precisely to avoid similar manoeuvres in future wars that the victorious powers, at the time of the Restoration, did not restore the Republic of Genoa, but gave Liguria to the Savoy.

Specialists in Alpine Warfare

During the wars in which the Piedmontese army was involved during the first half of the eighteenth century, military engineers often improvised Alpine field fortifications to counter the advance of French regiments. A solid experience of defence at altitude had thus been ingrained with no parallel in Europe. Always outnumbered and with an immense frontier to defend, once the main routes of penetration had been secured through the network of Alpine fortresses, it remained essential to protect them from being outflanked. It was essential to occupy all the prominent points from which the French artillery could fire into the interior of the fortresses themselves. An understanding of the basic rules for the construction and defence of Alpine field fortifications had spread, not only among military engineers and artillery officers who were well-trained in the techniques of fortification, but also among infantry officers.[5]

These criteria could be summarised as follows:

- Avoid dispersing your forces by splitting them up to defend each point, but only position them in places that cannot be avoided to block the enemy's progress.
- Create well-fortified strongholds using dry stones, logs and whatever is available locally.
- If possible, fortify all high points to prevent the enemy from swooping down from above or overwhelming the defenders with their own fire.
- Set up at least two firing lines, so that while half the defenders are reloading their *fucili*, the other half are firing continuously and accurately.
- Link the strongholds with protected and manned walkways to prevent them from being outflanked and to bring in reinforcements and supplies.
- Establish temporary fortifications from which to retreat, if necessary, with the intention of slowing or diverting the enemy's advance towards the main fortifications.
- Clear the ground around the main or temporary strongholds of trees and anything else that might impede the defenders' ability to fire.
- Finally, use the terrain to slow down the enemy attack by forcing them to attack uphill.

---

5   For a detailed discussion of the theoretical and practical evolution of the construction techniques of camp fortifications in eighteenth century Europe and Piedmont, see R. Sconfienza, 'I trinceramenti sabaudi del Piccolo San Bernardo nel XVIII secolo', *Annales Sabaudiae*, vol.1, 2005, pp.49–58.

A classic example of the last point was the defence of the main Piedmontese strongholds during the Battle of Assietta on 14 July 1747. The defenders placed their fortifications by making the most of the terrain: high points, accessible only after a steep climb, and where there was insufficient room for the French battalions to deploy. Their soldiers were so crushed together their fire could not affect the defenders, sheltered behind drystone walls, whose fire at the enemy mass caused carnage. The Austro-Piedmontese lost a few dozen men against several thousand French, including most of the officers.[6] Such a massacre, followed by other difficult Alpine attacks in 1743 and 1744, convinced the Franco-Spaniards to desist. This brought an end to the War of the Austrian Succession in Italy.

The victorious defence of the Authion plateau and its surrounding peaks in Val Roia, which took place in the summer of 1793 during the War of the Alps, is part of this experience. Although less bloody than the Battle of Assietta, it halted the French advance, at least for that year. Knowing that they would not be able to conquer Authion with direct attacks, in 1794, the French preferred to go around it, crossing the border of the Republic of Genoa without declaring war, to disrupt the Piedmontese defence with an attack from the rear.

The Piedmontese defensive technique still proved its worth, for example, when, in one of the most famous episodes, between 13 and 14 April 1796, a few hundred Piedmontese grenadiers from the *3° Battaglione* and a similar number of soldiers from the Austrian *frei corps Gyulay*, entrenching themselves in the ruins of Cosseria castle, managed to block three French demi-brigades with heavy losses. With their retreat routes blocked by the French and with only the ammunition in their cartridge boxes, the defenders were unable to hold out to the bitter end and were forced to surrender after running out of ammunition.

Again, the losses of the attackers were far greater than those of the defenders:

> In the second and bloodiest attack, according to French sources, the French had more than 1,000 dead and wounded, to which must be added the casualties of the first attack: an enormous figure … for their part, the Austro-Piedmontese lost 150 men between dead and wounded, including the commander, *luogotenente colonnello* Filippo *cavaliere* del Carretto di Camerano, a Piedmontese *capitano* Rubin and a Croatian captain.[7]

The survivors were taken prisoner and rendered harmless by the victors, while at Assietta, the defenders won and kept their fighting capacity almost intact. As far as the Piedmontese *3° Granatieri* are concerned, the *ruolini di rivista* (muster rolls) indicate that many of them managed to escape from captivity and rejoined the ranks a few days after the surrender of Cosseria. As they were unarmed, they had to be completely re-equipped and could not be employed before the end of hostilities and the battalion was disbanded.

In the wars that the Piedmontese army fought against France or Spain, there was always one constant: the impossibility of effectively defending the Duchy of Savoy and the city of Nice. It became impossible to defend to the bitter end beyond the peaks, usually against

---

6   G. Cerino Badone, *You have to die in Piedmont! The Battle of Assietta, 19 July 1747* (Warwick: Helion & Company, 2023).
7   G. Merla, *O bravi guerrieri! L'arrivo di Napoleone in Italia e la guerra delle Alpi* (Pisa: Del Cerro 1988), p.327.

larger armies, because to bring the Piedmontese army into Savoy or to entrench it around Nice would have meant risking the units. Unable to retreat or receive supplies or reinforcements until the spring, they would have been trapped. A small army like that of Savoy could not afford the luxury of sacrificing a large proportion of its regiments. It was, therefore, customary to surrender the transalpine possessions to foreign occupation, to preserve the army and then to form alliances for the purpose of victory. Whenever peace came, Savoy and Nice were always recovered somehow. The War of the Alps was not and could not be an exception, and, in 1792, the Piedmontese had to surrender Savoy to French occupation. In 1793, they attempted to regain it, as had been planned, but began their invasion in mid-August and were soon forced to retreat when the first snow fell at high altitudes in October. The situation in the County of Nice was different: after losing the city and its surroundings, the Piedmontese army established a line of defence on the slopes of the Maritime Alps and held most of the territory until the spring of 1794, when the French bypassed the Piedmontese defences by crossing the Riviera, forcing the Austro-Sardinians to retreat beyond the Colle di Tenda.

2

Vittorio Amedeo III's Army

As soon as he ascended the throne, Vittorio Amedeo III undertook a radical reorganisation of the army, giving the regiments new flags, uniforms and equipment. He was an admirer of the successes of the army of King Frederick II of Prussia (1740–1786), and loved to watch the units parade, accompanied by his sons. His love of fine uniforms meant that the new ones adopted by the army from 1775 were particularly elegant and sumptuous, probably the finest ever worn by Savoyard soldiers.

Despite the King's wishes, the recruitment of army officers from the bourgeoisie did not increase significantly before the War of the Alps. Exceptions were the positions in the *Corpo Reale d'Artiglieria* (Royal Corps of Artillery) and the *Legione Truppe Leggere* (Light Infantry Legion), where the nobility were reluctant to serve. Later, during the long war, the constant need to recruit new officers favoured recruiting members of the bourgeoisie. However, the opposite was also true: the nobles, eager to fight against France, were the promoters and commanders of the corps of *Cacciatori Volontari* (chasseur volunteers) formed, from the winter of 1792, to fight the adventurous war of outposts, patrols and raids.

The army continued to be a powerful economic engine with its orders for clothing, equipment and food. The strengthening of the production of artillery and firearms, in which Piedmont was now about self-sufficient, led to the definitive consolidation of Turin's arsenal.

The great reform of the army carried out by Vittorio Amedeo III and his officials in the early years of his reign, and perfected in the following years,[1] tended towards the preparation of a Prussian-style land army. The matrimonial alliances with the Bourbons of France, the reconstruction of the fortress of Tortona, the fortification of the Citadel of Alessandria, both close to Lombardy, and the augmentation of the number of cavalry regiments, clearly showed the Austrians in possession of northern Italy that the Savoyards were increasingly determined to secure and extend their dominions by garrisoning all the territories in their possession. The Habsburgs were, therefore, not unjustified in distrusting Vittorio Amedeo III, which would prove to be a major factor in their defeat in 1796.

Perhaps the strategic choices of the Savoy family in the third quarter of the eighteenth century were inevitable and seemed shrewd: no one could have imagined a revolution like

---

1   To delve deeper on the Piedmontese army reforms of the period see S. Ales, *Le Regie Truppe Sarde, 1773–1814* (Roma: Ufficio Storico dello Stato Maggiore Esercito, 1989) and the unsurpassed work of N. Brancaccio, *L'Esercito del vecchio Piemonte dal 1540 al 1861. Gli Ordinamenti*. (Roma: Ministero della Guerra, 1922).

the French one, with the people ousting the Bourbons and going so far as to guillotine the royal couple.

Concern about what was happening in France in 1789 and in the years that followed had alerted the European monarchies to the possible repercussions – at that stage mainly of an ideological nature – that could fall on their respective states. When the urge to export the Revolution by force of arms became apparent in France, it was the diplomacy to create alliances that struggled to get off the ground. Vittorio Amedeo III, the princes and his ministers were divided between those who thought it wise to mobilise the army and those who feared the French reaction to this move. The King of Sardinia feared, above all, the possible repercussions on the French royal family. This is why the French attack of September 17923 was so astonishing. It was launched against an unprepared army led by inexperienced commanders.

To face the French, the King of Sardinia had at his disposal nine weak national ordnance regiments (*Guardie, Savoia, Monferrato, Piemonte, Saluzzo, Aosta, La Regina, Lombardia* and *Sardegna*) of 1,150 men each. In addition, there were four Swiss regiments (*de Courten, Christ, Schmidt* and *Rochmondet*), one German regiment, *Reale Alemanno*, and the *Chablais* regiment, which recruited men of various nationalities. In addition, there were 14 provincial infantry regiments (*Genevois, Maurienne, Nizza, Ivrea, Torino, Vercelli, Mondovì, Asti, Pinerolo, Casale, Novara, Tortona, Susa* and *Acqui*) recruited in the provinces of the same names. They consisted of a first weak operational battalion of four *fucilieri* companies and one *granatiere* company, with a total of 483 men, and an even weaker second battalion for training and garrison duties.

In 1774, the cavalry of Vittorio Amedeo III consisted of eight regiments. Four of these were dragoons, three of which were old regiments: *Dragoni del Re, Dragoni di Piemonte* and *Dragoni della Regina*. The fourth, *Dragoni del Chablais*, was new and took this name because its nominal command was given to the *Duca* di Chiablese. The other three were line cavalry regiments: *Savoia, Piemonte Reale* and *Aosta Cavalleria*, the latter new, under the nominal command of the *Duca* di Aosta. The eighth regiment, *Cavalleggeri del Re*, was originally known as *Dragoni del Genevois*. Its honorary *colonnello* was Prince Victor Amadeus, who renamed the regiment *Cavalleggeri del Re* when he became king. However, despite the name change, it remained a line cavalry regiment. The Savoy cavalry also included a ninth regiment, *Dragoni Leggeri di Sardegna*, which carried out gendarmerie duties on the island, a role that did not exist on the mainland but was needed on that turbulent island. In 1795, to make the best use of the resources available, four companies of the island regiment were sent to the mainland, where they did not take part in the fighting but were very useful in carrying correspondence between Turin and the various armies.

The *Legione Truppe Leggere* was made up of four battalions spread throughout the country whose main task was to stop smuggling. Accordingly, they guarded both the borders and the main communication routes where government officials levied duties on goods moving from province to province. It was a corps that was useful for defence, but it had to be concentrated and properly trained. Due to the needs of the war, three battalions were made active, while the fourth was assigned to garrison duties.

The *Legione degli Accampamenti* (Legion of Encampments), made up of privates and specialists, was created to help the army march and camp on the plains. It was therefore of little use in the defence of mountainous territory.

At the beginning of the Alpine War, the *Corpo Reale d'Artiglieria* had four battalions totalling 2,604 men, including 448 provincial recruits. Each battalion was made up of four companies of gunners and a company of specialists. The *Compagnia Bombardieri* (Company of Bombardiers), who worked mainly in the Turin arsenal to produce ammunition, belonged to the first battalion. The second included the *Compagnia Maestranze* (artillery workers), whose men also worked in the Turin arsenal on the production of cannons, their barrels and carriages. The third included the *Zappatori* (sappers) company, which was responsible for repairing the roads along which the columns of artillery were to pass. It also helped to construct positions for the pieces along with the gunners at the front. Finally, the fourth included the *Compagnia Minatori* (miners).

Storm Clouds on the Horizon

Vittorio Amedeo III's position in the face of French revolutionary expansionism soon became untenable. Relations with Austria were not good: the Habsburgs had never fully tolerated the cession of the Lombard territories of Vigevanasco, Oltrepò Pavese and Vogherese to Piedmont in 1748; they also claimed rights over the entire territory between the Sesia and Ticino rivers. But above all, they weighed the knowledge that Piedmontese policy had gravitated towards French alliances for decades, with an unexpressed desire to appropriate other territories in Austrian Lombardy.

The King of Sardinia, unable to practise the traditional policy of counterweight between France and Austria and finding intolerable the hypothesis that an absolute monarch could ally himself with the French revolutionaries, had to somehow come to terms with the Austrians, the only power that could help his eventual military effort on the ground. Yet, in 1792, with Louis XVI still formally King of France, it is easy to understand how difficult it was for the King of Sardinia to enter the war and to comply with Austrian and Prussian demands to open a southern front against France. It was important not to exacerbate the already precarious situation of Louis and the queen, Marie Antoinette, who were both under close guard. Certainly, the wavering of the King of Sardinia did nothing to improve the already difficult and suspicious relations between Piedmont and Austria.

Even more embarrassing was the presence in Turin of a number of French nobles, led by the *Comte* d'Artois, the King's son-in-law, who had fled with vague ambitions of reclaiming France. It was inevitable that he would be accommodated, given the ties of kinship, but his presence further reduced the small margins of negotiation left with the French.

With the arrest of Louis XVI on 10 August 1792, events began to gather pace. On 21 September, the Republic was proclaimed in France and, on 22 September, the French invaded Nice and Savoy without a declaration of war, surprising the Piedmontese army that had not yet mobilised.

The wars that the Piedmontese were facing were quite different from those that had taken place throughout the eighteenth century. The *guerre en dentelle* opposed European dynasties against each other and served to settle dynastic issues. They were generally relatively unbloody affairs. The wars begun by the French in 1792, on the other hand, were of a new kind: of ideas and of people, expansionist not simply for territorial growth but, above all, for the desire to take their ideas beyond the frontiers and impose them on the whole of Europe.

The French revolutionaries hoped to achieve the collapse of Piedmont, whose army was supposedly made up of oppressed peasants eager to defect to the new ideas. On 10 August 1792, the enemy made a printed document titled *L'Avviso* (the notice) to be distributed to the Piedmontese. The document urged them to 'have the greatness of soul to leave a country where you are badly treated, badly fed and badly paid, to come under the flags of Liberty, enjoy its pleasures, receive good pay, and live under fair discipline and popular government'.[2] The French attempt to enlist Savoyards in their regiments had limited success. A short time later, compulsory military service had to be introduced.

Although there was undoubtedly some popular unrest during the war years, this was due more to the hardships caused by the burdens of war than to the spread of the new ideas among the people. More important was the penetration of the new ideas into the class that had produced them in France, the bourgeoisie. But the latter had very few officers in the army, and all were in the lower ranks. It could not, therefore, significantly influence the determination to fight that the Savoyard soldiers maintained to the last.

The Piedmontese army responded with a hard fight that would last several years: in the words of Giovanni Merla, 'The French will find a hard bone in the Alps'.[3]

Any state that had not been at war for decades would have had problems finding army commanders who could get up to speed quickly. In the Piedmontese army of 1792, there was an important aggravating factor. This was an army in which promotion was based not on merit but on length of service, and even more so on social position, which, apart from the occasional luck of having a talented superior, could not produce suitable senior commanders. The general officers of the army retained their rank and continued their careers for life. This system of privilege could only result in elderly, inadequate commanders unable to motivate their troops to fight. Thus, the supreme command of the defence of the two provinces beyond the Alps was given to aged, sometimes octogenarian, generals and, as one might expect, the start of the war was disastrous.

The army corps assigned to the defence of the two provinces was not inadequate. In Savoy, under the command of the 77-year-old *generale conte* Giovanni Battista Felice Lazzary, there were about 12,000 men (12 battalions of ordnance infantry, including two Swiss), nine battalions of provincial infantry (including two from the *Legione degli Accampamenti*), a battalion of the *Legione Truppe Leggere*, six squadrons of cavalry and dragoons and 16 field pieces. In the County of Nice, the command was entrusted to *luogotenente generale* Louis Eugène de Courten (1715-1802), commander of the Swiss-Valais Regiment of the same name. Some 9,000 men had been assembled (eight ordnance battalions, including two Swiss, four battalions of provincial infantry, two companies of the *Legione degli Accampamenti* and eight field pieces, three cavalry squadrons and most of the navy.[4]

While the loss of Savoy was complete because the defenders only held the Alpine passes, the defeat in the County of Nice was less bitter because the Piedmontese were able to hold the Val Roia blocking the French advance.

---

2   Merla, *O bravi guerrieri!*, Appendix, p.416.
3   Merla, *O bravi guerrieri!*, pp.111–112.
4   F. Pinelli, *Storia militare del Piemonte dalla pace di Acquisgrana al 1850* (Torino: De Giorgis, 1854), p.101. V. Ilari, P. Crociani, & C. Paoletti, *La guerra delle Alpi (1792–1796)* (Roma: Stato Maggiore dell'Esercito, Ufficio Storico, 2000), pp.25–27.

Vittorio Amedeo III was deeply disappointed in the behaviour of his generals and was forced to ask his Austrian ally to send a skilful general capable of commanding the joint Austro and Piedmontese army, he also hoped for massive military aid from the Habsburgs. But all he received was 60-year-old Walloon *Feldzeugmeister* Baron Joseph de Vins (1732–1798), who did have a good military reputation, and a few thousand Austrian soldiers.

The middle- and lower-ranking officers of the Piedmontese army, determined to defend their country, were inexperienced yet young and bellicose. They managed, with the exception of a few cowards and incompetents, to rally and motivate their companies, putting up adequate resistance that endured for a considerable time through hopes and disappointments.

The period between the autumn of 1792 and the spring of 1793 was a valuable opportunity for the Kingdom of Sardinia to mobilise and deploy its army, preparing it to garrison the Alpine passes as soon as the snow melted. During this period, the mountains were guarded by militias, including mountaineers familiar with the area and accustomed to the Alpine winter. The Piedmontese army's ability to resist French attacks within the first months depended on the aptitude of soldiers from Piedmont, Savoy, and Nice to replicate the achievements of their predecessors in the Alps. The tales of bravery told by their elders on long winter evenings inspired them to follow in their footsteps. It was clear that the French would eventually try to conquer Piedmont again, as they had done for centuries.

Recruitment was intense during the winter, and the influx of volunteers and provincial levies made it easy to bring regiments up to wartime strength. New battalions and specialist units were formed, and the artillery arsenal in Turin stepped up its purchase of the artillery components and *fucili* (muskets) it could not produce. By April, enough ammunition had been produced for the soldiers and the artillery.

The exigencies of war, the indispensable presence of experienced gunners in all the fortifications and the dispersal of batteries among the various army corps necessitated a massive increase in the manpower of the *Corpo Reale d'Artiglieria*. This was achieved not only by increasing recruitment but also by enlisting many provincial soldiers and entire companies of volunteer militiamen.

Since the batteries could not be used in the countryside, as the Piedmontese army generals had planned, the available 3- and 4-pounder mountain pieces and, above all, the 4- and 8-pounder field pieces

Grenadier pointing at two 8-pounders. Drawing by A.M. Stagnon, circa 1795. (Private collection)

were used when the conditions of the mountain roads and mule tracks made it possible. The War Regulations of 5 May 1792, which stipulated that each line infantry battalion should be provided with two 4-pounders, or, if of grenadiers of two 8-pounder light guns for every two battalions, could not be implemented, and the guns, especially the 4-pounders, were placed in tactically advantageous positions in the mountain entrenchments, while many more heavy 8-pounders and all the 16-pounders remained in reserve at the commands.

The Austrian Ally: Few Soldiers, No Artillery

By coincidence, on the same day that *lieutenant-général* Anne-Pierre, *marquis* de Montesquiou-Fézensac (1739–1798), commander of the invading French *Armée di Midi* crossed the Sardinian border without declaring war (22 September 1792), the King of Sardinia's plenipotentiary signed an agreement in Milan with the plenipotentiary of Holy Roman Emperor Francis II (1792–1806). The latter agreed to provide an auxiliary corps consisting of seven infantry battalions, four squadrons of light cavalry, and 22 artillery pieces. *Feldmarschall-leutnant* Leopold Lorenz Graf von Strassoldo (1739-1809) was appointed as the commander of this corps, with two *generalmajors*, *baron* Michelangelo Alessandro Colli Marchini (1736–1808) and *marchese* Giovanni Provera (1736–1804), both Italian subjects of the Habsburgs, serving as subordinates. Colli was a native of Vigevano. Since 1745, the city of Vigevano and the surrounding area (the Vigevanasco) had been under Savoy rule, but when Colli was born there (1738), it was under Austrian rule, so he joined the Austrian army and, although formally now a subject of Savoy, spent his entire military career there. Provera was probably a native of Pavia, a city in Lombardy, then under Habsburg rule.

Left with no alternative, Vittorio Amedeo III was forced to accept an alliance that provided him with derisory aid and jeopardised certain provinces of the kingdom that his father had acquired in return for the important assistance the Piedmontese army had provided to Maria Theresa of Austria during the War of the Austrian Succession.

In addition to the Austrian troops that arrived in Piedmont in the winter of 1792–1793, a further contingent of 31,240 men (20 infantry battalions and nine cavalry divisions) was expected to be sent in 1794.[5] It never arrived. This may have been part of the Austrian army stationed in Lombardy that was expected to assist in the reconquest of the lost provinces beyond the Alps. Instead, this Austrian corps was sent to fight against the French after the latter had defeated the Piedmontese and begun to invade the Po Valley. It was a strange strategy of Austria to allow a valuable ally to be defeated and to lose the contribution of its 25–30,000 remaining combatants. The result was that Bonaparte beat the Austrians at Lodi on 10–11 May 1796 and entered Milan on the 26th of the same month.

As always, not all the mistakes were made by the Austrians. Their overriding tactical objective was the defence of their Lombard possessions, and the fear that the French might use the Ligurian Riviera as a direct route to Milan led them to block further aid. On 5 January 1793, Vittorio Amedeo III wrote to Luigi Giuseppe Arborio-Gattinara *marchese* di

---

5   AST, Ufficio Generale del Soldo, Ordini Generali e Misti (OGM), mazzo 69: Stato delle Truppe Austriache destinate per il Piemonte per l'anno 1794, undated, but October 1792.

Breme, his representative at the Court of Vienna, noting that the Austrians had pledged to provide it (the new contingent) only when there was nothing more to fear for Lombardy.[6]

Austria's fears were not absurd, and, in 1796, they were realised, but only when the Piedmontese army corps, left alone to defend the area between Ceva and Mondovì, was attacked by Bonaparte's troops and defeated after a fierce rearguard action. If the Austrians, instead of retreating towards Lombardy, had linked up with the Piedmontese for defence, there would have been a chance of victory. But it must be remembered that the opponent was the rising genius of Napoleon Bonaparte.

At the end of February 1793, the Austrian contingent was finally in place in Piedmont. A contemporary Piedmontese document lists the units that were sent to support Vittorio Amedeo III, and they are as follows:

> Two battalions of infantry regiment *IR 48 Caprara* (2,027 men).
> The same for regiment *IR44 Belgioioso* (2,027 men).
> The grenadier companies of the two infantry regiments formed as *Wolust* Grenadier Battalion (458 men).
> The *IR5 Erstes Garrison Regiment* (1,020 men).
> The *IR6 Zweytes Garrison Regiment* (1,013 men)
> Two divisions of *Stabs-Dragoner* (613 men).

For a total of 7,952 men, all told.

Twenty-two pieces of artillery were also to be sent to Piedmont (three small field pieces, 12 of larger calibre, seven 'big cannons or howitzers') served by 634 artillerymen, but these never reached Piedmont. To the contingent was added in June 1793, the *Gyulay* (elsewhere Giulay or Gyulai) *Freikorps* of 815 men, bringing the theoretical total of the contingent to 8,767 men.[7]

When planning began for the distribution of troops for the resumption of hostilities in the spring, it was immediately clear that, in the absence of a large Austrian expeditionary force, it would be impossible to go on the offensive. The French could attack anywhere, choosing from the many Alpine passes available, while the Piedmontese army was forced to spread its forces all over the frontier and wait for the attacks. De Vins could not have been of much help in these decisions since he did not know the characteristics of the territory except from the inaccurate maps of the time, and he certainly had orders from Vienna to prevent the ambitious Victor Amadeus III from attacking. Weakened in this way, the King of Sardinia would have more easily agreed to surrender his western territories to the Habsburgs!

It was necessary to distribute the available combat troops among the various army corps and, to free the second provincial battalions from garrison duties as soon as possible, a reserve company was established in each regiment. Its purpose was twofold: to train and equip the recruits before they were sent to the active companies and to contribute to public order and the suppression of insurrectionary attempts by the Piedmontese Jacobins, incited by the French.

---

6   Ilari et al, *La guerra delle Alpi*, p.50.
7   AST, OGM, mazzo 71: Letter of Di Cravanzana, 7 June 1793.

The King and Princes at War

The King, who loved to wear fine uniforms and to parade, did not have the warlike temperament of his ancestors but decided to go to the troops to make them feel close to him. The King's *Guardie del Corpo* (Household Guards), although they had not fired a shot outside of celebrations for decades, organised themselves to follow and protect him.

On 9 January 1793, they were informed of the King's decision to leave Turin for the front, giving them plenty of time to prepare to accompany him. However, the sovereign waited until the summer to leave the city.[8]

Finally, on 7 July, Vittorio Amedeo III issued detailed instructions for mobilising the *Guardie del Corpo*, and how to select them. In 1793 there were three companies of *Guardie del Corpo*, commanded by officers from the leading noble families of the kingdom. They were recruited mainly from among the gentlemen. The first company was composed mainly of Savoyards, the second of Piedmontese and the third of Sardinians.

Two squadrons were to be prepared for the expedition, for a total of 150 men, including a *maggiore* (major), an *aiutante maggiore* (aide major), two *capitani* (captains), two *luogotenenti* (lieutenants), seven *marescialli d'alloggio* (maréchal de logis, a squadron sergeant major), one of whom was always present at the King's side, a *chirurgo maggiore* (surgeon major) and a *cappellano* (chaplain) were to follow the squadrons. Each squadron was made up of a *primo brigadiere* (corporal major), an acting *brigadiere* (corporal), three *sotto brigadieri* (lance corporals) and 67 guards. Of these, 120 men formed two fully operational squadrons, while the remaining 30 were to perform various services closer to the King. These included two *trombettieri* (trumpeters), a *maniscalco* (farrier) and a *sellaio* (saddler). The 30 also included the standard guards, who remained with the monarch. Each company was equipped with a beautifully embroidered cavalry standard.[9] The king ordered the two squadrons to take those of the first two companies with them while those of the third and the *timballiere* (kettle drummer) remained in Turin. Before the departure of the two companies, 30 new guards were recruited to provide a more adequate service.

The two squadrons, having laid down their parade swords, were provided with another suitable for possible combat to protect the monarch, and all were equipped with two pistols and a *fucile* each.

However, after a few visits in July 1793, the shortest at Susa and the longest between Cuneo and the Colle di Tenda, the King always remained in Turin. Every spring thereafter, the *Guardie del Corpo* continued to prepare for the campaign, but in vain.

As the King had decided to send two of his sons (the *duchi* d'Aosta and del Monferrato) and the *duca* del Chablais to lead the army corps assigned to them, small detachments of the *Guardie del Corpo*, commanded by a *maresciallo d'alloggio*, accompanied them and were adequately equipped to carry out their duties. The *duchi* d'Aosta and del Chablais, however, were rarely seen by the troops. The only member of the royal family present with any continuity in his corps was the *duca* del Monferrato, who even asked the King to stay in Aosta

---

8   AST, OGM, mazzo 71. Determinazioni di Sua Maestà per abilitare le Guardie del Corpo a entrare in Campagna, 7 July 1793.
9   E. Ricchiardi. *Bandiere e stendardi dell'Esercito Sardo, 1713–1802* (Torino: Centro Studi Piemontesi, 2006), pp.125–131.

with the troops for the winter instead of returning to the comfort of the palace, but it is not certain that Vittorio Amedeo III agreed.

The *duca* d'Aosta was present with the 3rd Corps for at least a few days in 1793. On 5 July 1793, he ordered that the troops under his nominal command be provided with 12-seater carriages for transporting the wounded, like those already provided for the 4th Corps, and six stretchers per battalion for transporting the wounded to field hospitals. To solve the serious problem of having to detach soldiers from the lines, thus reducing their defensive capacity, he ordered that before each battle 100 peasants be made available to carry stretchers. To cheer up the troops waiting for the French to attack, the Prince ordered brandy to be distributed to the soldiers before the battle. Finally, to reduce illness and following the dictates of the limited medical science of the time, vinegar was to be distributed to the soldiers at least once or twice a month.[10]

As was the case with Vittorio Amedeo III's regulations on the organisation of the army and its preparation for battle on the plains, the progression of higher command from the established regimental ranks was not feasible in the Alpine War. In May 1792, a series of higher ranks was established: Three *capitani generali* (captain generals – a rank reserved for the princes, the *duchi* del Chablais, d'Aosta and del Monferrato), 16 *generali* (generals – 10 of infantry and six of cavalry), 21 *luogotenenti generali* (lieutenant generals – 17 of infantry and six of cavalry), 50 *maggior generali* (major generals – 39 infantry and 11 cavalry), and finally 48 *brigadier generali* (brigadier generals – 41 of infantry and seven of cavalry). In other words, an overabundance of old officers from the nobility, inexperienced in command. The large number of cavalry generals in relation to the size of the army should not be surprising, as they were officers from the nobility, in a world where the highest aspiration was to wear the cavalry uniform and rank. Very few of them were able to command during the War of the Alps, which instead saw resourceful officers emerge from the lower ranks.

Before the war, there were only two king's *aiutanti di campo* (aides de camp): the *conte* Gio Batta Delfino di Triviè and the *nobiluomo* (nobleman) Filippo d'Ormea, who did not play an active role in the War of the Alps.

In 1793, the King appointed other officers to join his aides de camp. But some of them, eager to play an active role in the war, asked the King to assign them to a fighting unit. *Luogotenente colonnello* Giuseppe Faussone, *cavaliere* di San Germagnano (1757–1793),[11] was sent to command the *2° Battaglione Cacciatori*. He was a good commander and led his battalion in the Toulon expedition, where he was killed on 18 September 1793.[12] Other members of the King's entourage who asked to be assigned to a fighting unit were Pietro Ignazio Asinari di Bernezzo, known as the *marchese* di Brezé, commander of the *Legione degli Accampamenti* in 1789, *brigadiere generale di fanteria* and *gran mastro* (grand master) of the House of Chablais, then *maggior generale* of infantry. At Nice, during the French attack in September 1792, he tried unsuccessfully to halt the hasty retreat of the Sardinian

---

10 AST, Ufficio Generale del Soldo, Intendenza d'Armata (IdA), mazzo 4: letter to the Ufficio Generale del Soldo, 5 July 1793.
11 In the Savoy nobility the title of *Cavaliere* indicated a second-born son who was not entitled to the family fief.
12 A. Lo Faso di Serradifalco, *La difesa di un regno. Il sacrificio dell'esercito del Regno di Sardegna nella guerra contro la Francia, 1792-1796* (Udine: Gaspari, 2009), pp.339–340.

troops.[13] For a short time, the *marchese* Giuseppe Enrico Costa di Beauregard (1752–1824) was *Aiutante di Campo del Re*, then he was allowed to join the *Granatieri Reali* (Royal Grenadiers) as a volunteer. He was a *gentiluono di camera* (Gentleman of the Chamber) at the Court of Savoy and a *maggiore* of the *Legione degli Accampamenti*. On 13 May 1794, Beauregard was appointed to the staff of *Baron* Colli with the rank of *maggiore di battaglione* (battalion major or battalion assistant). On 14 March 1795, he became *quartiermastro generale* (quartermaster general, equivalent to the chief of staff) in the same army corps with the rank of *luogotenente colonnello*. Finally, on 22 March 1796, he was promoted to the rank of *colonnello*.[14] Among the aides of Vittorio Amedeo III was the *cavaliere* Filippo del Carretto of Camerano. On 12 March 1793, he was appointed *capitano* of the *1° Corpo Franco*, at the head of which he performed bravely in the Battle of Authion (8–12 June 1793), where he was wounded. As a result of his conduct, he was appointed *maggiore* of the *Corpo Franco* on 10 October, *aiutante maggiore* of the army staff on 26 November 1793 and King's *aiutante di campo* on 21 December. On 24 June 1795, while serving as *aiutante di campo* to *feldzeugmeister* de Vins he was again wounded while taking part in an action involving Austrian troops. On 29 March 1796, he was appointed commander of the *3° Granatieri* and promoted to *luogotenente colonnello* on 5 April, being killed in action on 12 April 1796 during the defence of the castle of Cosseria.

Generals at War

The senior officers who served at the front were mainly *luogotenenti generali*, *maggior generali* and *brigadieri generali*, the latter sometimes also in actual command of a regiment. Advancement between these ranks was the prerogative of the King and, in peacetime, was reserved for members of the nobility. Even during the War of the Alps, higher ranks remained the prerogative of the nobility, but promotions and their frequency often depended on the merits of the person being promoted rather than their position within the nobility. Unfortunately, however, even in the case of reprimand, except in rare cases of cowardice or blatant disobedience, officers who belonged to the general staff were almost always relegated to non-operational duties or retired with a promotion to a higher rank with increased financial benefits and salary.

By order of 26 June 1784, general officers wore rich uniforms that were clearly distinguishable by their special lace.[15] Their coat was blue, with wide lapels and red lining. The tricorn hat was edged with gold lace, as was the lace that held the blue cockade. The epaulettes were of gold lace, with a *graine d'épinarde* bullion fringe. Their sash, worn at the waist below the coat, was almost completely golden, only edged in blue/gold, with golden tassels and spinach-grain fringe.

The rank distinctions were: *generale*, three lines of the general's lace on the cuffs and one line on the collar; *luogotenente generale*, two lines of the same lace on both collar and cuffs; *maggior generale*, two lines of the same lace on the cuffs and a single line on the collar. A *brigadiere*

---

13 Lo Faso di Serradifalco, *La difesa di un regno*, p.195.
14 Lo Faso di Serradifalco, *La difesa di un regno*, pp.306–307.
15 AST, OGM mazzo 64: Regolamento per le uniformi dei Generali, 26 June 1764.

generale was not entitled to the special general's chevron and was distinguished with more richness than the chevron of the officers below him: five lines on the collar and two on the cuffs.

The *aiutanti generali* wore a coat in the same colours as the generals, with the distinctions for their actual rank, but if they were army-level adjutants, their pocket flaps were edged both inside and out with two stripes of gold lace.

Infantry generals wore white waistcoats and breeches without distinction, while cavalry generals wore them in chamois and artillery generals in blue.

In addition to the main uniform, officers of the general staff were allowed to wear a *piccola uniforme* (an easier uniform for everyday uses) of the same colours, but with the general's lace confined to the collar and lapels, and with the addition of embroidered frogs.

The same regulation stipulated that the *aiutanti di campo* wore the uniform of the unit to which they belonged, with the insignia of their rank and their role identified by a blue plume, the stalk of which was placed under the cockade of the tricorn hat.

Medals to Reward Valour

De Vins was undoubtedly the one who proposed to Vittorio Amedeo III the creation of the Piedmontese army medal for Military Valour, on the grounds that a similar decoration had already been introduced in the Austrian army on 19 July 1789 by order of Emperor Joseph II. *Der Tapferkeit* (Bravery) was a medal struck in two versions, gold or silver, the former intended for officers, the latter for NCOs.

Vittorio Amedeo III, who understood the idea, but remained concerned about the motivation of the troops, introduced the medal with different intentions. It was promulgated on 27 May 1793 with the publication of the 'Regulations for the badge of honour established by His Majesty for the NCOs and Soldiers of the Royal Troops'.

The title alone indicates an important difference between the Piedmontese medal and the Austrian one: it was intended only for the troops, while meritorious officers continued to be rewarded with the award of a dynastic order or promotion, not to mention cash bounties. Not only that, but a fifth article clearly stated that being an NCO did not confer the privilege of receiving the medal since, 'if both are involved in the same act of arms, a soldier may be awarded the Gold Medal for having distinguished himself most and the NCO who commanded him may only be awarded a silver one'. Moreover, the regulations stated that:

> … acts of outstanding bravery are those of a person who has contributed in a special way to the success of an event, to save from some danger a body of troops, officers, NCOs or soldiers, colours, the money chest, military equipment and artillery, and provided that such actions are confirmed by witnesses and are not judged to be reckless or produced by the desire of glory, shall entitle him to the award of the badge of honour.

Once the medal had been awarded, it remained the property of the soldier, who could pass it on to his heirs, provided that his conduct, even after his discharge, was not criminal.[16]

---

16   AST, Segreteria di Guerra, Miscellanea I, mazzo 1: Regolamento per il distintivo d'onore, 27 May 1793.

The medals, most of which were silver, were seen as carefully awarded, rewarding acts of bravery that were documented. There were also a few rare cases where a soldier decorated with the Silver Medal was awarded the Gold Medal for a second act of bravery. In that case, he had to return the silver medal in accordance with the regulations.

A little more than 200 medals for bravery were actually distributed (see Table 1), 81 of them to national ordnance infantry regiments (five to the *Reggimento Guardie*, 15 to the *Savoie*, 17 to the *Monferrato*, six to *Piemonte*, two to *Aosta*, 12 to *Saluzzo*, three to *La Marina*, four to *La Regina*, 13 to *Sardegna*, and one to *Oneglia*), 14 to regiments of foreign ordnance regiments (three to the *Reggimento Reale Alemanno*, one to *Christ*, three to *Stettler*, three to *de Courten*, four to *Chablais*) and 65 to the Provincial Infantry (six to *Granatieri Reali*, two to *Guastatori*, nine to *Acqui* regiment, two to *Asti*, three to *Casale*, six to *Genevois*, two each to *Ivrea* and *Vercelli*, five to *Mondovì*, as many as 14 to *Maurienne*, nine to *Nizza*, one each to *Novara*, *Pinerolo*, *Susa*, *Torino* and *Tortona*, and two to *Vercelli* (although the medals were mostly earned by *granatieri* or *cacciatori* in the élite battalions). The *Legione Truppe Leggere, 1°* and *2° Reggimento Truppe Leggere* received seven medals, while the NCOs and soldiers in the volunteer light infantry companies received 15. The *Corpo Reale d'Artiglieria* received 16 medals, the militias five, and the cavalry only three, awarded to the dragoons (one each to *Dragoni di Piemonte*, *della Regina's* and *Chablais* regiments).[17]

Silver Medals for Valour. (With permission, collection of A. Brambilla, Milan)

Table 1 Medals for Valour Awarded.

	Medals
National line infantry	81
Stranger line infantry	14
Provincial line Infantry	65
Truppe Leggere	7
Volunteer light troops	15
Artillery	16
Cavalry	4
Militia	5
Total	207

---

17 Brancaccio, *Gli ordinamenti*, pp.395–396.

3

The Piedmontese Army in Action

Getting the Ordnance Infantry Ready to Fight

In September 1792, when the French attacked the Kingdom of Sardinia, Victor Amadeus III had at his disposal nine regiments of ordnance infantry, to which were added four Swiss, one German and one of mixed nationality, making a total of about 30 professional infantry battalions.

Each battalion of about 600 men consisted of four companies of *fucilieri* (infantrymen),[1] and one company of *granatieri* (grenadiers). It was planned that, in the event of war, the regiment's two *granatieri* companies would join with those of two other regiments to form an independent grenadier battalion of six companies. The *cacciatori* (light infantrymen), who in peacetime were distributed among the fusilier companies, were to form one company per battalion. This company would, in turn, be combined with others to form autonomous light infantry battalions.

The French attack finally led to a reinforcement of the ordnance infantry regiments on 11 January 1793. The two battalions now had 694 men each, and the regiment, including the staff, had 1,385 men. With this increase, the theoretical strength of the national ordnance infantry was 16,755 men, all volunteers.[2]

The national ordnance regiments took their name from one of the provinces of the Kingdom. The exceptions were the *Reggimento Guardie*, nominally under the command of the sovereign, and *La Regina*, dedicated to the royal consort. The other seven regiments were *Savoia*, *Monferrato*, *Piemonte*, *Saluzzo*, *Aosta*, *Lombardia* and *Sardegna*, to which the *Oneglia* regiment was added in 1793. The Swiss ordnance regiments took their names from their colonel proprietor. In January 1793, they were *de Courten* (*Streng* in 1795) from the

---

1 In the Piedmontese eighteenth-century army, the infantryman of the ordinary companies was called a *fuciliere* (fusilier) because he was equipped with a *fucile* (musket). The name *fucile* came from latin *focile*, that meant the way to fire the charge. In the Piedmontese army there were no regiments of fusiliers. The same weapon was also used by the elite soldiers, the *granatieri* (grenadiers) and the *cacciatori* (light infantrymen). The rare rifles, with a rifled-barrel that equipped the light infantrymen, were called *carabina a canna rigata*. In the same army the term musket was in use until the seventeenth century for the serpent musket, an infantry weapon equipped with an S-shaped metal arm, or serpent, bearing the fuse that ignited the charge.
2 AST, OGM, mazzo 70: Aumento di 203 uomini in ogni reggimento di fanteria d'ordinanza, 11 January 1793.

canton of Valais, *Christ* and *Shmidt* from Graubünden, and *Rochmondet* (*Steller* from 13 September 1794) from Bern. The German ordnance regiment was called the *Reale Alemanno*, while the mixed foreign ordnance infantry regiment, but officered by Savoyards and nominally under the command of the *duca* del Chablais, was *Chablais*.

An infantry regiment normally had 48 officers: a *colonnello*, a *luogotenente colonnello*, a *maggiore di reggimento* (regimental major or regimental adjutant), a *maggiore di battaglione* (battailon major), a *quartiermastro* (quartermaster) eight *capitani*, five *luogotenenti capitani*, 12 *luogotenenti*, 12 *sotto luogotenenti* (second lieutenant), two *aiutanti* and four *insegna* (ensigns). There were 52 NCOs: two *sergenti maggiori* (sergeants major), a *tamburo maggiore* (drum major), four *furieri* (*fourrier* or quartermaster sergeants), 12 *sergenti di compagnia* (company sergeants), 13 *sergenti di plotone* (platoon sergeants) and 20 *sergenti sovrannumerari* (supernumerary sergeants).[3] Approximately one officer to every 13 men, including *caporali* (corporals), a good leader-to-troop ratio, indicating well-commanded companies.

In peacetime, officers rarely changed regiments and were slow to rise in rank. It was also common for officers to be given a higher brevet rank than they actually held, for example a *capitano* with the rank of *maggiore*. This gave them slightly higher pay and a better position for future promotion. This approach, however, tended to keep officers in their ranks without age limits, with the result that some occupied intermediate ranks when they were well advanced in years. With the outbreak of the war, the lower ranks, as well as the generals, underwent a rapid ageing process, with older but better officers being assigned to non-operational troops and *compagnie di riserva*, and the others being retired.

At the other end of the age spectrum, it was customary for aristocratic boys to be rewarded for successful service at the *Accademia Militare di Torino* (Turin Military Academy) by receiving lower ranks in the regiments. They entered the academy as children. In addition to the basic subjects, they learnt horse riding and fencing and the rudiments of military science. The academy also had a special category of very young boys who usually belonged to the most established families at court, the pages. These young men would alternately serve the sovereign, the princes or queens and princesses, learning the difficult art of living among the powerful, in addition to their studies at the academy. When they had finished their training, they also became junior officers in the regiments, often advancing faster than their peers because of their kinship.

With officers sometimes too old and worn out by the tedium of garrison life, or too young and lacking in experience and influence over their subordinates, the real effectiveness of the company lay in the hands of the NCOs. With the outbreak of the war, the latter factor became apparent: clever officers, able to understand and enhance the role of their NCOs, were able to lead fierce companies into battle. In other cases, it could spell disaster.

An analysis of the muster rolls preserved in the State Archives of Turin shows that during the War of the Alps, the experienced NCOs were more stable in their company than the officers, as they were the real soul of the unit. The lists also show that it was not uncommon for newly promoted NCOs to be removed from their ranks shortly after appointment because they had proved unsuitable. NCOs who could no longer cope with the rigours of life

---

3   AST, OGM, mazzo 70: Aumento di 203 uomini in ogni reggimento di fanteria d'ordinanza, 11 January 1793.

at the front were retained in rank but sent to the *compagnia di riserva* (reserve company) to use their experience in training recruits. This loss of company personnel was compensated for by the selection of the best of the veteran supernumerary NCOs, thus ensuring that the officers had good control of the company through subordinates who had been tested in the many battles of the long war.[4]

A lucky few NCOs were appointed as a *sergente maggiore* on the staff of one of the regimental battalions. These NCOs were of vital importance to the battalion and would remain with the unit for a long period of time. The *sergenti maggiori* could also be sent to a carefully chosen location for a period to encourage men to join the battalion voluntarily, without the coercion typical of other armies. An NCO's career could culminate in the rank of *insegna*, of which there were two in each battalion, who had the privilege of carrying one of the battalion's two flags. An *insegna* ranked the same as a *sotto luogotenente* but, with rare exceptions for special reasons, could not be promoted further.

Among the NCOs, the *tamburo maggiore* was responsible for recruiting and instructing the company's musicians (drummers, fifers, hunting horn players or trumpeters) and leading them, following the regimental band when present, which in turn was led by a more senior and experienced musician in the role of *capobanda* (music leader), who in the Savoyard army was ranked as private. The *tamburo maggiore* served with the *1° Battaglione*, but the nature of mountain warfare meant that the two battalions rarely operated together. It was therefore necessary to have a senior and experienced drummer, with the rank of *caporale tamburino* (corporal drummer), to perform the duties in the *2° Battaglione*.

The regimental medical staff consisted of a *chirurgo maggiore* (surgeon major) and a *garzone chirurgo* (assistant surgeon). They worked in the regimental hospital, which was usually in the second line but close to the troops. The *frater*, one per company with the rank of private, was a medically trained soldier who, with the limited resources available at that time, stabilised the wounded and transferred them to the hospital to be handed over to the surgeons.

Religious services were performed by the regimental *cappellano* (chaplain), assisted by a *sotto cappellano* (sub chaplain). In infantry regiments of German or Swiss German nationality, since the soldiers were Protestants, the chaplain and assistant chaplain were ministers of that religion. In the camps, to be close to the troops for the administration of the sacraments, a special tent was used as a chapel to house the field altar, which followed the regiment on the back of a mule. This location, however, was not without risk. Often enough, a sudden enemy attack and the retreat of the unit would force the two clerics to leave the tent, resulting in the loss of the field altar, which then had to be replaced by the *Ufficio Generale del Soldo* (Paymaster General).

Each infantry battalion had one *armaiolo* (armourer) for the maintenance of weapons and two *falegnami* (carpenters) for the repair of carriages. As a rule, these specialists were privates, but it was possible for one of them, with experience and seniority, to reach the rank of *corporale* or *sergente*.

The *furieri* (quartermaster sergeants), usually *sergenti*, performed administrative functions, kept the company's books up to date and kept the muster rolls. These latter were

---

4   AST, Info's from various Ruolini di Rivista [Muster rolls], 1792–1796.

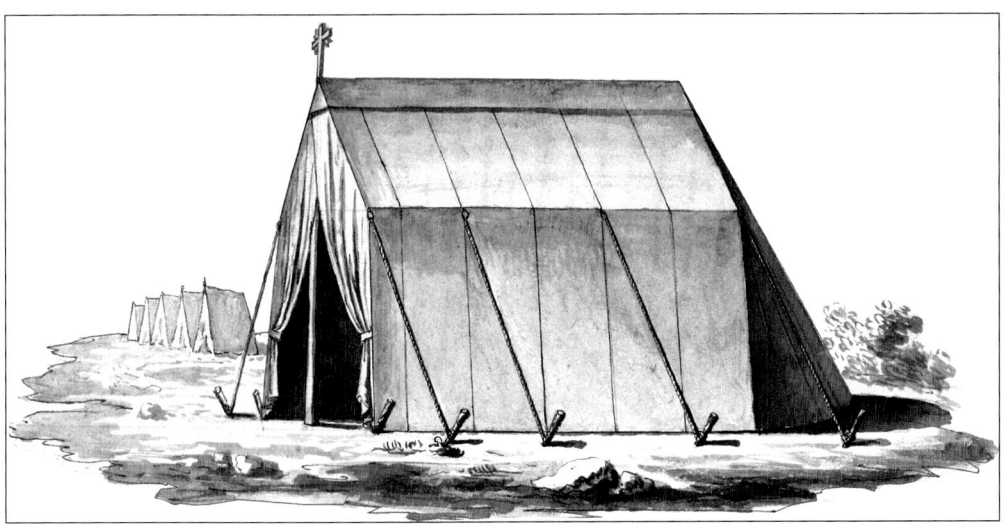

Tent used as a regimental chapel. (Anne S.K. Brown Military Collection)

compiled during the monthly inspections of the *ufficiale del soldo* (pay officer) and were necessary to count the men actually present in order to pay them, provide them with the provisions and what was stipulated in the clothing regulations. The rosters also identified those absent for any reason, and those who were not entitled to either pay or food. The sick and wounded housed in regimental hospitals were counted, but those who were admitted to other hospitals still had to receive money and food.

The monthly inspection of the company was carried out by an *ufficiale del soldo*, who was shown the previous month's roster by the *furiere*, and the changes recorded in the days since the last inspection, and verified them. To correct any mistakes made by the *furiere* or to check for any attempt at deception, the inspection was carried out in the presence of the company. During the war, the inspection was particularly difficult because the *furiere* could not give precise information about each member of the company, for example, if their fate were unknown after a clash with the enemy.[5] We can imagine the hard life of these employees of the military administration who, protected from the weather by a cloak, on the back of a mule and carrying boxes containing documents, trudged along mule tracks to reach the mountain pastures where the companies to be inspected were waiting.

In each company, a private was appointed as the *vivandiere* (sutler). His job was to provide the soldiers with extra food and drink, in addition to their normal supplies. These comforts had to be paid for directly by the soldier at favourable prices agreed with the *colonnello*, who received a percentage of the income. When the company was in the mountains, the *vivandiere*, usually equipped with a cart, also had to find a mule to carry his food, cook it every day, and set up a place where the soldiers could stay dry and, if possible, warm. It was, therefore, his responsibility to stock up as best as he could. Due to the difficulties of procuring what

---

5   The muster rolls of the Piedmontese army from the last decades of the seventeenth century to 1864, when the capital of the Kingdom of Italy was transferred to Florence, are preserved in the AST.

he wanted in the mountain valleys, he was not always able to keep to his daily schedule. The *vivandiere* likely handled the mail for the officers and men of his company, taking it to the positions to cheer up their hard lives.

When the company was on the march, the *furiere* and the *vivandiere* had to be at the forefront, as they were responsible for providing their company with food and lodging.

A document from the Swiss *Reggimento Rochmondet*, sets out the rules to be followed by the company *vivandieri* and *furieri* on transfer marches. The *vivandieri* had to prepare food for the soldiers. To do this, they had to provide themselves with a cart to transport the food and everything needed to cook and eat it. A good legume soup, half a Piedmontese *libbra* (369g) of beef and a quarter of a *libbra* of bread every other day was the daily meal. The *furiere* had to give him a daily list of the rations to be prepared so that he could buy the necessary quantities. Early in the morning, the *vivandiere* was allowed to set off in his cart for the next stage of the journey. They both had to find a suitable place to cook, and provide the soldiers with food and drink. The *furiere* would also have to check that what the *ufficiale del soldo* had prepared for the next stage would be sufficient to accommodate the troops and officers for the night.[6]

A small nucleus of *cannonieri ausiliari* (auxiliary gunners) had been trained in each infantry battalion to use the two 4-pounder guns provided for the planned campaign in the Po valley, but the reality of the Alpine War made these specialists less useful. Looking through the muster rolls of the *fucilieri* companies of the spring of 1793 and later, it is still possible to find soldiers with a small separate entry indicating that they were *cannonieri ausiliari,* and sometimes a *caporale* appears among them. Three or four per company, or 15 per battalion, were still listed in the War Organisation of 11 January 1793, but fewer appeared in the muster rolls. On the other hand, the needs of mountain warfare made 4-pounders indispensable, as they could be easily transported by mule once dismantled, but the firing was done by *cannonieri* (gunners) of the *Corpo Reale d'Artiglieria* (Royal Artillery Corps). However, the trained auxiliary gunners were happy to act as matrosses to help their sometimes-understaffed *Corpo Reale d'Artiglieria* colleagues in firing the pieces.

The problem of how to train the new recruits, who were fortunately arriving in large numbers, soon arose. The solution was to create a new independent company in each infantry regiment, dedicated to training. The *compagnia di riserva* was made up of officers and NCOs who were no longer able to cope with the rigours of the front line, as well as *caporali* and experienced soldiers in the same condition. Some of them were sent to the company on a temporary basis to await their full recovery so that they could return to their original company. The recruits underwent accelerated training but were not sent to their company until they were deemed fit. While in the company, recruits were also assessed by instructors and surgeons for physical fitness and mental toughness. If they were deemed unfit, they were discharged.

To recruit new soldiers, especially during the winter break, but at other times as well, the units sent an officer, a *sergente* and a *corporale* to the places where volunteers were concentrated to recruit them to their regiment, always in competition with other units. Recruits

---

6   AST, Ufficio Generale del Soldo, Livre des orders du Régiment Rochmondet, mazzo 74: Instruction provisional pour les Vivandiers, undated.

with military experience, which was not uncommon in the Kingdom of Sardinia given the large number of young men who had served in provincial regiments or veterans who had received a royal pardon for desertion, did not go through the reserve companies but were sent directly to the regiment, where they received the enlistment bonus.

The recruitment of Swiss troops was common in almost all European armies. In the Duchy of Savoy, the tradition had begun at the end of the sixteenth century, when *Duca* Emanuele Filiberto, unable to raise a large army, decided to bind the Swiss cantons to him with a non-aggression pact and the creation of a company of *Alabardieri Svizzeri* (Swiss halberdiers), within the Household troops of the Court of Turin.[7] The treaty of the following century also allowed the Dukes of Savoy to hire Swiss infantry as reinforcements for their army. From the beginning of the eighteenth century, some Savoyard-Swiss regiments became permanent, and they were not dismissed at the end of hostilities.

In 1791 there were three Swiss infantry regiments. The *de Courten* regiment (*Streng* from 1795) was recruited in the Catholic canton of Vallais. The other two were recruited in the Protestant cantons: the *Rochmondet* regiment (from 1794 *Stettler*) was the only one made up of three battalions, and the *Christ* regiment. Just before the war, a fourth regiment was raised, the *Schmidt* regiment, which was assigned to the garrison on the island of Sardinia and took virtually no part in the Alpine War. After various vicissitudes, the *Schmidt* regiment, made up of a single battalion, was on its way to the mainland from Sardinia and was shipwrecked in Corsica after a storm, where the British Army, always short of men, recruited its soldiers.

In 1793, proposals to raise new regiments were made by various Swiss officers following the news that the King of Sardinia intended to recruit more Swiss regiments. Three new regiments were raised from 1793 to 1794. The *Bachmann* regiment was the first. It was commanded by Nicolas Bachmann an der Lenz, baron of Näfels. Because of the Swiss reaction to the massacre of the Swiss Guards defending the Tuileries Palace in Paris, the regiment was able to recruit many men. Later, however, the *Zimmermann* regiment, under the command of Christian Emanuel Zimmermann of Hilferdingen in the canton of Lucerne, and the *Peyer-Imhof* regiment, commanded by Jean Conrad Peyer-Imhof of Schaffhausen had more difficulty in recruitment.

The role played by the six Swiss regiments in the Alpine War was not as decisive as that of the regiments of their fellow countrymen in the previous wars. The last two always had recruitment problems, to the point where they were relegated to defending the valleys inhabited by their Protestant co-religionists. The *11° Granatieri* was also deployed in the same valleys. It was made up of the grenadier companies of the last three regiments. In May 1794, about a hundred grenadiers of the *11°* were captured at the surrender of Fort Mirabocco, a small fortress for the defence of the Luserna valley, and their commander, *maggiore* Giorgio Mesmer, was prosecuted and shot for surrendering the fortress without a fight.[8]

---

7   E. Ricchiardi, 'Uniformi della Guardia Svizzera 1740–1831', *Armi Antiche*, 1985, pp.107–128.
8   P. Bianchi, *La guerra franco-piemontese e le valli valdesi (1792–1799)* (Torino: Claudiana, 2001), pp.73–117.

Getting the Provincial Infantry Units Ready to Fight

There were 14 provincial infantry regiments, each named after a province of the Kingdom, and the *Legione degli Accampamenti*. All were formed from the soldiers of the provincial levies. The latter were to be replaced by two battalions of *Granatieri Reali* and one of *Pionieri*, as they were unsuited to mountain warfare. The 14 provincial line infantry regiments were: *Genevois, Maurienne, Nizza, Ivrea, Torino, Vercelli, Mondovì, Asti, Pinerolo, Casale, Novara, Tortona, Acqui* and *Susa*.

The peculiar Piedmontese conscription of the time had different characteristics from the modern conscription that was abolished in Italy about two decades ago. According to it, men who were considered able-bodied made a personal commitment to serve in the army for a certain period of time. On the other hand, in the Kingdom of Sardinia of the eighteenth century, municipalities had to provide a certain number of conscripts in proportion to the number of male inhabitants. The obligation was not personal. It was communal. In times of peace, the conscripts had to join the regiment once or twice a year for a few days of training. In times of war, they served full-time. It was the responsibility of the communes to maintain the contingents assigned to them by replacing those who were discharged, died or deserted. Conscripts joined the regiment of their province, which was where most officers also came from. Often, officers from the nobility would ask to join a provincial regiment after a few years of service in an ordnance regiment. The lesser commitment required allowed them, while still strutting around in uniform, to have plenty of free time to look after their families, marry and manage their estates. In time of war, however, they too became fully operational. The system was well established and allowed for aggressive infantry regiments in the event of war, greatly limiting the cost of maintaining them in peacetime.[9]

On 11 July 1792, just before the outbreak of war, it was planned that the provincial regiments would be structured into a war battalion of 483 men and a second battalion, known as the garrison battalion, of only 356 men. In all, the strength of a provincial regiment in 1792 was 854 men. It was soon clear that these regiments would have to be reinforced in the face of the French.[10] This took place on 4 February 1793, bringing the strength of the provincial regiments up to par with the regiments of the ordnance.[11]

The sense of defending one's country and one's king with which these loyal troops went to fight the French is well documented by their bravery. They, too, were a thorn in the side of the French. While there are a few documented episodes of low morale, many others bear witness to their fighting spirit.

Of the 14 provincial infantry regiments, two, *Genevois* and *Maurienne*, were recruited in Savoy. With their recruitment area under the yoke of the enemy, hopes of maintaining their numbers were limited. Contrary to the King's fears, however, the Piedmontese regiments remained strong throughout the war, even with the contribution of volunteers. Many Savoyards, especially peasants and mountaineers, continued to fight for their king and, deeply Catholic, came to hate the French, who took pride in persecuting the clergy and

---

9   E. Ricchiardi, *Da milizia scelta a reggimenti provinciali: il potenziamento dell'esercito sabaudo dopo l'acquisizione della Sicilia (1713–1737)* (Torino: Centro Studi Piemontesi, 2014), pp.135–182.
10 AST, OGM, mazzo 69: État du Regiment Provincial, 11 July 1792.
11 AST, OGM, mazzo 70: Nuovo piede dei Reggimenti Provinciali, 4 February 1793.

turning monasteries into barracks or stables. These sentiments are borne out by the no less than 20 medals for valour to the soldiers of these two regiments: around 35 percent (20 out of 56) of all the medals awarded to the 14 provincial infantry regiments.[12]

A similar example of loyalty to the crown was provided by the youth of the County of Nice. After the occupation the city and its immediate surroundings, the regiment *Nizza* retreated with the rest of the army to the heights of the Val Roia, which they defended with particular bravery because, from the heights, many could see their villages occupied and harassed by the French. The regiment recruited most of the *1°* battalion in Nice, while the rest of the *1°* and *2°* battalions were recruited in the most populated province of Cuneo, on the other side of the Colle di Tenda. After the loss of Val Roia, the conscript contingent of the *Nizza* regiment was maintained by the voluntary enlistment of militiamen from Nice, who took an active part in the defence of the southern front.

In total, the provincial units had a wartime strength of almost 20,000 men. With the addition of a few thousand *Granatieri Reali* and *Pionieri*, the total number of provincial soldiers was around 22,000.

The *Reggimento Maurienne* Legend

Thanks to Charles-Albert Costa di Beauregard, who in 1878 published the memoirs and correspondence of his ancestor Henri Joseph Costa di Beauregard, who had written a diary of his personal impressions of the War of the Alps, we know the exciting story that circulated in the Piedmontese army in the spring of 1793 about the loyalty of the soldiers of the *Reggimento Maurienne* to the House of Savoy. Writing to his wife, who had left Savoy for Lausanne in Switzerland, Henri-Joseph told her the beautiful story of the restoration of the *Maurienne* after it had been disbanded during the retreat from Savoy in the autumn of 1792:

> By a misunderstood order, the *Maurienne* had been disbanded during the defeat that led to the invasion of our country last year. The men had returned to their homes and promised to assemble at Susa on 1 January of this year 1793. But it must be said that we [the Savoy officers who had retired to Piedmont] hardly expected them to keep their word after four months of Republican rule. But their *colonnello* had gone to Susa on the appointed day. He had marked out a bivouac in the snow, made fires and had some barracks built. Then, despite the terrible cold, the *colonnello* went for a walk in the Susa parade ground. My love, he did not wait long. At ten o'clock in the morning, the first soldier arrived. His name was Grillet and he came from Lanslevillard, one of the villages closest to Moncenisio. This brave boy had left home the day before on paths that could break his neck … He was followed by two *caporali* from Epierre, who had turned their uniforms inside out so as not to be recognised. After them, others appeared in groups of three or four from the most distant paths … it was wonderful to see the companies reforming. After five days, the regiment had regained two-thirds of its strength. When I learned all this,

---

12 Brancaccio, *Gli ordinamenti*, p.396.

I said to myself that if the King believed me, he would deprive certain nobles of my acquaintance of their honours and their cords, to adorn their breasts where the noblest hearts I know beat.[13]

Henri (1752–1824) was a Savoyard who belonged to the less wealthy nobility. In April 1792, when the situation in France deteriorated, he resumed his duties as an officer in the *Legione degli Accampamenti*, in which he had once served. In the late winter of 1793, when the Legion was disbanded, he became an officer in the *Granatieri Reali*. In the summer of 1793, he became *Baron* Colli's *aiutante maggiore*. In 1795, still with Colli, he was promoted to *luogotenente colonnello* and then to *colonnello*. He served as *quartiermastro* of the army corps.

The antecedent of the story he reported to his wife was the order he received on 23 September 1792, during the retreat from Savoy, from *conte* Sebastian de Villette de Chevron, *colonnello comandante* of the *Reggimento Maurienne*, to return to his home. He was warned to assemble in Susa in November. For this order, issued without prior authorisation, Chevron de Villette was brought before the Council of War on 8 December 1792. He was sentenced in absentia on 26 January 1793 to two years imprisonment in a fort and deprived of his rank for failing to return from Savoy. Seven other officers of the regiment, a *capitano luogotenente*, two *luogotenenti*, the same number of *sotto luogotenenti* and an *alfiere* were also stripped of their rank for failing to report to Susa in January 1793. The *alfiere* was a young cadet officer who entered the regiment in this role while awaiting promotion to *sotto luogotenente*.

The position of the troops was more complex: only 14 had obeyed the colonel's order to assemble at Susa in November 1792. Seven more hurriedly arrived in December. It was then that *luogotenente colonnello* Giuseppe Gioacchino Passerat, *marchese* di San Severino, commander of the *2° Battaglione* of the *Maurienne*, was promoted to *colonnello comandante* of the regiment (12 February 1793), with the task of rebuilding the regiment itself. He was the officer described by Henri as nervously walking around Susa in the cold of January 1793, waiting for his soldiers.

This is the story, but fortunately the muster rolls of the *Maurienne* from the first half of 1793 have been preserved and allow us to reconstruct what really happened.[14] The heroic soldier Grillet de Lanslevillard, who had arrived in Susa at ten o'clock in the morning, the brave boy who had left home the day before on a dangerous journey, and the two *caporali* of Epierre cannot be found in the muster rolls. It is easy to imagine how, as the story spread among the officials, the news was embellished and distorted. By the time it reached Henri Costa de Beauregard, it had reached epic proportions.

In fact, the reorganisation of the *Maurienne* took place at a time when the order to transform the garrison battalion into an operational battalion was about to be issued, increasing the number of men the regiment had to reach. The reorganisation also provided for the garrison battalion, now under the command of the new *colonnello*, to become the *1° Maurienne* and the old *1°* battalion to become the *2° Maurienne*. For these reasons, the soldiers returning from Savoy were reassigned to companies other than their original

---

13   C.A. Costa de Beauregard, *Un homme d'autrefois* (Paris: E. Plon, 1878), p.146.
14   AST, Ruolini di rivista, Reggimento Provinciale di Maurienne, mazzi 4 e 5.

ones, making the reconstruction of the facts more complicated. On 30 June 1793, the new strength of the *Maurienne* had not yet been reached. However, the regiment still numbered 933 men, most of them Savoyards, who had been able to cross the Alps thanks to the melting snow. In the meantime, however, the regiment was also in the process of recruiting soldiers from Piedmont and Valle d'Aosta. Recruitment continued, however, and by the summer, the regiment had reached a strength above that required, so much so that a company of *cacciatori* was formed to take part in the Siege of Toulon as part of the *2° Cacciatori*, and the companies of grenadiers reached sufficient strength to be included in the *7° Granatieri*. The regiment fought throughout the war on the northern front, mainly in the defence of the Moncenisio Pass and the Susa and Chisone valleys, and the *Maurienne* light infantrymen and grenadiers distinguished themselves in the elite battalions.

Always on the Front Line: The *Granatieri Reali*

The *Granatieri Reali* was an elite corps established on 21 January 1793. They were formed from the most aggressive provincial soldiers of the suppressed *Legione degli Accampamenti*. It was conceived as a line infantry regiment, and the men who had to form it were divided into two battalions of four companies of grenadiers, for a total of 872 men. However, the muster rolls of 1793 show that five companies were raised for each battalion instead of four, as the number of men was too high. From 1794 onwards, however, the number of companies returned to the number provided for in the founding document.

Throughout the war, *colonnello* Federico, *marchese* di Bellegarde, successfully commanded the *Granatieri Reali*. He continued to command them even when, on 16 February 1796, he was promoted to the rank of *brigadiere generale di fanteria* and given command of a division of the army corps sent to defend Ceva. Bellegarde's division included, in addition to the *1°* and *2° Granatieri Reali*, five other grenadier battalions and two fusilier battalions of the provincial *Reggimento Asti*.[15] *Luogotenente colonnello* Michele Angelo Rossi di Santarosa, *conte* di Pomerolo, commanded the *2° Battalion Granatieri Reali*, in place of the *luogotenente colonnello* Amedeo Ricci, *conte* d'Andon, who was mortally wounded on 29 June 1793 while leading the counterattack at Colle delle Traversette, near the Petit Saint Bernard pass.[16]

The two battalions included their respective staffs and an eleventh company of *cacciatori*. The latter had a contradictory role: the instruction of recruits and, in battle, the supply of men for advanced posts, a task typical of light infantrymen. It consisted of 127 men: a *capitano*, a *luogotenente*, a *sotto luogotenente*, two *trabanti* (officer's assistant), a *furiere*, a *sergente di compagnia*, a *sergente di plotone*, a *sergente sovrannumerario*, four *caporali*, two *caporali sovrannumerari* (supernumerary corporals), a *tamburino*, a *vivandiere*, 10 veteran privates and 100 recruits. The instruction of the recruits was the responsibility of the 10 veterans. As required by the charter, the company was certainly not qualified to act as a light force in the advanced posts. The mistake was rectified, and the *cacciatori* company was then called the *compagnia di riserva*, and a twelfth *cacciatori* company was created. It was

---

15 Lo Faso di Serradifalco, *La difesa di un regno*, pp.214–215.
16 AST, Ruolini di Rivista, Granatieri Reali, mazzo 1.

composed of the same commissioned officers and NCOs as infantry companies but it also included a *vivandiere*, a *frater* and 80 *cacciatori*.

The staff of the *1° Granatieri Reali*, which also acted as the regimental staff, consisted of 17 men: *aiutante maggiore di reggimento*, two *alfieri*, *quartiermastro*, *cappellano*, *sergente maggiore*, *tamburino maggiore*, *caporale maggiore* (corporal major – somewhere between the corporal and platoon sergeant), two *armaioli*, *falegname*, *prevosto* (regimental provost) and *arciere* (battalion or company provost). The staff of the second battalion consisted of the following men: *aiutante maggiore di battaglione*, two *alfieri*, *furiere*, two *assistenti del quartiermastro*, *scrivano* (clerk), *sotto cappellano*, *garzone chirurgo*, *sergente maggiore*, *caporale maggiore*, two *armaioli*, *falegname*, and *arciere*. In total, at their creation, the *Granatieri Reali* were to have a force of 1,069 men.[17]

Henri Costa de Beauregard, whom we have already met for the legend of the *Reggimento Maurienne*, was authorised by the sovereign to serve as a warrant officer in the *Granatieri Reali* to be at the side of his very young son Eugéne, who was commissioned as a *sotto luogotenente* and promoted to *luogotenente* on 14 October 1793.[18]

In his diary, Henri Costa vividly describes, in one of the rare testimonies of the period, the hardships of the precarious life of the *Granatieri Reali* during the bad weather of the spring season, camped at the best of times in the defensive positions located at over 2,000 metres on the Piccolo San Bernardo Pass. In a letter written towards the end of February 1793, he tells us that the *Granatieri Reali* were ordered to take up defensive positions on the pass while it was snowing. As quickly as possible barracks were erected in the positions for the protection of officers and men from the weather, but the accommodation was limited. There were 13 of them in the small one-room barrack allocated to the officers. But at least they stayed warm and, according to the diary, only went out when on duty. Soldiers in other barracks did the same, only going out to walk along the snow-covered paths leading to the outposts for sentry duty.

It was difficult to transport supplies from the village of La Thuile, where the corps headquarters was located, and only mules could be used. As a result, the companies on the line often went hungry and spent periods without any comfort. The column carrying the supplies had to cover almost 20 kilometres in the snow and on steep paths, climbing 500 metres. It was at least half a day's march. The food arrived frozen, and it was not easy for the soldiers to prepare it. Sometimes, the sutlers and their mules would manage to reach the companies in the line, but this was only a sporadic source of comfort. Henri Costa reports that sometimes the troops had to reach the outposts with only a little bread, which, if frozen, had to be broken with a *fucile* butt, and the ice melted to provide drinking water. Only the sentries had coats, and the officer on duty and his soldiers were hungry and shivering, the cold freezing their beards. But the *Granatieri Reali* stood their ground, in a demonstration of love for their country.[19]

Even the rest stops at La Thuile (1,492m) were spent in very cold conditions with lots of snow, but at least the rustic accommodation was more comfortable and the food more regular. Despite this, the muster rolls do not show many casualties that winter; these

---

17 AST, OGM, mazzo 70: Determinazioni di S.M. per i Granatieri Reali, 21 Jan 1793.
18 Lo Faso di Serradifalco, *La difesa di un regno*, pp.306–307.
19 Costa de Beauregard, *Un homme d'autrefois*, pp.14–15.

would come as the season improved and the French attacked, but deaths from disease were numerous. Abbot Fenoil, who was in charge of the church at La Thuile, reported that there were many sick and that many of them could not be saved by the *chirurgo maggiore* and his assistant, at a time when treatment was still sketchy, and antibiotics were not yet discovered. The small local cemetery was overflowing, and a new cemetery had to be opened to bury the dead.[20]

In August 1793, the *Granatieri Reali* took part in the unsuccessful attempt to invade Savoy. After returning to the Valle d'Aosta, they were sent to the Piedmontese plains to winter and reorganise. Their behaviour during the advance and the subsequent retreat from Savoy was reported to the King. This was probably done by the *duca* del Monferrato himself, who commanded the army corps. On 19 December 1793, Vittorio Amedeo III was in receipt of the report and praised the corps for its behaviour.[21] Moreover, on 22 February 1794, when the *Granatieri Reali* received the order to leave their winter headquarters in Asti to take part in the defence of the Val Roia, the route was slightly extended so that they would pass by the Royal Castle of Moncalieri, a few kilometres from Turin, where the King had gone to inspect and congratulate them. We can imagine that the grenadiers, having rested and re-equipped themselves during the winter break, proudly paraded, preceded by the Turkish band and the flags.

The corps resumed its march and by 9 March had already reached the threshold of the Val Roia, the Colle di Tenda, still covered in snow. From the colle, the corps moved on to the mountains of the valley, where the lines were laid out to be fully operational in the spring.

Again, Henri Costa gives us an insight into the life of the *Granatieri*'s in these mountains: 'We arrived at Authion in the pouring rain and found no wood for heating or houses to live in.' It was a situation very similar to the one that the *Granatieri Reali* had already experienced in the Valle d'Aosta. They had been among the first to be sent to the positions to be defended. At that time, the supply and accommodation situation was still precarious. Henri went on to describe his situation: 'I have a door, a window and a path that leads to my cave; my hole is big enough for my bed.' But he was an officer, and of course the soldiers were organised as best they could. They were waiting for the mules to arrive with tents, provisions, ammunition and all the necessary equipment.[22]

Thus continued the difficult life of the *Granatieri Reali*, who fought on the southern front until the end of the war, taking part in the last resistance between Ceva and Mondovì in April 1796.

---

20 Fenoil, *La Terreur sur les Alpes*, pp.12–16.
21 OGM, mazzo 71: Letter from the King to the Granatieri Reali, praising them for the way they had behaved, 19 December 1793.
22 Costa di Beauregard, *Un homme d'autrefois*, pp.210–211.

4

Infantry Uniforms, Flags and Equipment

The colourful uniforms of Vittorio Amedeo III's reign were probably the most elegant worn by the Piedmontese army in the eighteenth century. Obviously, exposed to the weather and mostly without overcoats, dusty or muddy, the soldiers of the War of the Alps must have looked very bedraggled most of the time. But they looked better than their enemies. According to the sources, the French soldiers lacked everything and were often described as starving and shoeless, and perhaps because of this, they fought with an irrepressible fury. They were eager to clothe themselves and to plunder what they could. It was a fury that baffled the enemy and was often a guarantee of victory.

We will, however, describe the Piedmontese army uniforms as they were laid down in the regulations. We will also show them as they were depicted in the numerous figures drawn by private artists in the patriotic frenzy of the war.[1]

Vittorio Amedeo III's basic uniform was inspired by that of the Prussian army. It consisted of a dark blue coat, tight but not too tight, as worn by Frederick II's soldiers. The two tails of the coat were so long that they were four fingers off the ground when the soldier knelt. Other basic features of the uniform were a turned collar, cuffs that narrowed according to the fashion of the time, and the presence of lapels and pocket flaps, which were always horizontal and had three buttonholes. Regiments differed in the colour of collar, cuffs, lapels and turnbacks, and the metal of buttons: tin or brass, or silver or gold for officers and *sergenti*. The buttons were arranged with seven for each lapel, the row continuing below the right lapel with three more, three under each pocket flap, two at the kidneys, five perpendicular to the sides of each sleeve (two to button the cuffs, and another three in a row above the cuffs themselves to close the opening). A smaller button held the blue epaulette strap near the neck, which was sewn to the left shoulder. It kept the cartridge box bandoleer, of those equipped with it, secure across the shoulder.

The turnbacks, with a small heart-shaped head covered with fabric in the colour of the lining or the cuffs, were held in the corners by two hooks (*crochet*). If the lining was white, the turnback ornament was dark blue.

The *Reggimento Guardie* was distinguished by frogs ending in a tassel. They were made of white wool for *caporali* and enlisted men, and of silver and silver silk for *sergenti* and officers.

---

1   Ricchiardi, *Iconografia militare sabauda*.

The coats of the soldiers of the provincial infantry regiments were identical to those of the ordnance. The only difference was that the six lower buttons of the seven that adorned the lapel were arranged in pairs.

The black felt tricorn the troops wore had a reduced front point, in keeping with the fashion of the time. Depending on the metal of the buttons, the wings were bordered with a narrow lace of white or yellow goat's hair for the troops, or silver or gold lace for officers and *sergenti*. On the left of the tricorn was a blue cockade, held in place by a white or silver lace sewn on top and buttoned at bottom with a regimental metal button. Soldiers wore a black neckcloth around their necks, but for aesthetic reasons this was red for regiments with a black collar. The only exception to this rule was the red neckcloth of the *Reggimento Reale Alemanno*, which had a white collar but was allowed to wear red neck cloths.

Line infantry waistcoats and breeches were white, with regimental buttons. The breeches reached just below the knee. They were buttoned at the sides of each leg with three small uniform buttons. The long black gaiters had a white knee pad and were buttoned at the side with small uniform buttons.

Where troops were allowed to serve in white waistcoats, the regiment to which they belonged was identified by the collar being the colour of the coat's lining or blue if it was white. The cuffs were the same colour as the coat, but, again, blue if the coat was white. When serving in a waistcoat, soldiers could take off the tricorn hat and wear a woollen cap called a *bonetto*, the colour of which was not regulated but was probably decided by the *colonnello*, who chose one of the distinctive colours.

The shoes were made of leather, with a relatively high heel and brass buckles on the front. The latter were protected and covered by the gaiters, which were fastened under the shoes with a strap.

The uniform was supplied and renewed every three years by the tailor who had the periodic contract. Usually, the most worn parts, such as the waistcoat and especially the breeches, were provided more frequently. The old uniform remained with the soldier, who wore it in ordinary service and kept the new one for exercises and parades. During the war, the accelerated wear and tear of wartime activities often led to deviations from these rules. It was not uncommon to read urgent requests from *colonnelli* complaining about the poor condition of uniforms, which soldiers often had to wear for long periods of time, even at night when they were resting, without being able to change or wash them while they were near the front. The military administration responded to the requests as best it could, with one eye on cost and the other on urgency.

The distinctive colours of the regiments, both national and foreign, and of the provincial infantry regiments are summarised in the colour plates. In a few cases during the war, difficulty in obtaining cloth of a particular colour for the linings forced some regiments to change their colours on a temporary basis, but this did not become a permanent change.

The officers did not receive their uniforms from the *Ufficio Generale del Soldo* but had them made at their expense by a tailor who was familiar with the regulations and, therefore, able to provide uniforms that were perfectly in keeping with their requirements. They were made of finer fabrics than the plain cloth used for the troops. If the officer was garrisoned in Turin or another important city, he would go to the tailor personally. Alternatively, officers garrisoned in smaller towns could have their uniforms commissioned by relatives. They would know the officer's measurements and send them by courier.

During the War of the Alps, the officers also had a pair of identical uniforms, one new and in better condition and the other older and worn out, for use in everyday life and on the campaign. As far as the line infantry were concerned, the only exception was the *Reggimento Guardie*, whose officers had a full uniform with embroidered frogs ending in a tassel, and a pair of identical small frog-and-gallon uniforms for the same purposes as their colleagues in the other regiments. The full uniform was reserved for service with the King or at court, and in most cases the officers probably did not even wear it on campaign.

Clothed in the best quality and with rank distinctions and gold or silver buttons, the officers were also clearly distinguished from their subordinates by the sashes and epaulettes that adorned both shoulders of the coat. For all ranks, the epaulettes were formed with gold or silver lace in four rows, at the outer edge of which a *graine d'èpinard* bullion fringe one and a half *ounces* long (about 6.5cm; the Piedmontese *ounce* was approximately 4.3cm) fell from the shoulders. Commissioned officers' coat rank distinctions are shown in Table 2.

Table 2 Officer Rank Distinctions.

Rank	Facing	Collar	Pocket flap
Colonnello	Five lace rows border	Two lines border	No laces
Luogotenente colonnello	Five lace rows border	One line border	No laces
Maggiore di brigata	Single-line lace border and then a separate double-line lace	One line border	No laces
Maggiore di battaglione	Three lace rows border	One line border	No laces
Capitano	Two lace rows border	One line border	No laces
Luogotenente	No laces	One line border	No laces
Sotto luogotenente and insegna	No laces	No laces	No laces
Aiutante maggiore di brigata	Bordered by its own rank	One line border	Two lines border
Aiutante maggiore di battaglione	Bordered by its own rank	One line border	One line border

Another distinction of the officers was the heart-shaped turnback ornaments that were the same colour as those of the troops but edged in gold or silver. Finally, when on duty, officers wore a rich gold and blue sash around their waists, with the amount of gold increasing with rank.

NCO rank distinctions were formed with simple gold or silver laces, like those used to distinguish officers, and are summarised in Table 3.

Table 3 *Sergente* Rank Distinctions.

Rank	Collar	Facing	Pocket flap
Sergente maggiore	Single lace row border	Single-line lace border and then a separate double-line lace	Single lace row border
Sergente di compagnia	Single lace row border	Single-line lace border and then a separate double-line lace	No laces
Sergente di plotone	Single lace row border	Three lace rows border	No laces

The *sergenti maggiori*, who were part of the battalion staff and whose duties were mainly administrative and educational, were important NCOs whose uniforms were decorated with gold or silver rank laces but differed from other *sergenti* in that their coat pocket flaps were trimmed with a single line of lace. As they did not carry out operational duties, they were not armed with a *fucile* and the necessary accessories to use it. A *sergente maggiore* of the *Reggimento Guardie*, thus equipped and dressed in the rich regimental uniform, is shown in colour plate 5. He is armed with a *sergente*'s sabre and carries a walking stick with a silver knob and a blue dragoon knot. This was not official issue but followed the fashion.

The *sergenti di compagnia* and *sergenti di plotone* had the same weapons as the troops. They did not carry a bandoleer cartridge box, but a small *patrona* (small cartridge box) worn at the waist with no ornaments, which contained eight cartridges. The *sergenti*'s cartridge boxes in grenadier companies had a brass bursting grenade in the centre of the lid as a symbol of distinction. In addition to the grenade, the *sergenti* of the *Reggimento Guardie* had a row of silver lace around their cartridge box to further distinguish them. The company and platoon *sergenti* wore a short cane as a symbol of their authority, which hung by a sword knot at the second button of the left lapel. This cane was probably a remnant of the *sergentina*, the short halberd with which *sergenti* were equipped in the past.

The appearance of a *caporali* is clearly seen in colour plate 5. As shown in Table 4, they were distinguished by yellow or white lace. The *caporale maggiore* shared administrative and training duties with the *sergente maggiore* and because of that his uniform included a border on the pocket flaps of the coat and a walking cane.

Table 4 *Caporale* Rank Distinctions.

Rank	Collar	Facing	Pocket flap
Caporale maggiore	Single lace row border	Single-line lace border and then a separate three-line lace	Single lace row border
Caporale	Single lace row border	Three lace rows border	No laces
Caporale Sovrannumerario	Single lace row border	Two lace rows border	No laces

Granatieri, including officers, were distinguished by a line of wavy lace, the *serpentou* (serpentine chevrons) on the facings, yellow or white for the troops, gold or silver for *sergenti* and officers. The wavy lace embroidered in silver on the officers of the *Reggimento Guardie* was the only exception.

Granatieri sometimes wore a blackened bearskin cap instead of the tricorn. The back of the bearskin cap was lined with a blue piece of cloth. At the back, the cap ended in a cloth tail. The colour of the tail was chosen by the *colonnello* from those of the cuffs or the lining of the coat. Depending on the metal of the regimental buttons, the lace used to decorate the tail of the cap and the terminal tassel was white or yellow. The tails of *sergenti* and officers were usually decorated with gold or silver lace. To protect the cap from the elements, it could be covered with a waterproofed, waxed canvas cover with a bursting grenade painted on the front.[2]

---

2 AST, Ufficio Generale del Soldo, Contratti provviste diverse (Cpd), Mazzo 113: Contratto con il pellicciaio Chinet per la fornitura di bonetti ai granatieri, 22 April 1791.

There are no precise specifications for the officers' bearskin caps. The latter were probably supplied by the royal furrier Gio Batta Chinet (sometimes Quinet), who was the supplier of the soldiers' bearskin caps and knew their required form and ornamentation. All bearskin caps were decorated on the front with a stamped brass plate, gold for officers, surrounded by a double relief border with the Savoy spread eagle in the centre. The eagle is surrounded by flag trophies. The regimental arms, identical to those on the flags, were stamped on the eagle's breast.

A distinctive feature of the grenadiers was the *cache-mêche* (matchbox) attached to the front of their belt, which contained the slow match used to light the fuse of the hand grenade from which they took their name. These grenades had long since fallen into disuse due to their ineffectiveness, but the grenadiers had kept the matchbox as another symbol of their status. An additional distinctive feature of the grenadiers' equipment was the small axe that hung from their belt. It could be used during attacks to break down enemy defences, to prepare defences – cutting logs to build obstacles to the enemy's advance and shelter the defenders – or to provide wood for the daily fires.

The *cacciatori* were also equipped with a small axe attached to their belt and wore a wavy lace, identical to that of the grenadiers, but placed on the sleeves facing the cuffs.

Specialists such as armourers, carpenters and a platoon of auxiliary gunners were assigned to the infantry battalions. The first two of these wore the regimental uniform of a private soldier but with a few peculiarities. Like the grenadiers, they wore a bearskin cap. The only difference was the design of the brass plate on the front, which showed two crossed axes. They were armed with a pistol, carried at the bottom of a long, narrow bandolier from the left shoulder to the end of the left tail of the coat. On their front, they wore a large apron of natural leather with an irregular lower edge and a pouch at the waist to carry what was needed to fire the pistol. In addition to the sabre, the carpenters were equipped with a large axe, which they carried on the right shoulder during parades, with the edge of the iron facing forward.

The auxiliary gunners wore the regimental uniform. However, they had blue waistcoats and breeches, the colour of the *Corpo Reale d'Artiglieria*. In addition to the sabre, they wore a long, narrow, white bandoleer, like those worn by carpenters. It held the *polverino*, a blackened leather powder holder with a brass mouthpiece and spring lid that contained the gunpowder. They were also equipped with the *buttafuoco*. This was a wooden stick to which the fuse was attached, ready to be lit for firing the artillery piece. It is probable that during the war the auxiliary gunners abandoned the special bandoleer and carried the powder over their shoulder by means of a blue cord.

The *prevosto* wore the regimental uniform but without lapels.

The *tamburo maggiore* of the *Reggimento Guardie*, a *sergente*, wore a richly chevroned regimental coat. It was decorated with a blue bandoleer bordered with silver laces, which ran from the right shoulder to the left side of the body. It ended with a drumstick holder, which held two small drumsticks as a symbol of their function. Finally, at chest height, the bandoleer bore a silver brass plate with the regimental emblems. Their counterparts in the other infantry regiments decorated their coats less conspicuously due to the absence of the embroidered silver frogs.

When the two battalions of a regiment operated in different locations, which was the norm during the Alpine War, the *tamburo maggiore* remained with the first battalion, while a senior drummer with the rank of *caporale tamburino* took his place in the second battalion.

The drummers of the fusiliers and grenadiers wore a regimental uniform decorated with a drummer's lace (white with a blue wavy lace in the middle) bordering the collar, the cuffs and the lapels. Pointed frogs without tassels were formed on the three buttons under the right lapel and the corresponding loops on the left, three on the pocket flaps, three on the sleeves on the three buttons that closed them and probably two on the back buttons at waist level. Grenadier drummers and fifers also wore a bearskin cap identical to that of the grenadiers but with a drummer's laces instead of the simple one worn by their peers.

Before the war, it was decided that drums should be made of brass. This produced a more audible sound than wooden drums. Brass proved to be a good compromise between lightness and strength. With the war and the increased need for brass plates for the rapid mobilisation of all European armies, these became difficult and too expensive to obtain. So, the Piedmontese army resumed the supply of wooden drum shells, of which local production was sufficient. Of course, the brass drums that had already been in circulation were still being used. They had wooden hoops that were painted with alternating diagonal lines in blue and white. The wooden cases had blue shells with the regimental crest painted in oil in the centre.

Fifers were also found in the ranks of both the fusiliers and the grenadiers. In addition to the fife, the fifers of the grenadiers were sometimes given flutes, for reasons we do not know. The uniform of the fife players was identical to that of the drummers but with the addition of a swallow's neck ornament made of drummer's lace on the shoulders. Curiously, this ornament was soon adopted by the drummers and became known as the *tamburine* (drummer's shoulder ornament).

It was envisaged that hunting horn players would be attached to the companies of the light infantrymen. These wore the regimental uniform, with sleeves decorated with the special white and blue wavy lace, and collar and cuffs bordered on one side by a half a chevron.[3]

In 1774, while maintaining the traditional distinction between the *colonnella* (colonel's flag) and the *ordinanza* (ordnance flag), the King decided to replace the flags of the infantry regiments with new ones. The first battalion of each regiment was given two flags, one, the colonel's, with the symbolism of belonging to the King of Sardinia's army and the other with the regimental colours and badges. The second battalion, however, received two identical battalion flags.

The new flags were smaller in size than those previously in use, from 220 to about 180cm. The colonels' flags maintained the Savoy eagle surmounted by the royal crown of Sardinia, but with downturned wings. They were surrounded with the ribbon of the Sovereign Order of Saints Maurice and Lazarus, and those of ordnance had a white border decorated with a blue wavy ribbon. All the flags were divided into four quarters by the large white Savoy cross, which reached to the edge. The first and third corners were blue, the second and fourth the colour of the lapels. The wavy flames, rising from the outer corners of the colonels' flags and from those of the cross of the ordnance flags, were the colour of the coat's lining. The flames were edged with a narrow band of gold or silver, depending on the metal of the regimental

---

3　E. Ricchiardi, *Musicisti in uniforme. L'arte dei suoni nell'esercito sabaudo* (Lucca: Lim, 2019), pp.33–60.

buttons. The eagle of the colonels' flags showed the regimental arms on its breast. That of the *Reggimento Guardie* showed the great arms of the Kingdom of Sardinia, while the colonel's flag of the *Reggimento La Regina* the same great arms flanked by the arms of the Royal House of Bourbon, the queen's house. The other regiments showed the regimental arms, quartered with the old Savoy eagle with the modern Savoy arms in the breast. The flags were surrounded by a large white band with inside the blue *gallone ondeggiante alla Sarda* (Sardinian-style wavy chevron).

The King also decided to distinguish the flags of the provincial infantry regiments with small wavy flames of the colour of the background of the quarter placed inside the larger ones.[4]

The staffs were wooden, about 310cm long, including the brass end, and covered with crimson velvet. The latter was fixed to the staff by means of brass-headed nails arranged in three vertical lines and protected by a brass ring in the part that rested on the ground. The finial was a small spearhead, measuring about 17cm (see colour plate 9). The cord knotted under the spearhead was made of blue interlaced gold or silver threads and was about 120cm long, including the tassels at each end. Finally, a blue taffeta cravat, without fringes, measuring about 110cm in length was also tied under spearhead.

Granatieri Reali Uniforms, Flags and Equipment

The *Granatieri Reali* uniforms were initially the same as those of the *Legione degli Accampamenti*, with the addition of wavy lace on the cuffs and the grenadier's bearskin cap with white tail and regimental plate. As in the original corps, the buttons were alternately brass and tin (gold and silver for officers and NCOs). However, it was planned that the first issue of new uniforms would have brass, or gold plated. The same was done with the laces, white/yellow for the soldiers and silver/gold for NCOs and officers, which became yellow or gold.

The esteem in which Victor Amadeus III held the corps was also reflected in the numerous distinctions awarded over time, which were rare in the Piedmontese army. On 29 July 1793, the King approved two of these special distinctions. The grenadiers' cartridge box was decorated with four brass exploding grenades in the corners and a stamped brass plaque in the centre. We have no drawings or illustrations of the latter, but it probably bears in relief the letters G.R. for *Granatieri Reali*, as we see on the brass plate of the bearskin cap (colour plate 10). Like their colleagues in the line infantry, the elite company of the corps, the *cacciatori*, were distinguished by the wavy lace on their sleeves. However, as a special distinction, they wore a hat with a high crown, of which we again have no drawing or representation. They also decorated their cartridge box with four brass hunting horns with the same plaque in the centre as the grenadiers.

Finally, a further specific adornment was granted to the *Granatieri Reali* on 16 May 1795: a brass grenade surmounted by a red tassel on the tricorn cap, often worn as an alternative to the bearskin cap.[5]

---

4   Ricchiardi, *Bandiere e stendardi*, pp.151–231.
5   S. Ales, *Le regie truppe sarde*, p.145.

The *Legione degli Accampamenti*, from which the *Granatieri Reali* originated, was made up of three battalions, each of four companies. In 1777, Vittorio Amedeo III decided that each company would have a guidon, flame edged in white with a wavy ribbon in the middle. The ribbon was the colour of the tassel of the tricorn that distinguished the company. However, a finial in the shape of an eagle adorned the *1a Compagnia* of each battalion. The flame of the *1a Compagnia* of the *1° Battaglione*, which acted as the *colonnella*, had a completely red edge and no wavy ribbon to distinguish it.

The *Granatieri Reali*, formed in 1793 from two battalions of four companies each, joined together two by two in *centuria*, were allowed to choose four of the Legion's guidons, one for each *centuria*. We do not know which ones the *colonnello* chose, but we can assume that three were eagle finials and the fourth, which was the grenadiers' characteristic colour, was the red wavy ribbon guidon. It is likely that the cravats of three of the cornets were kept in the colour of the wavy ribbon, while the *colonnello* wore a blue cravat knotted under the finial (colour plate 10).

In fact, these guidons were used in battles. This is confirmed by the Silver Medal for Military Valour awarded on 3 June 1794 to *sergente sovrannumerario* Teobaldo Dadone, for his heroism on 27 April of the same year. During the French attack on the summit of Monte Saccarello (2,200m), a peak in the Val Roia, he recovered the guidon that had already been taken by a French officer, killing him.[6]

Regimental Bands

The King encouraged the formation of military bands in all national ordnance infantry regiments because of his passion for parades. Each band was made up of eight musicians. They were called hautboists, although they actually played oboes, bassoons and hunting horns. They would be joined in the parades by the musicians of the various companies to increase the number of musicians.

Later, *bande turche* (Turkish bands), also called *bande albanesi* (Albanian bands), were formed, which included trumpets, cymbals, bass drums, rolling drums, triangles and other instruments. This kind of rhythmic band, which was typical of the Islamic world and which was unknown in Piedmont until then, became very popular.

In the Piedmontese army, the *tamburo maggiore* was the leader of companies' musicians and, when it existed, the leader of the *banda turca*. When the *banda turca* played together with the hautbois band, they formed the *grande banda* (great band), led by the regimental *capo musica* (music leader) and subordinated to the *tamburo maggiore*.

There were also regiments that did not have a hautbois band and only had the *banda turca*. As we have seen, this was the case with the *Granatieri Reali*. There were also special cases. Instead of the traditional band, the *Reggimento Savoia* was authorised to adopt a *piccola banda* (small band), consisting mainly of clarinettists. In line with a European trend that had developed in the last quarter of the eighteenth century, this instrument began to replace the oboes in Piedmont too.[7]

---

6 LUF, OGM, mazzo 72: Award of silver medals for valour, 3 June 1794.
7 Ricchiardi, *Musicisti in uniforme*, pp.33–60.

Browsing through the muster rolls of the War of the Alps era, one reads that in the bands, even in the Turkish ones, men belonging to families of musicians, such as the Avenati, who included many skilled players, came gladly to enrol. The musicians also came to contribute to the defence of Piedmont, accepting the uncertainties and inconveniences of military life.[8]

Before the war, the provincial infantry regiments did not include a band in their personnel, as it was considered expensive and unnecessary, as they only met for a few weeks a year to practise and be inspected. However, during the Alpine War, these regiments were active, and some *colonnelli* asked for permission to organise a band. The King agreed, knowing that it was necessary to maintain the morale of the troops who were working hard in the conflict. And so, on 18 March 1793, the commander of the *Granatieri Reali* was authorised to set up a Turkish band consisting of 15 musicians.[9]

It took more than a year for the King to agree, on 30 May 1794, to the unusual request of the officers of the provincial *Reggimento Mondovì*, who asked for permission to form a small Turkish band of eight volunteers at their own expense but who asked the military administration to pay their salaries, the soldiers' food and a contribution towards their uniforms.[10] Once the proposal had been approved, the regiment began to recruit musicians, which exceeded the most optimistic expectations as 10 musicians presented themselves, allowing the *colonnello* to choose the best eight. A few months later, the request was repeated by the officers of the provincial *Reggimento Asti*, who, on 14 February 1795, obtained the sovereign's permission for a Turkish band like that of the *Reggimento Mondovì*.[11]

The most precious decoration that adorned the fine uniforms of band musicians was no longer issued during the War of the Alps. It was absurd to spend money on fine uniforms that could rarely be worn by musicians placed at the rear of their regiments. It was instead decided to use uniforms with simplified decorations that could be easily maintained and replaced when worn. However, even these were probably only worn for concerts or important occasions and were replaced daily by a simple soldier's uniform. This was at least the case for the bands formed during the war. The earlier bands, which had the richer uniforms distributed before the war, would have used them in the towns where their unit was stationed during the winter breaks, playing for the regiment, but also in theatres and at gatherings for the entertainment of the citizens.

---

8   AST, Ruolini di rivista. Several mazzi 1792–1796.
9   AST, OGM, mazzo 70: Turkish band granted to the *Granatieri Reali*, 18 March 1793.
10 AST, OGM, mazzo 72: Turkish band granted to regiment *Mondovì*, 30 May 1794.
11 AST, OGM, mazzo 74: Turkish band granted to regiment *Asti*, 14 February 1795.

Colour Plate 1.
A: *Luogotenente Generale*. **B:** *Maggior Generale*. **C:** *Brigadiere Generale*. **D:** *Ufficiale del Soldo* in 1793 pattern uniform. **E:** *Palafreniere* of *Treno di Provianda*. **F:** *Milizia valdese* (Waldesian militia), *barbetti*. **G:** *Cacciatori di Camoscio*. **H:** Generals' lace. (Anne S.K. Brown Military Collection)

Colour Plate 2.
Fucilieri of national regiments. **A:** *Guardie*. **B:** *Piemonte*. **C:** *Monferrato*. **D:** *Lombardia*. *Fucilieri* of foreign regiments. **E:** *Reale Alemanno*. **F:** *Peyer-In-Hof*. (Anne S.K. Brown Military Collection)

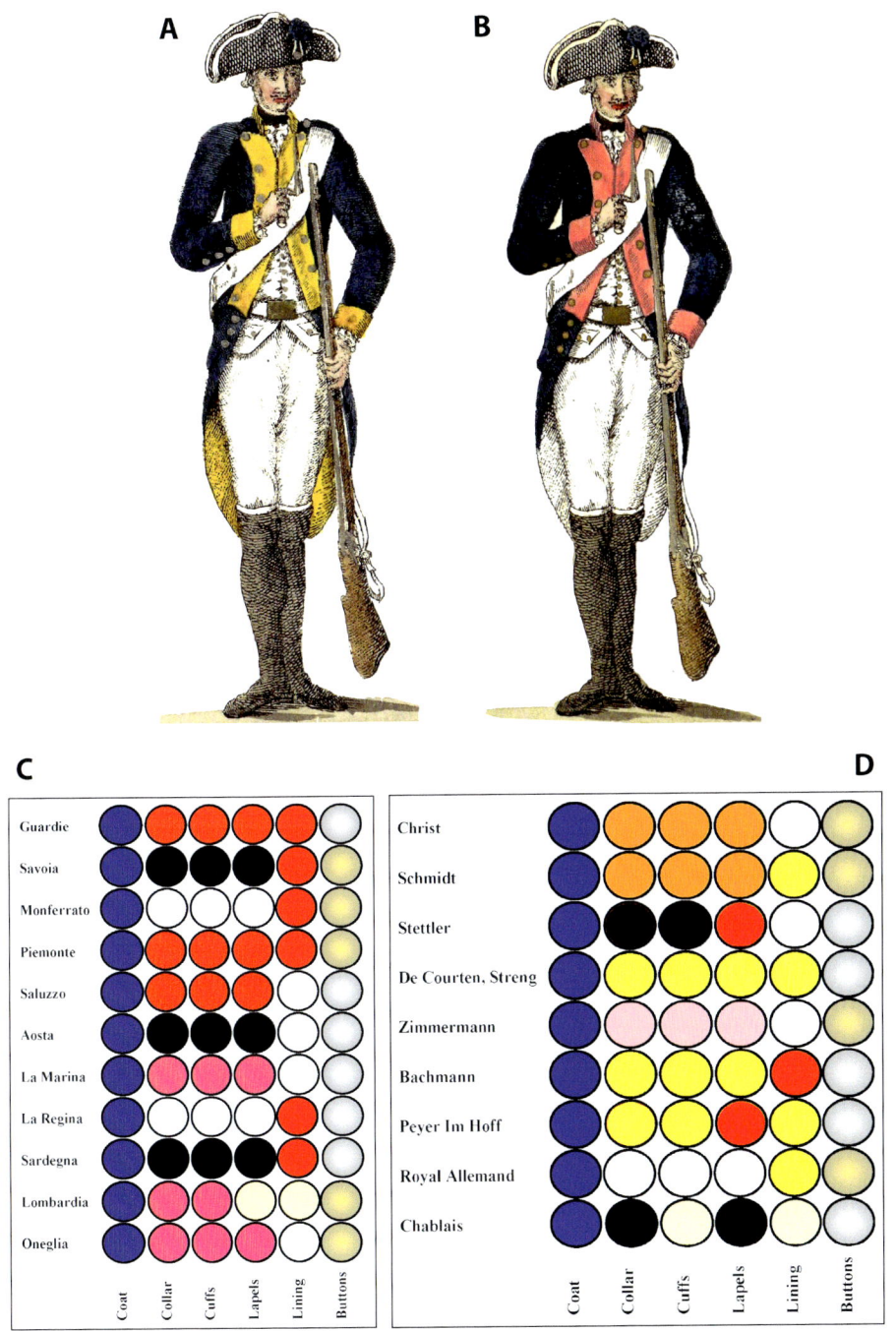

Colour Plate 3.
Fucilieri of foreign regiments. **A:** *Streng.* **B:** *Zimmerman.* (Anne S.K. Brown Military Collection) **C:** Distinctive colours of the national regiments. **D:** Distinctive colours of the foreign regiments. (Author's illustration)

Colour Plate 4.
Fucilieri of provincial infantry regiments. **A:** *Susa*. **B:** *Torina*. **C:** *Maurienne*. **D:** *Nizza*. **E:** *Vercelli*. **F:** *Casale*. **G:** *Novara*. **H:** *Genevois*. (Anne S.K. Brown Military Collection) **I:** Distinctive colours of the provincial regiments. (Author's illustration)

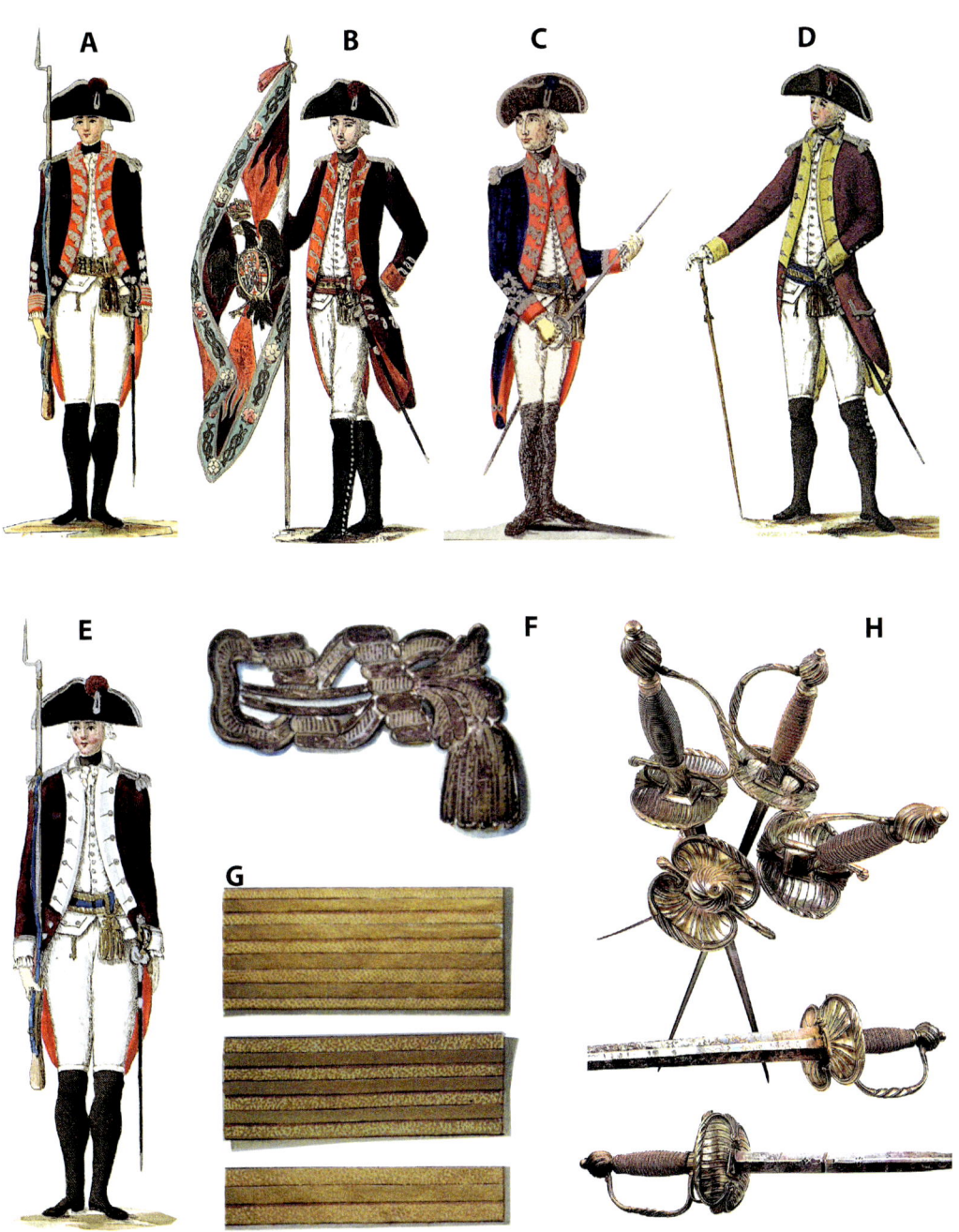

Colour Plate 5.
National regiment infantry officer's uniforms. **A:** *Colonnello, Guardie.* **B:** *Insegna, Guardie.* **C:** *Capitano, Guardie.* **D:** *Aiutante Maggiore di battaglione, de Courten.* **E:** *Capitano, La Regina.* **F:** Silver frogs, *Guardie.* **G:** Rank laces. (Anne S.K. Brown Military Collection) **H:** Infantry officers' sword, 1774 pattern. (With the kind permission of the Centro Studi Piemontesi)

Colour Plate 6.
Line infantry NCOs **A:** *Sergente maggiore, Guardie*. **B:** *Sergente, Savoie, granatieri*. **C:** *Sergente, Monferrato, cacciatori*. **D:** *Caporale maggiore, Saluzzo*. **E:** *Caporale, Real Alemanno, fucilieri*. (Anne S.K. Brown Military Collection) **F:** NCO and bandsman sabre, *Guardie*. **G:** NCO, or possibly bandsman, sabre, other line infantry regiments. (With the kind permission of the Centro Studi Piemontesi)

Colour Plate 7.
Infantry bandsmen's and company musicians' uniforms. **A:** *tamburo Maggiore, Guardie.* **B:** *Tamburino, Saluzza, granatieri.* **C:** *Tamburino, Saluzza, fucilieri.* **D:** *Piffero, Piemonte.* **E:** *Corno da caccia, Savoie.* **F:** *Oboe, Piemonte* **G:** *Oboe, Monferrato.* (Anne S.K. Brown Military Collection)

Colour Plate 8.
A: *Granatiere, Guardie.* **B:** *Falegname, Savoie.* **C:** Relationship of infantry flag colours to regimental uniforms. (Anne S.K. Brown Military Collection) **D:** Grenadier's matchbox and bearskin cap brass plates of *La Regina* and *La Marina*. (Private collection)

Colour Plate 9.
Line infantry 1774 pattern *bandiere*. **A:** *Colonnella* and *ordinanza*, *La Regina*. **B:** *Colonnella* and *ordinanza*, *La Marina*. **C:** *Colonnella* and *ordinanza*, *Maurienne*. **D:** *Colonnella* and *ordinanza*, *Nizza*. (Anne S.K. Brown Military Collection) **E:** Reproduction bronze finial, 1774 pattern. (Author's collection)

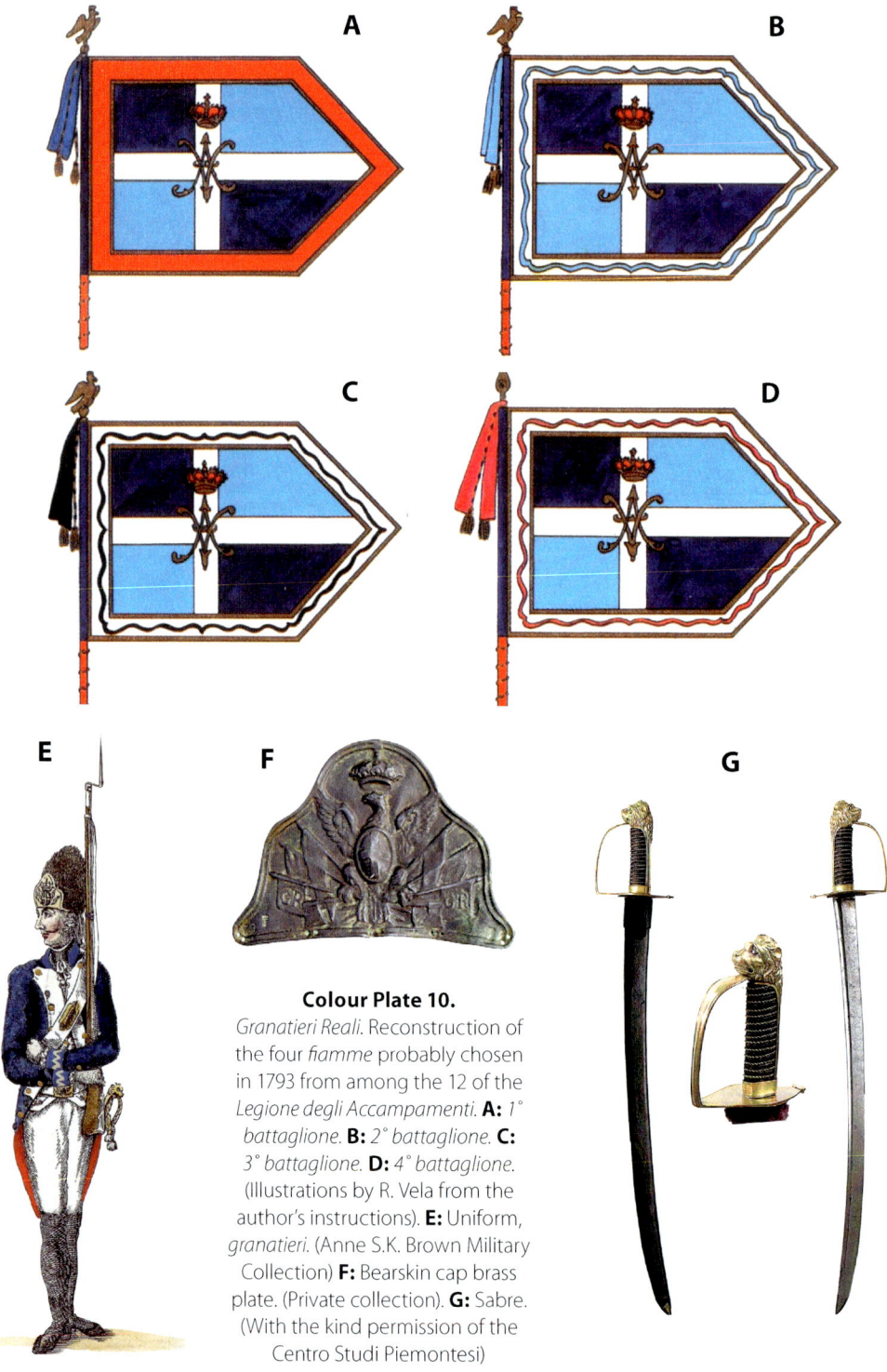

Colour Plate 10.
Granatieri Reali. Reconstruction of the four *fiamme* probably chosen in 1793 from among the 12 of the *Legione degli Accampamenti*. **A:** *1° battaglione*. **B:** *2° battaglione*. **C:** *3° battaglione*. **D:** *4° battaglione*. (Illustrations by R. Vela from the author's instructions). **E:** Uniform, *granatieri*. (Anne S.K. Brown Military Collection) **F:** Bearskin cap brass plate. (Private collection). **G:** Sabre. (With the kind permission of the Centro Studi Piemontesi)

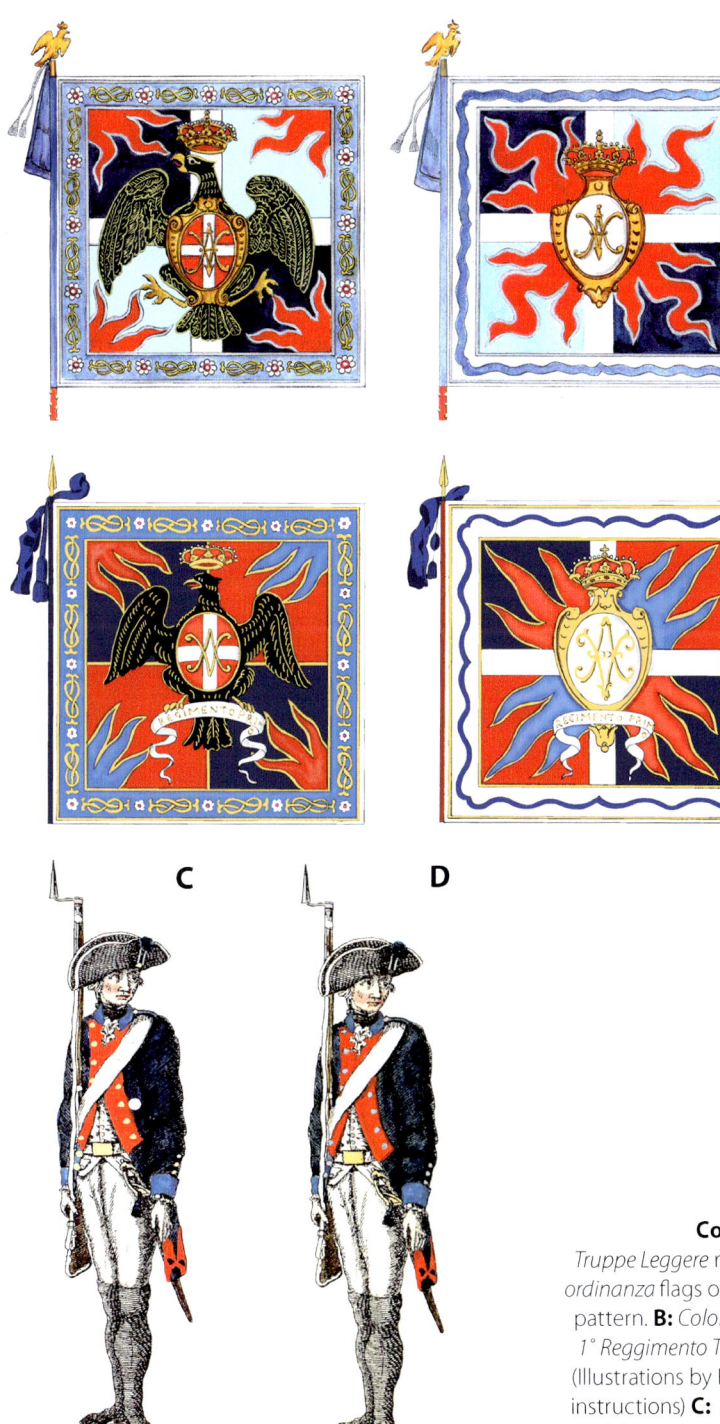

Colour Plate 11.
Truppe Leggere regiments. **A:** *Colonnella* and *ordinanza* flags of Legione Truppe Leggere, 1774 pattern. **B:** *Colonnella* and *ordinanza* flags of 1° Reggimento Truppe Leggere, 1795 pattern. (Illustrations by Roberto Vela on the author's instructions) **C:** *1° Reggimento Truppe leggere.* **D:** *2° Reggimento Truppe leggere.* (Anne S.K. Brown Military Collection)

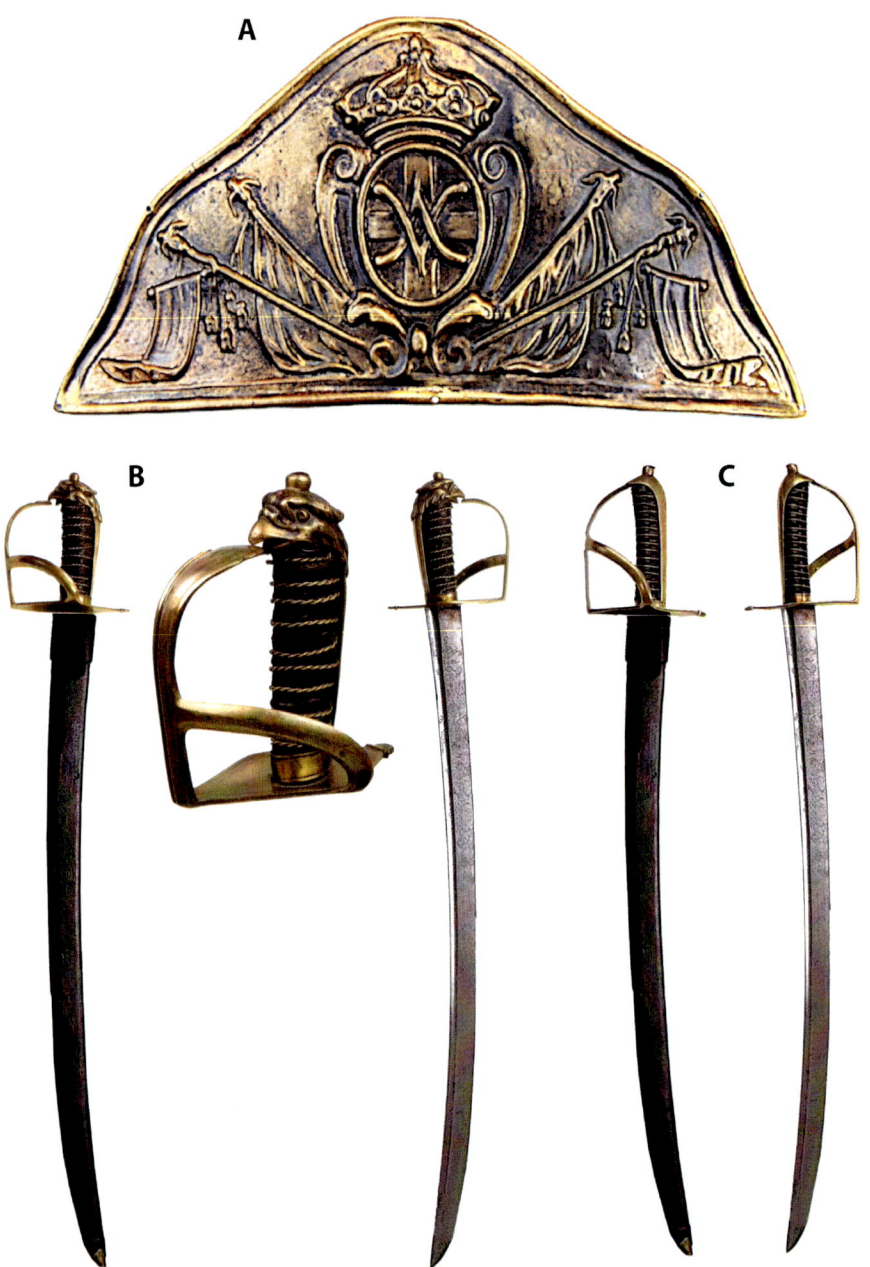

Colour Plate 12.
Truppe Leggere regiments. **A:** Grenadiers' Bearskin cap brass plate with the VA monogram of the King in the middle, surmounted with the royal crown and surrounded with an ensign's panoply. (Private collection) **B:** *Legione Truppe Leggere* sabre, 1774 pattern for *sergenti* and *tamburino Maggiore*. **C:** *Legione Truppe Leggere* sabre, 1774 pattern for *caporali*, musicians, specialists and privates. (With the kind permission of the Centro Studi Piemontesi)

COLOUR PLATE SECTION 1 67

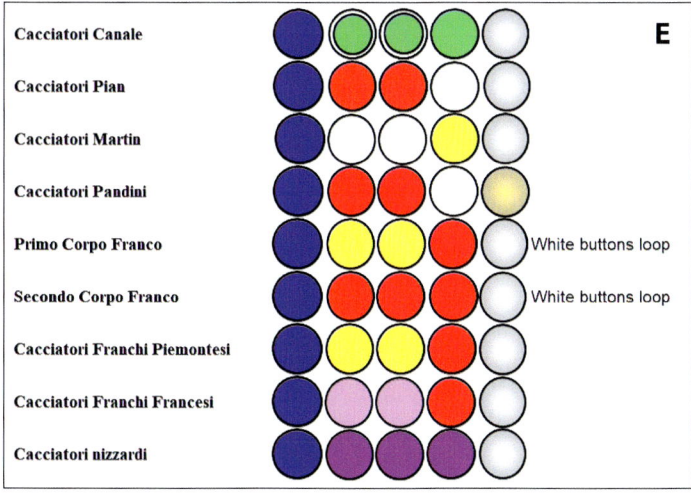

Colour Plate 13.
Uniforms of the *cacciatori volontari* corps. Comparison of Austrian and Piedmontese army uniforms. **A:** *Cacciatore* of the *Corpo Franco*, Piedmontese companies. **B:** Soldier of the Austrian IR56 *Colloredo* Regiment. **C:** Private of the Austrian *Grenzinfanterie Zweiter Banal* Regiment. **D:** Uniform of the *Cacciatori di Canale*. (Anne S.K. Brown Military Collection) **E:** Distinctive colours of the *cacciatori volontari*. (Author's illustration)

Colour Plate 14.
Uniforms of the *cacciatori volontari* corps: **A:** *Cacciatori Carabinieri di Canale.* **B:** *Cacciatori Pian.* **C:** *Cacciatori Martin.* **D:** Detail of figure C. **E:** *Cacciatori Nizzardi.* **F:** *1° Corpo Franco* (Piedmontese). **G:** *Cacciatori Scelti di Nizza.* H: Detail of figure G. (Anne S.K. Brown Military Collection)

Colour Plate 15.
Uniforms of the cacciatori volontari corps: **A:** *1° Corpo Franco* (French). **B:** *2° Corpo Franco*. **C:** Detail of figure B. **D:** *Cacciatori Franchi Piemontesi*. **E:** *Cacciatori Franchi francesi*. **F:** Detail of figure E. (Anne S.K. Brown Military Collection)

Colour Plate 16.
Uniforms of other corps. **A:** *Guastatori*, 1793 pattern. **B:** *Guastatori*, overcoat. (Private collection). **C:** *Guastatori*, 1795 pattern (C). **D:** Military engineer (on right) flanked by a *luogotenente generale*, probably Spirito Benedetto Nicolis, *conte* di Robilant, commander of the *Corpo Reale degli Ingegneri*, presenting a project to the King. Reworked and coloured by the author. **E:** *Chirurgo Maggiore*, 1793.
(Anne S.K. Brown Military Collection)

Colour Plate 17.
Uniforms of *Corpo Reale d'Artiglieria* and *Treno d'artiglieria*: **A:** *Auitante maggiore.* **B:** *Caporale.* **C:** *Cannoniere.* **D:** *Cannoniere ausiliario, Reggimento Piemonte.* **E:** *Palafreneire, Treno d'Artiglieria.* (Anne S.K. Brown Military Collection)

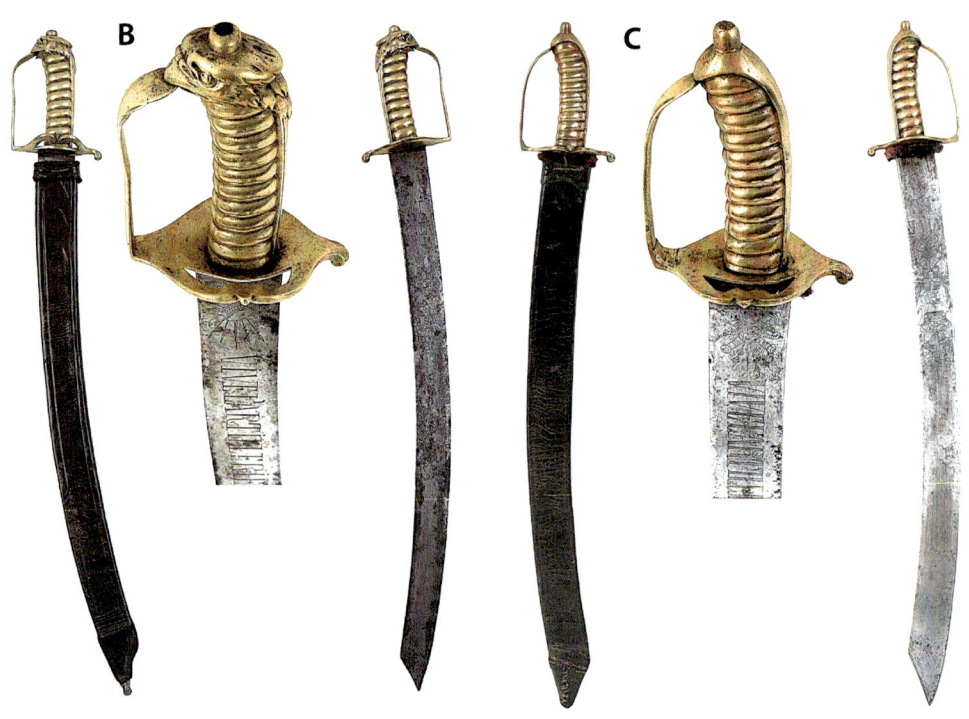

Colour Plate 18. *Corpo Reale d'Artiglieria* and *Treno d'artiglieria*: **A:** *Corpo Reale d'Artiglieria*'s *bandiere colonnella* and *d'ordinanza*. (Anne S.K. Brown Military Collection) **B:** *Sergenti* sabre, 1775 pattern. **C:** *Caporali* and *cannonieri* sabre, 1775 pattern. (With the kind permission of the Centro Studi Piemontesi)

Colour Plate 19.
Uniforms and ensigns of mounted regiments. **A:** *Cavalleggeri del Re.* **B:** *Dragoni del Re.* **C:** *Piemonte Reale Cavalleria.* (Anne S.K. Brown Military Collection)

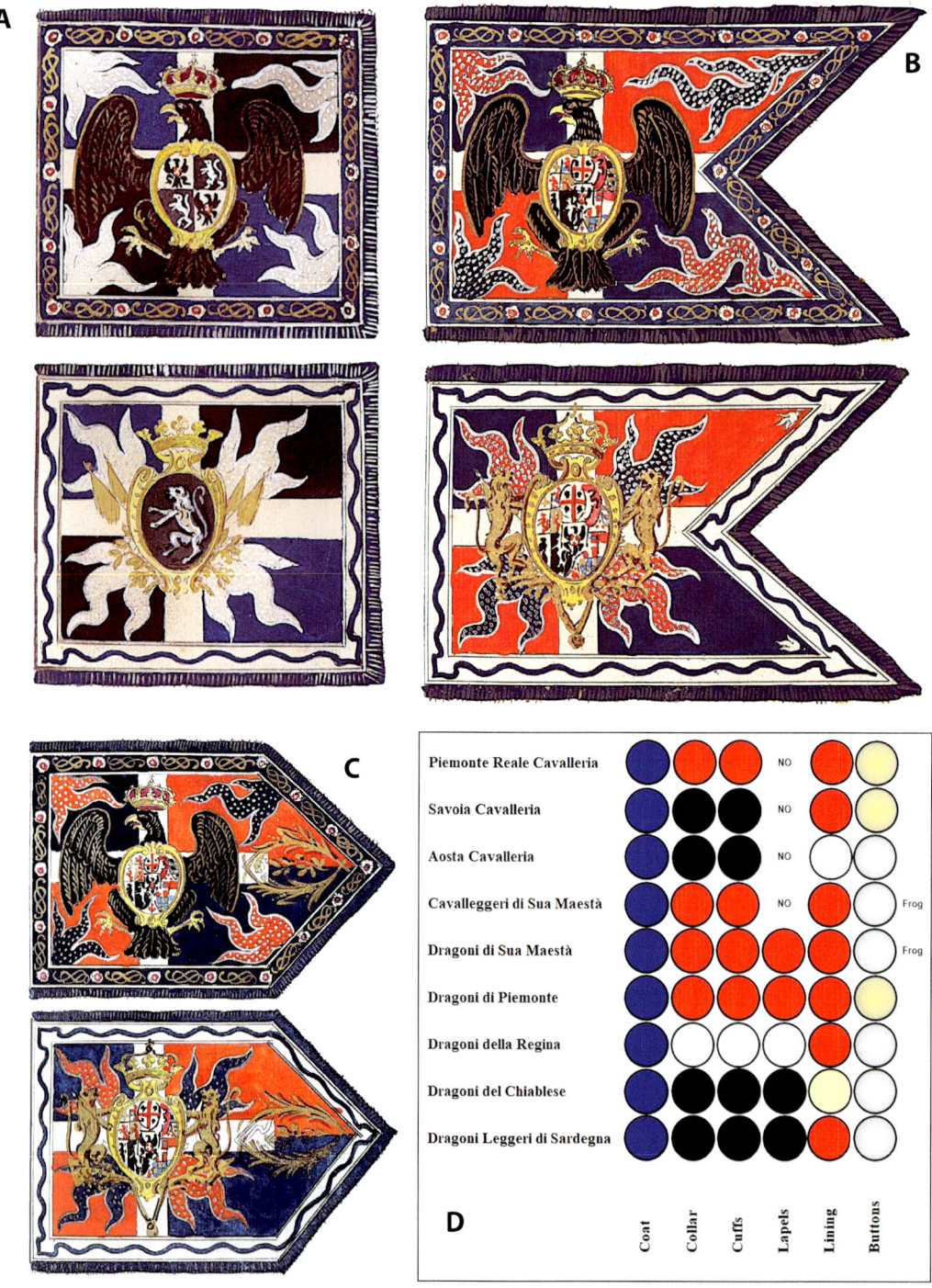

Colour Plate 20.
Mounted regiments **A:** *Stendardo colonnello* and *d'ordinanza* of *Aosta Cavalleria*. **B:** *Cornette* of *Dragoni del Re*. **C:** *Fiamme* of *Cavalleggeri del Re*. (Private collection) **D:** Distinctive colours of the mounted regiments. (Author's illustration)

Colour Plate 21.
Uniforms and ensigns of the Savoyard *Corpo Reale di Marina*. **A:** *Capitano comandante di bordo*. **B:** Sailor. **C:** *Granatiere delle Fregate*. (Anne S.K. Brown Military Collection) **D:** Savoyard naval ensign in use during the War of the Alps. (Author's illustration) **E:** *Coltellaccio* (cutlass) used by sailors and *Granatieri delle Fregate*. (With the kind permission of the Centro Studi Piemontesi)

5

The Militia

On 10 October 1792, just days after the devastating French assault, Vittorio Amedeo III ordered the mobilisation of all the municipalities of the Kingdom's continental provinces. The *milizia volontaria* (volunteer militia) recruited volunteers between the ages of 16 and 60, who were placed in companies consisting of a minimum of 36 and a maximum of 48 men. In the first case the company was commanded by three officers, in the second by four.

By the end of 1792 there were 35,602 men in the militia, but due to a shortage of arms and control of costs, the government decided that call-ups would be for limited periods and in accordance with local needs.[1] In the years that followed, however, most of the militias played an important role in supporting the few troops that guarded the territory against Jacobin infiltration and widespread banditry. Many militias, such as those of the Langhe and the Alpine valleys, played an effective military role, supporting and protecting the flanks of the army. In addition, entire volunteer companies of militiamen were incorporated into the *Corpo Reale d'Artiglieria* as *cannonieri ausiliari* (auxiliary gunners or matrosses) – initially 16 companies from the Nice militia, and later numerous companies from other provinces.[2] Subsequently, to maintain the numbers of the provincial infantry regiments, various militia companies were incorporated, usually with the obligation to serve for 12 months, after which they were regularly discharged.

A large part of the Savoy population was dismayed by the defeat of the Piedmontese army in 1792, by the clumsy attempt by Savoy to regain the province in 1793, and by the French occupation. In 1814 part of Savoy reverted to the kingdom, but the two most important towns in the province, Chambéry and Annecy, were only recovered in 1815. However, many Savoyards did not suffer passively under the French occupation. In 1793, some companies of militiamen from the Maurienne followed the retreat of the Piedmontese army after the failed invasion and later settled in the Piccolo San Bernardo and on the Moncenisio passes. On 23 January 1794, these companies were reorganised into a *Corpo di Milizie Savoiarde* (Corps of Savoy Militiamen) to serve on the borders of Savoy. These were companies of 114 men (a *capitano*, a *luogotenente*, four *sergenti*, six *caporali*, a *tamburino* and 100 militiamen). To protect them from the cold, they wore a coat, probably grey, with a coloured collar to

---

1 Ilari et al, *La guerra delle Alpi*, p.57.
2 Brancaccio, *Gli Ordinamenti*, p.359.

distinguish the companies, turquoise for the first, red for the second, yellow for the third, etc., as other companies came into being.³

There is little surviving information on these militiamen, who were still active in the Susa valley in the summer of 1794. It is probable that those of them who decided to stay and fight were later absorbed into one of the Savoyard line infantry regiments – *Savoia*, *Maurienne* or *Genevois*.

Most writers, even Italians who do not come from Piedmont and therefore do not know the local dialect, have mistakenly considered the term *barbetti* to be synonymous with militiamen. In reality, the term was used to refer to Waldensian believers and, therefore, to the militiamen of the valleys where these Protestants lived: Val Pellice, Germanasca and the lower part of the Val Chisone.

Persecuted by the French and Piedmontese until the end of the seventeenth century, the Waldensians were later tolerated by the Savoy family, starting with Vittorio Amedeo II (1685–1730). It was for this reason that the *barbetti* were constantly used as a militia for the defence of their valleys, alongside the Piedmontese army. Throughout the eighteenth century, the Waldensian militia were an effective vanguard of the Piedmontese troops. Experienced mountaineers, they understood that French soldiers feared them because they knew how to exploit the terrain and could suddenly appear and, because they were skilled marksmen, cause casualties in their ranks with well-aimed shots.⁴

Of course, as always, not everyone in the valley community was of the same opinion during the War of the Alps, and some sided with the Jacobins. This was the case for Gio Albarea, a *sotto luogotenente* in the Waldensian militia, who was dismissed by Vittorio Amedeo III on 2 June 1794 because he had never actually served with his company and, more seriously, because he had appeared before the municipal council wearing the French tricolour instead of the Savoy blue.⁵

In the winter of 1793–1794, four companies of *barbetti* were used in the defence of their valleys, two from the Pellice valley, one from the Germanasca valley, and the fourth from the lower Chisone valley. They consisted of a total of 394 men which included two *cappellani cattolici* (catholic chaplains) and two *ministri* (protestant chaplains), one *chirurgo maggiore*, four *capitani*, four *luogotenenti*, 16 *sergenti*, 32 *caporali*, four *tamburini* and 330 militiamen. About 50 of them contributed, with regular soldiers, to the defence of the modest Fort Mirabocco, located in the upper Pellice valley.

On 1 December 1792 a detailed regulation was issued for the militia of the Duchy of Aosta. A force of 1,000 men was planned, divided into two battalions of five companies each. A company was made up of 100 men (a *capitano*, a *luogotenente*, a *sotto luogotenente*, four *sergenti*, eight *caporali*, a *tamburino* and 84 militiamen). The battalion was commanded by a *luogotenente colonnello*, who had a *maggiore* and two of the *capitani* on his staff.

Within each company, seven volunteers were detailed to form a *cacciatori* company, which might or might not operate separately, depending on the circumstances. The *sergenti*

---

3 AST, Regia Segreteria di Guerra, lettere all'Ufficio Generale del Soldo (LUF), mazzo 273: Determinazioni di S.M. per un Corpo di Milizie Savoiarde, 24 January 1794.
4 Bianchi, *Le valli valdesi*, pp.97–98.
5 AST, LUF, mazzo 274: Letter dated 2 June 1794.

were to be chosen from among the members of each company, bearing in mind that there should be a few from each parish.

NCOs and militiamen of the battalion were provided with *fucili*, bayonets and bandoleers, and, to the former, sabres of the militia *sergente* model. The soldiers of the *cacciatori* company were also provided with a similar sabre, while the drummers were provided with drum cases and bandoleers.

The *cacciatori* company was employed throughout the winter of 1792–1793 to guard the Col du Mont (2,632m), a pass that separated Val Grisanche from Tarantasia occupied by the French and only passable by men and mules. Having conquered the Col, the French could have swooped in behind the Piedmontese defences of La Thuile and the Piccolo San Bernardo Pass, and caused the abandonment of at least the upper part of the Valle d'Aosta. The company carried out their task effectively. In this regard, F. Fenoil wrote that as the *cacciatori* of the Valdostan militia wore waistcoats of red, it was a curious sight to see them stand out when they were scattered amidst the white snow.[6] On 9 May 1793, it was decided to replace this company with another called *Cacciatori di Camosci* (Chamois hunters' company). It was recruited from among the valley inhabitants of Val Grisanche and neighbouring villages and excellent mountaineers who were perfectly skilled in guarding the mountains where they hunted. Commanded by officers from outside the valley, it was made up of 130 Valle d'Aosta natives (a *capitano*, a *luogotenente*, a *sotto luogotenente*, six *sergenti*, 12 *caporali*, two *tamburini* and 107 militiamen).[7] The unit normally assisted the regular troops garrisoning the Valgrisenche and was on the front line during the coldest and snowiest months between mid-October and the end of March to contest the pass for the French. If necessary, they would alert the army's wintering units in the more accessible parts of the valley. These would then rush to the Col du Mont to prevent the French from occupying it as soon as the snow began to melt. The only time the *Cacciatori di Camosci* took part in fighting outside the Valle d'Aosta was when they were included in the vanguard of the Piedmontese expeditionary force that attempted to recover Savoy in August-October 1793. After a while, the company's commander was the valuable *Capitano* Jean-François Chamonin (1762–1828), a native of Valgrisenche, who commanded the company for the rest of the war.[8]

Among the abundant documentation on the War of the Alps preserved in the State Archives and the Royal Library of Turin, detailed regulations assigning each of the numerous militias a uniform have yet to be found. Fortunately, in the numerous albums that collect figures of the uniforms of Sardinian army regiments, the various militias are also represented in their uniforms, characteristic of the province or locality of recruitment. It is certain that this uniform clothing was not provided by the *Ufficio Generale del Soldo*, which merely supplied armament and old drums. The uniform was optional, and it was left to the militiamen to purchase it. Probably only officers and perhaps a few *sergenti* had enough money to acquire the uniform to strut around their village on festive days.[9]

---

6   F. Fenoil, *La Terreur sur les Alpes, avec l'histoire des deux premiers Règiments des Soques* (Aoste : Éduard Duc, 1887), pp.97–98.
7   AST, OGM, mazzo 70: Determinazioni di S.M. per i Cacciatori di Camosci, 9 May 1793.
8   Fenoil, *La Terreur sur les Alpes*, pp.101–106.
9   E. Ricchiardi, 'Iconografia militare sabauda. L'Esercito Sardo attraverso la figurinistica militare', in Gustavo Mola di Nomaglio (ed.), *1416, Savoye Bonne Nouvelle* (Torino: Centro Studi Piemontes, 2021), vol.II, pp.1059–1172, < https://doi.org/10.26344/CSP.SBN/RIC>, accessed 19 November 2024.

6

The Elite Units: Forge of Heroes

Light Infantry

In Europe, light infantry had become an established operational necessity in regular infantry battalions and various free corps had been created to provide light forces. In Piedmont, on the other hand, Carlo Emanuele III (1730–1773) was satisfied with the conquests of the first decades of his reign and did not introduce any new changes to the infantry organisation of his army, nor did he show any interest in light infantrymen. Vittorio Amedeo III, however, demonstrated his openness to foreign experiences by deploying regular light infantrymen. The establishment of the *Legione Truppe Leggere* did not follow the same pattern, however. Despite its name, the unit was organised and armed like the line infantry but equipped with the lighter Model 1759 *fucile da dragone* (dragoon musket), 147.7cm long, and initially with a long ring bayonet (measuring 642mm in length and weighing 430g), later replaced by the lighter Model 1731 dragoon bayonet (measuring 364cm in length and weighing 215g). As this was more suited to the type of service to which the Legion was dedicated, a lighter weapon was provided.[1] In the reorganisation of the line infantry regiments in 1786, the King decided that in each of the eight *fucilieri* companies several light infantrymen were to be placed, with their officers, *sergenti* and hunting horn players, making a regimental total of 59 men.[2]

At the beginning of the War of the Alps, it became clear that the use of the regimental light infantrymen was inadequate and inappropriate. It was not effective to distribute them among the companies. Therefore, on 20 February 1793, an independent company was formed by uniting the regimental light infantry, consisting of 60 men, with the addition of a sutler. The order was carried out without delay, so that the companies would be ready to occupy the forward posts as soon as the snow permitted.[3] However, on 22 March 1793, the light infantry companies were separated from their regiments to form two autonomous battalions, the *1°* and *2° Cacciatori*. It is important to note that although this approach was

---

1 F. Sterrantino, *Le armi da fuoco del vecchio Piemonte (1683–1799)* (Lorenzo, Torino 2002), pp.140–144.
2 AST, Stabilimenti Militari (StM), mazzo 4. Nuova formazione dei reggimenti di fanteria d'ordinanza, 22 June 1786.
3 AST, OGM, mazzo 70: The regimental *cacciatori* grouped together in two autonomous companies, 20 February 1793.

effective in combat, it reduced the effectiveness of the infantry regiments by depriving them of their light infantry companies.[4]

The *1° Cacciatori* was formed from the light companies of the *Guardie, Saluzzo, Aosta, de Courten, La Regina, Christ, Sardegna,* and *Lombardia* regiments. *Colonnello* Eustachio Luserna Roringo, *conte* di Campiglione, commanded the battalion and led it in a series of battles in Val Roia. He also directed it during the first part of the Siege of Toulon. He was later relieved of his command by the Council of War, for reasons we do not know, and later left the army at his request. In Toulon, he was replaced by the *maggiore di battaglione*, suddenly promoted to *luogotenente colonnello*, Carlo Incisa, *cavaliere* di Santo Stefano Belbo. He returned to his homeland at the end of the expedition and died in April 1794 from the wounds he had received in the siege. On 24 April 1794, the command of the *1° Cacciatori* was entrusted to *luogotenente colonnello* Maurizio Pastoris *cavaliere* di Saluggia, who commanded it until the end of the war.[5]

The *2° Cacciatori* initially consisted of only seven companies, which came from the *Savoia, Monferrato, Piemonte, Reale Alemanno, La Marina, Chablais,* and *Rochmondet* regiments. On 6 November 1793, the latter company was replaced by the newly formed light infantry company of the *Novara* provincial regiment. The *Maurienne* provincial regiment's new light company was added to complete the *2° Cacciatori*. The *2° Cacciatori* was entrusted to *Cavaliere* Pietro Fatio, who died on 22 June 1793. He was replaced by Giuseppe Faussone, *cavaliere* di Germagnano, *luogotenente colonnello* and *aiutante di campo* to the King, who was quickly sent by Vittorio Amedeo III to Susa to take command. However, this senior officer also perished from a blow to the head in the bloody Siege of Toulon during his battalion's defence of the redoubt of Fort Faron on 18 December 1793. On 10 April 1794, the battalion's new commander was *maggiore* Luigi Colli Ricci, *marchese* di Felizzano. The military career of Luigi Colli Ricci, who had been appointed *capitano* of the grenadiers in the provincial *Acqui* regiment on 7 Aug 1792, accelerated during the war. On 22 Jan 1793, he was made *maggiore* in the *Mondovì* provincial regiment, moving with the same rank on 10 April 1794 to the *2° Cacciatori*. A year later, on 2 May 1795, we find him *luogotenente colonnello* and on 5 December 1795 *colonnello* of the same unit. In view of the difficult defence of the following year, with the French approaching Ceva, on 20 March 1796, Luigi Colli Ricci's experience and valour were put to good use by placing him in command of the newly formed regiment composed of the *1°* and *2° Cacciatori*.[6]

The rapid succession of commanders of the two light battalions gives an idea of the bravery of those senior officers who set an example by fighting at the head of their unit. Unfortunately, it is not so easy to reconstruct the vicissitudes of the troops, as not all muster rolls have survived, and incomplete information is taken from the others. For example, muster rolls rarely record wounds, but only their possible consequences, such as transfer to a reserve company, to a *Battaglione di Guarnigione* (Garrison Battalion) or *Corpo degli Invalidi* (Invalid Corps), or discharge. Casualties are also not always accurately reported, largely due to the nature of the warfare these units fought. The rapid retreats at the end of

---

4 AST, OGM, mazzo 70: The regimental companies of *Cacciatori*, grouped in the *1°* and *2° Cacciatori* battalions, 22 March 1793.
5 Lo Faso di Serradifalco, *La difesa di un regno*, p.391.
6 Lo Faso di Serradifalco, *La difesa di un regno*, pp.294–295.

firefights often did not allow the *sergenti* compiling the lists to know whether the soldier absent from the roll call had deserted, been captured, or had died and been buried by those in control of the position.

A rare document gives us an insight into the great difficulty of keeping a battalion like the *2° Cacciatori*, which required men of physical strength in fighting condition, endurance and fighting spirit. It lists the soldiers that the regiments would have had to provide to keep the *2°* up to strength and standards as it prepared to go to Toulon. More than 35 men, including NCOs, *caporali* and privates, were deemed unfit to serve as light troops for various reasons. A company *sergente* from the *Reggimento Monferrato* was deemed unfit because of his poor health. A *sergente* of the *Reggimento La Marina* was nearly blind, a *corporale* was asthmatic, a hunting horn player of the *Reggimento Piemonte* had fallen ill in Sardinia when the regiment left the island and never re-joined the corps. Finally, some of the light infantrymen could not march for long periods, while others could no longer stand the rigours of the light infantrymen's life. The regiment also had to replace at least three *caporali* and nine soldiers who had been taken prisoner or killed in action and, finally, a *cacciatore* of *Reggimento La Marina* was in prison for murder.[7]

Replacing these soldiers was troublesome because their home regiments, which were also grappling with similar problems, found it difficult to deprive themselves of their best men and compromise was not easily achieved.

Despite everything, what is certain is that the two battalions fought effectively against the French throughout the course of the war and were invaluable in mountain fighting for their recklessness.

The two light battalions were deployed where they were most needed as the war progressed. Initially, the *1°* was sent to Val Roia, from where it was detached in the autumn of 1793 to reach Oneglia, the only mainland embarkation point still under Savoy control, to be transported to Toulon. It returned in December 1793, spent the winter in Oneglia and after that returned to Val Roia. The *2°* was initially deployed in the defence of the Moncenisio Pass as part of the second corps. It then took part in the unsuccessful attempt to retake Savoy (August–October 1793). It also then left for Toulon. On its return, it remained with the fourth army corps, where it actively participated in the recovery of Ormea in Val Tanaro and in the defence of the French incursions in Liguria. Finally, in April 1796, to give some consistency to its deployment, and when, like all the army's divisions, it was severely under-strength at the time, it was reunited with the *1° Cacciatori* to form a regiment.

The two battalions that paraded for inspection had a multi-coloured appearance. The officers and men wore the uniforms of their home regiments, with no other distinctions or special headgear, and the companies deployed were thus a complete palette of colours. All were united by the wavy lace on their sleeves, which they proudly displayed as a sign that they belonged to an elite unit. We can imagine that even those for whom the wavy lace was not prescribed, such as the *chirurgo maggiore* and the *arciere*, proudly added it to their uniforms.

---

7 AST, OGM, mazzo 71: Difficulties in finding suitable men for enlistment in the *2° Cacciatori*, 23 October 1793.

The 11 Grenadiers' Battalions

The infantry regiments' grenadier companies were also to be grouped in sixes to form independent battalions in case of war. Ten battalions were thus formed from the available companies. An eleventh was added shortly afterwards by combining the grenadier companies of the three new Swiss regiments, *Bachmann*, *Peyer-Imhoff* and *Zimmerman*.

With a strength of 87 men each, all included, the six companies made up a battalion of 522 men, so the total number of grenadiers available from the 11 battalions was theoretically 5,742. In practice, however, the grenadier battalions, like the light infantry ones, suffered heavy casualties, aggravated by disease and the same difficulty in maintaining their numbers, and rarely reached two-thirds of their strength. They were used to defend critical points or in bloody attacks and counterattacks. To provide the battalions with the expected services, each had its own staff in which the commander was nominally included, and that also included the *maggiore di battaglione* for administrative and training management, the *cappellano* and the *chirurgo maggiore*.

Described below is the succession of the battalions' commanders and which companies were included in any battalion during the War of the Alps.[8]

1° Granatieri

This battalion's composition remained unchanged throughout the war, and it was formed by combining the companies of the *Guardie*, *Asti* and *Casale* regiments. The battalion was commanded by *luogotenente colonnello* Jean-Gaspard Dichat, *vassallo* di Toisinges (1740–1796). He took part in the Battle of Authion (8–12 April 1793) and remained in command until 6 January 1795. Dichat was one of the most competent and courageous officers in the Piedmontese army. Originally *luogotenente colonnello* of the *Reggimento Aosta*, he was appointed commander of the *1° Granatieri* and promoted to *colonnello* on 20 May 1794. He gave up command of the *1°* when, on 6 January 1795, he was appointed to the command of the regiment formed by the merger of the *8°* and *9° Granatieri*. Unfortunately, he was killed on 21 April 1796 in the Battle of Brichetto, during the last fighting near Mondovì.

2° Granatieri

The *2° Granatieri* combined companies from the *Savoia*, *La Marina* and *Torino* regiments. In January 1796, the two companies of *La Marina* were transferred to the *3° Granatieri* and from then on, the battalion had only four companies. Throughout the war, the *2°* remained under the command of the Piedmontese *maggiore nobiluomo* Gaspare *marchese* del Carretto.

3° Granatieri

This battalion included the grenadier companies of the *Monferrato*, *Piemonte* and *Rochmondet* regiments. In January 1796, the two companies of the *Rochmondet* regiment were replaced by those of the *La Marina* regiment, and later, in January 1796, those of the *Susa* regiment replaced those of the *Piemonte* regiment. For a short time, this battalion was

---

8   N. Brancaccio, *L'Esercito del vecchio Piemonte (1560–1859)*, *Sunti Storici* (Ministero della Guerra, Roma 1923), pp.108–114, and https://en.wikipedia.org/wiki/Jean-Gaspard_Dichat_de_Toisinge, (accessed 19 November 2024).

under the command of *maggiore* Silvio Ballard, *vassallo* di Roccafranca. After his resignation on 24 February 1793, he passed the command to *luogotenente colonnello* Alfonso del Carretto, *conte* di Monfort. On 2 November 1794, del Carretto was replaced by *luogotenente colonnello* Carlo Caissotti, *conte* di Chiusano. Finally, on 29 March 1796, Di Chiusano was relieved by *luogotenente colonnello* Filippo del Carretto, *conte* di Camerano, the heroic commander who was killed on 13 April 1796 during the defence of the castle of Cosseria, where the 3° was heavily involved.

4° Granatieri
Established with grenadier companies from the *Saluzzo*, *Vercelli* and *Tortona* regiments the *4° Granatieri* was placed under the command of *luogotenente colonnello* Maximilian Adamo, *barone* de Reinbach, who commanded it until 21 February 1795. He was replaced by *maggiore* Luigi Bongiovanni, *cavaliere* di Castelborgo, who was in turn replaced by the *nobiluomo* Enrico Francesco de Ruphy on 12 March 1796.

5° Granatieri
This battalion was made up of the grenadier companies of the *Aosta*, *de Courten* and *Mondovì* regiments. Its first commander was Luigi Gabaleone di Salmour, *conte* d'Andezeno, who commanded it briefly. He was replaced on 22 July 1793 by *maggiore* Giovanni Dattili, *conte* di Torre del Monte. He left the command on 27 February 1796 to *luogotenente colonnello* Giuseppe Rebuffo, *conte* di San Michele, who commanded it until the end of the war.

6° Granatieri
The *6° Granatieri* consisted of the grenadier companies of the *Reale Alemanno*, *Chablais* and *Genevois* regiments. It was commanded for a long time by *luogotenente colonnello* Joseph François De Conzier, *marchese* d'Allemagne, who was released from service on 17 February 1796. It is not known by whom he was replaced.

7° Granatieri
This battalion included the companies belonging to the provincial *Maurienne*, *Ivrea* and *Pinerolo* regiments under the command of *maggiore* François Joseph, *vassallo* Du Magny, who seems to have commanded it throughout the course of the War of the Alps.

8° Granatieri
The *8° Granatieri* included the grenadier companies of the *Nizza*, *La Regina* and *Sardegna* regiments, under the command of *maggiore* Carlo Francesco Giacinto Caissotti, *conte* di Chiusano. He was replaced on 9 April 1794 by *maggiore* Carlo Felice Biscaretti, *cavaliere* Di Ruffia, who was released from service on 12 February 1795 due to a disastrous fall from his horse. The name of his replacement is not known.

9° Granatieri
Composed of companies from the *Christ*, *Lombardia* and *Acqui* regiments the *9° Granatieri* was placed under the command of *maggiore* Benedetto Biscaretti, *cavaliere* da Ruffia, who led it until 29 November 1794. He was replaced by *maggiore* Remigio *conte* Panissera and later by *maggiore* Luigi Perachino, *marchese* di Cigliano.

10° Granatieri

This battalion was formed from the companies of the *Novara* and *Susa* regiments, to which the companies of the *Oneglia* regiment were joined on 10 May 1795. In January 1796 it remained with just four companies because the two from the *Susa* regiment were transferred to the *3° Granatieri*, in which they performed heroically at the Siege of Cosseria Castle. It has not been possible to find the names of the officers who commanded this battalion.

11° Granatieri

The *11°* were formed on 19 March 1794 from companies of the Swiss *Peyer Imhoff*, *Zimmermann* and *Bachmann* regiments under the command of *maggiore* Zimmermann, *Baron* de Reding. On 12 February 1796, the battalion was disbanded, and the companies returned to their respective regiments.

To give greater consistency to the grenadier formations, it was also decided to group them into regiments of two battalions, although individual battalions often operated independently. The regiments, which did not have their own numbering, were:

Regiment formed by the *1°* and *3° Granatieri*, throughout the war under the command of *colonnello* Carlo Caissotti, *conte* di Chiusano.

Regiment formed by the *2°* and *10° Granatieri*, throughout the war commanded by *colonnello* Giuseppe Bertone, *cavaliere* di Sambuy. Retired with the rank of *maggior generale* on July 1, 1794, it is not known by whom he was replaced.

Regiment formed from the *4°* and *5° Granatieri*. On 1 March 1793, it was placed under the command of *colonnello* Policarpo Cacherano d'Osasco, *cavaliere* di Cantarana, replaced on 14 October 1794 by *colonnello cavaliere* Nicolao Ratti and then, on 31 May 1794 by *luogotenente colonnello*, later *colonnello*, Francesco Giuseppe, *cavaliere* De Varax.

Regiment formed by the *6°* and *7° Granatieri*. The regiment on 25 March 1793 was under command of *luogotenente colonnello* Maurizio Pastoris, *cavaliere* di Saluggia, replaced on 6 August 1794 by *luogotenente colonnello*, later promoted to *colonnello* on 11 April 1795, Francesco Regard, *conte* di Clermont, who commanded it until the end of hostilities.

Regiment formed by the *8°* and *9° Granatieri*. Placed on 12 February 1793 under command of *colonnello* Giuseppe Solaro, *marchese* della Chiusa, it then passed on 6 January 1795 under the orders of *colonnello* Gaspare Dichat, *vassallo* di Toisinge, another of the most valuable commanders of the War of the Alps, who led it for the remainder of hostilities.[9]

The *Legione Truppe Leggere*

The *Legione Truppe Leggere* (Light Infantry Legion) was a unit established in 1776 to guard the Kingdom's borders and combat smuggling. For this reason, it was distributed throughout the territory. Although wearing shorter uniforms than ordinary infantry uniforms and a special helmet, the Legion was never armed with rifled carbines or trained for combat in open order. On 7 July 1786, the Legion was reorganised into four battalions organised and

---

9   Brancaccio, *Sunti Storici*, pp.108–115.

outfitted like the rest of the infantry, while the characteristic helmet was also abolished and replaced by the tricorn hat for the light companies and bearskin caps for grenadiers.

With the outbreak of the War of the Alps, the Legion abandoned its function as border guards, was replaced in these tasks by the local militia, and mobilised its battalions. Having four battalions was the only peculiarity of its organisation compared to that of the line infantry regiments, which consisted of only two battalions. Deployment in the field, as with the line infantry, was by battalion and their placement varied greatly during the war. Another specificity of the Legion was the fact that the four companies of light troops, one per battalion, had buglers instead of hunting horn players as signal musicians.

Put on a war footing during the winter of 1792–1793, an *état* of 18 February 1793 set an establishment for the Legion of 2,133 men distributed in four battalions, which in turn were in 1795 divided into the *1°* and *2°* regiments to form a brigade. The *1° Truppe Leggere* consisted of the *1°* and *2°* battalions, the *2° Reggimento Truppe Leggere* of the *3°* and *4°*. Each regiment's two battalions personnel were the same as that of the line infantry: battalion staff, four *fucilieri* companies of 106 men each, and one of 60 *cacciatori*. The only difference was the presence of two grenadier companies of 65 men each. The Legion's total, therefore, now amounted to 16 *fucilieri*, four *cacciatori*, and two *granatieri* companies.[10]

The distribution of the Legion's companies did not always allow the unity of the battalions to be maintained due to the dispersed nature of the front. For example, in a document dated 10 March 1795, shortly before the division into two regiments, the Legion was divided as follows *2°* battalion and *1ᵃ* and *2ᵃ cacciatori* companies in the Valle d'Aosta. *1°* and *4°* battalions, *3ᵃ* and *4ᵃ cacciatori companies* in the fourth corps together with *1ᵃ* and *2ᵃ granatieri*. The *3°* battalion, not mentioned in the document and without its élite companies, was probably used in the plains for public order duties and as a recruitment centre for the unit.[11]

In the spring of 1795, *colonnello* Alessandro Malabaila, *conte* d'Antignano, wrote a report in which he pointed out the fact that with the dispersion of the four battalions over the various theatres of operation, it was difficult for a single *colonnello*, who was also engaged in fighting with the *1°* battalion, to maintain an effective command of the Legion. So, on 7 April, the King therefore decided to split the Legion into two autonomous regiments, called the *1°* and *2° Reggimento Truppe Leggere*, thus effectively putting into practice what had already been planned but never implemented by the February 1793 order, comprising the number of elite companies. The only change was that a reserve company was added to each of the two regiments, as usual, with training duties. Each regiment thus consisted of nine *fucilieri* companies (one of which was the reserve company), two of *cacciatori*, each with a bugler, and one of *granatieri*, the latter now increased to 87 men. The staff of each regiment was to include a *quartiermastro*, a *cappellano* and a *chirurgo maggiore*. All in all, each regiment was to consist of 1,319 men.[12]

Malabaila d'Antignano retained command of the *1° Reggimento Truppe Leggere*, while the *2°* was entrusted to the newly promoted *colonnello* Onorato Leotardi, *barone* di Sant'Alessandro, who was before then in charge of the *4°* battalion. Subsequently retired

---

10 AST, OGM, mazzo 70: Aumento della forza della Legione Truppe Leggere,18 February 1793.
11 AST, OGM, mazzo 75: Quartieri d'inverno, 10 March 1795.
12 AST, OGM, mazzo 74: Formazione di 1° e 2° Reggimento Truppe Leggere, 7 April 1795.

at his request, Leotardi was replaced on 27 February 1796 by *brigadiere generale* Giovanni Battista, *cavaliere* Civalieri, who commanded the 2° until the end of hostilities.[13]

The two regiments kept the same uniforms as the Legion, but at the first distribution of the new ones in January 1795, to distinguish the two from each other, the *2° Reggimento* changed the buttons from brass/gold to tin/silver and the badges from yellow/gold to white/silver. As the old Legion flags had become outdated and worn out, it was decided to manufacture eight new flags, one *colonnella* and three *d'ordinanza* for each regiment, this was in keeping with the line regiments. There are no documents confirming the retention of the eagle-shaped finials on the *colonnelle*'s flags, as a reminder of their original legion designation, but it is likely that this was the case. To distinguish the two regiments, a wavy ribbon was embroidered below the *colonnelle*'s eagle and regimental coat of arms with the inscription *Reggimento Primo* or *Reggimento Secondo* (first or second regiment), respectively. Finally, to conform with the metal of the buttons, the edging of the flags of the 2° became silver.

---

13   Lo Faso di Serradifalco, *La difesa di un regno*, p.410.

7

Infantry Weaponry

Sabres

In the army of Vittorio Amedeo III, the shape of the *sabro* (sabre) guard and the tip of their blades helped to show the rank and affiliation of the NCOs and specialists of the various corps. Between 1775 and 1795, the King approved various sabre models to equip the line infantry corps, including the *Legione Truppe Leggere* and the *Granatieri Reali*.[1]

The first sabre model was designed for the *sergenti* of the *Reggimento Guardie*, *tamburo maggiore* included, and also distributed to the regimental band. This weapon had a two-branched brass guard, with a cast eagle head cap. The grip was of wood covered with blackened leather, wrapped with interlocked silver wire. The blade was curved, with a single cutting edge, grooved and pointed. This sabre had a total length of 17½ *ounces* (about 75cm) and was fitted with a blackened leather scabbard that also covered the tip because the iron tip protector was hidden inside (see colour plate 6). The sword knot and terminal tassel were made of silver wire.

The second sabre model was assigned to the *sergenti* and band musicians of all other line infantry regiments, including the provincial ones. The two-branched brass guard terminated in a button cap. The grip was of wood covered with blackened leather. bound with interlocked brass wire. The blade was curved, with a single cutting edge, grooved and pointed. The weapon had a total length of 18 *ounces* (about 77.4cm) and was fitted with a leather scabbard, similar to the one described above.

The third sabre model was intended for *caporali*, soldiers and all specialists of the *Reggimento Guardie*. It was later extended to *caporali* and soldiers of the other line regiments as well, but only to those belonging to the light or grenadier companies, as the *fucilieri* companies were only armed with bayonets. *Falegnami* and *armaioli* were also equipped with it because they were linked to the grenadiers, whose bearskin cap they also wore. This pattern of sabre had a two-branched brass guard surmounted by a button cap, a wooden grip covered with leather, bound with interlocked brass wire, a curved, single cutting edge, grooved blade and a scabbard like the previously described pattern and the same length. It was the most widespread pattern of sabre, of which 55,431 examples were produced.[2]

---

1 Sterrantino, *Le armi da fuoco del vecchio Piemonte*, p.77. P.E. Fiora, 'Origini dell'artiglieria da montagna. Secoli XVII e XVIII', *Armi Antiche*, 1974, pp.99–118.
2 M. Lupo, *Le lame del Re. Sabri e spade dell'Armata Sabauda dal 1560 al 1831* (Torino: Centro Studi Piemontesi, 2007), pp.326–339.

The sabre model established in 1794 for the *Granatieri Reali* used a grooved, single cutting-edge blade with a pointed apex, and guard like that of the previous model but surmounted by a cast brass lion's head cap. There is no evidence that the band's musicians, *sergenti* and company musicians carried a sabre of a different model. Initially, however, between 1793 and 1794, the *Granatieri Reali* carried on using the sabres of the *Legione degli Accampamenti* from which they originated. This weapon consisted of an un-grooved, single cutting-edge blade with a truncated apex, a single branched guard with a brass grip and a button cap.[3]

Finally, the sabres of the *Legione Truppe Leggere* had two different types of guards on the grooved blade with a pointed apex. The *sergenti* and the *tamburo Maggiore*'s sabre was brass, had two branches, the wooden grip was lined with blackened leather, bound with interlocked brass wire, all surmounted by an eagle's head cap. All others carried a sabre of the model adopted for the troops of the line regiments.

On 13 November 1774, Vittorio Amedeo III decided to adopt a new sword model for infantry officers with a silver or silver-plated brass *alla moschettiera* hilt, worked in fillet form and mounted on double-edged blades with a sharp point. The grip consisted of a wooden spindle around which was wound a spiral of silver or gold-plated copper wire. The sword had a total length of 102.9cm. Depending on the depths of the pockets of the customer, and the skill of the craftsman who produced the weapon, it could be more or less richly ornamented, but always according to the pattern approved by the King. Some examples of the decoration of the officer's sword of the time can be seen in colour plate 5.[4]

Such a valuable weapon had to be replaced during the war by a poorer, more robust weapon, and certainly sometimes by one's own regiment's robust and deadly *sabro*.

Muskets

At the beginning of the War of the Alps *fucilieri* and *granatieri* of some national and foreign infantry regiments were armed with the Model 1782 infantry *fucile*. The others and all provincial infantry, including the *Legione degli Accampamenti*, were armed with the excellent Model 1752 infantry *fucile*. At the same time, a different weapon had been issued to the light infantry companies. After it was realised that an efficient rifled-barrel carbine was not available, they were equipped with the same *fucili* as the line infantry, but with a modified butt to aid targeting. The unreliability of rifled-barrel carbines also limited their use by the French and Austrian revolutionary armies.[5]

The quality of the two models of Savoyard infantry *fucili* was sufficient to equip soldiers effectively. Francesco Sterrantino, an expert on Savoyard firearms, was authoritative following a thorough study. He wrote that 'the 1752 *fucile* was an excellent weapon, while the 1782 *fucile*, although the result of countless trials and research into the best solutions for the construction and assembly of its various parts, was of inferior quality'. He also wrote that 'the 1782 *fucile* hardly compares with the Prussian 1782 and Austrian 1784 patterns, but

---

3   Lupo, *Le lame del Re*, pp.326–344, 389–392.
4   Lupo, *Le lame del Re*, p.321.
5   For the French army, G. Ruello, *La fanteria francese nella guerra delle Alpi* (Torino: Acta, 2007), pp.103–123, for the Austrian army, D. Del Monte et D. Toso, *Le truppe leggere imperiali durante la guerra delle Alpi. Frei Corps, Grenzen, Jäger* (Torino: Acta, 2007), pp.124–131.

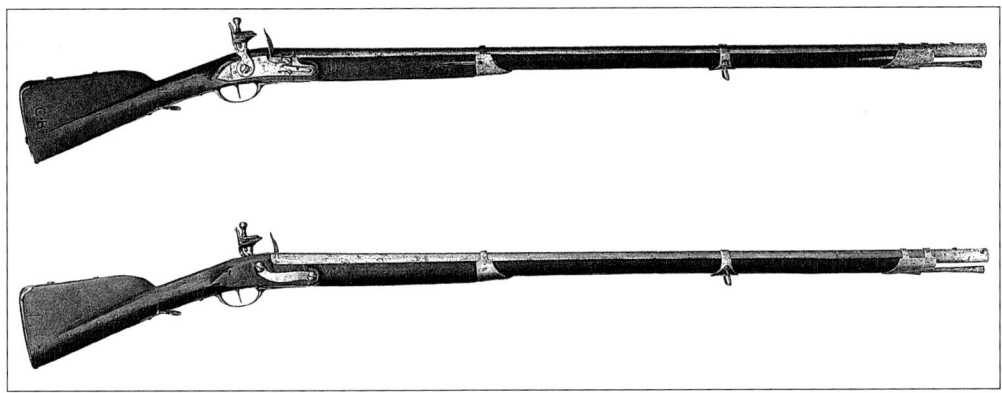

Modified *fucile* 1782 pattern, used by the line infantry light infantry companies. (Sterrantino, *Le armi da fuoco del vecchio Piemonte*, Fig. 72).

is surpassed by the French 1777, a new and evolving weapon' and was inferior to the British Army's 1792 musket.[6]

In any case, the production capacity of the Turin arsenal was insufficient to produce enough *fucili* for the rapid increase in the number of infantrymen in the winter-spring of 1793 and to compensate for the losses due to various causes, including casualties and those damaged in the fighting. It was, therefore, necessary to purchase large quantities of weapons abroad. These were generally of high quality and did not pose any problems in terms of cartridges and bullets, as they were always ordered in the 17.3mm calibre used by the Piedmontese infantry.

The *Granatieri Reali* were also equipped with Model 1752 infantry *fucile*, while the *Legione Truppe Leggere* was equipped with a shorter and lighter weapon, the *fucile da dragoni* model 1759.[7]

---

6   Sterrantino, *Le armi da fuoco del vecchio Piemonte*, p.159.
7   Sterrantino, *Le armi da fuoco del vecchio Piemonte*, pp.194–196.

8

Volunteer Light Troops

The need for light infantry in the Alpine campaigns led Pietro Francesco Zaverio Malabaila, *cavaliere* di Canale, to make a proposal to the King in October 1792. He suggested organising a *centuria* of volunteer light infantry, which could guard dangerous posts or attack the French rear. In the Piedmontese army of the time, a *centuria* was an assembly of two infantry companies, the term having been borrowed from the ancient Roman army. Malabaila, a *capitano* in the *Reggimento Guardie*, may have been inspired by the lightly equipped volunteer companies that were set up by both the British and the French in the second half of the eighteenth century to fight in North America. These units operated without heavy baggage or other impedimenta and were led by an officer experienced in fighting *la petite guerre* (the small war), as the combat of outposts and patrols was termed. Malabaila aspired to that role. Initially, the companies in North America were dressed like line troops, but for reasons of practicality the volunteers soon removed the tails from their coats and modified the tricorne, removing most of the wings. This was the birth of the ancestor of the felt helmet, or at least one of its forerunners.

On 28 October 1792, the King gave his approval, and promoted Malabaila to the rank of *maggiore*, giving him command of the *centuria*. Malabaila concentrated the volunteers in Carmagnola and was able to make the unit operational in the early spring of 1793. It took the name *Centuria Cacciatori Carabinieri di Canale*. On the same day that he approved Malabaila's project, the King also ordered the creation of a small reserve company in the new corps, consisting of a *sergente*, two *caporali*, a *caporale sovrannumerario* and 40 recruits. According to established practice, this company was to act as a recruitment and training centre for volunteers. However, it does not appear that this company was ever formed, as it does not appear in the muster rolls of the *centuria*.[1]

The first regulations issued for Malabaila's *centuria* set a strength of 338 men. There were six in the staff: *luogotenente aiutante maggiore*, *furiere*, *cappellano*, *chirurgo maggiore*, *sergente maggiore* and *arciere*; and 167 men in the *1ª Compagnia*, led by *maggiore comandante* Malabaila di Canale, with a *capitano*, a *capitano luogotenente*, a *luogotenente*, a *furiere*, two *trabanti*, a *sergente di compagnia*, two *sergenti di plotone*, three *sergenti sovrannumerari*, two *caporali*, a *suonatore del corno da caccia* (hunting horn player), a *frater*, a *vivandiere* and 150 light infantrymen. Finally, a *2ª Compagnia* of 165 men was created identical in

---

1   AST, Ruolini di rivista, Compagnie Canale, Pian, Pandini, mazzi 1–3.

establishement to the *1ª*, except that there was no *maggiore comandante*, and, accordingly, there was only one *trabante*.²

The recruitment process, which Malabaila himself had started on the day of the royal approval, proceeded apace despite the difficulties caused by the fierce competition from all the other corps in the army who needed to increase their numbers. In order to have administrative and medical support for the selection of candidates, it was essential to find the *sergente maggiore* and the *chirurgo maggiore* as soon as possible. For the first role, *sergente* Gioacchino Vignole from Turin was chosen. A *sergente* in the *Reggimento Novara*, he was immediately promoted to *sergente maggiore*. Secondo Truchi, a doctor from Montà d'Alba was appointed *chirurgo maggiore*. Carlo Madio, from Murisengo, was also immediately recruited as an *arciere*. He was to check the candidates' conduct and any previous convictions or desertions.

Recruiting officers was equally difficult because of the fierce competition. This was not least because partisan warfare required an iron will, excellent health and the right kind of leadership to inspire soldiers with a mentality of personal initiative. The corps also needed officers who could deal positively with forms of combat that were unusual for the Piedmontese army. In 1792, all that remained of this type of warfare were the records of the mountain battles of the War of the Austrian Succession (1741–1748), but no training documentation at all.

Malabaila di Canale, who remained in command of the *1a Compagnia* was assisted in his activities by lower-ranking officers, and he entrusted the *2a Compagnia* to *cavaliere* Rodolfo de Tscharner shortly before the resumption of hostilities. On 5 April 1794, the latter handed the company over to *capitano* Nicola Giuseppe Galleani, *cavaliere* d'Agliano.

On 8 September 1793, Galleani d'Agliano, then a *luogotenente* of the *Reggimento Guardie*, was wounded in the arm while fighting in Val Roia. After he had recovered, Malabaila, who knew him personally from his service in the same regiment, persuaded him to join his corps in April 1794 and had him appointed *capitano*.

The rapid turnover of officers in the *2ª Compagnia* shows the harshness of the type of warfare they fought, in which they rarely lasted more than a year. Recruitment became easier, although the two companies were unable to raise the two horn players they had planned. It was difficult to find horn players willing to enlist and share the poor and precarious lives of their comrades because of the small number of horn players in Piedmont. Only the *2a Compagnia* had its own horn player for one year, from 19 February 1793 to 1 March 1794.

By the end of 1792, Malabaila had done a fairly good job of recruiting the two companies. On 31 December, he was still far from the establishment strength of the *centuria* of 336 men. Nevertheless, no fewer than 247 men had applied in just two months and were carefully selected for their determination and physical fitness. This careful selection meant that as many as 50 men were deemed unsuitable, and even some officers had to be replaced as early as February 1793. The reasons for the exclusion of candidates from the muster rolls compiled at the Carmagnola recruitment centre are difficult to reconstruct. Most of them were probably excluded after screening by the *chirurgo maggiore*, since the standard entry

---

2   AST, StM, Vol. 5, Pag. 203: Regolamento per una Centuria di Cacciatori, 28 October 1792.

simply read, 'found unfit for military service'. In a few cases, the reasons were more precise: 'having been found guilty of misconduct' or 'for having hernia and being unfit for service'. Moreover, some candidates were found not to have been discharged from the regiment in which they were serving and had to be returned. They had tried to enlist fraudulently, to collect the *premio d'ingaggio* (enlistment bonus), and then to desert again.

The new speciality attracted youths, not veterans. Of the 180 or so volunteers accepted, about a third were very young, aged between 15 and 18. Another third were older but not over 21. The remaining third were between 22 and 30, perhaps with some military experience in a provincial regiment.

By encouraging each other, the volunteers presented themselves in groups. On the same day we find men from the same village enlisting, and we can imagine the disappointment of those of them who were found unfit. There were also cases of brothers or cousins rushing to enlist together. For example, the two d'Andriano brothers from Diano d'Alba. Carlo, who claimed to be 18 years old, was of robust build and was enlisted on 10 December 1792. He was judged suitable, and this perhaps favoured his brother Giuseppe, who was only 15 years old. He was also accepted and enlisted in the same company as Carlo. They both enlisted for two years, but in December 1794, they preferred to reenlist and face a third war campaign in their company, which had merged within the *Cacciatori Franchi* by then. Three campaigns were perhaps too many, and Giuseppe, the youngest, decided to desert and was declared such at the inspection review on 30 October 1795. He left fully clothed and armed with a sabre, leaving behind his *fucile* and cartridge box. Charles held out for another month but was also declared a deserter on 1 December 1795. Like his brother, he had taken care to leave his *fucile* behind. The Andriano brothers were lucky enough to pass through countless fights unscathed and unwounded.[3]

Spring was approaching, and in the Maritime Alps it arrived earlier than in the mountains further north. On 4 March 1793, Malabaila received the order to march the *Centuria* from Carmagnola to Breglio, in Val Roia, where the commander of the army corps of the County of Nice would assign them their final destination. In the muster rolls, there is a table summarising the force that Malabaila had managed to assemble in just four months. It was nearly full, with only the *cappellano* missing from the roll call. The *1a Compagnia*, commanded by Malabaila, assisted by *luogotenente* Blanchi d'Agliano and the *sotto luogotenente* Diego Visconti di Breme who died in combat on 7 August 1793, consisted of 144 men: three officers, six *sergenti*, two *caporali* and 136 light infantrymen. The *2a* was made up of 139 men: three officers, three *sergenti*, two *caporali*, one horn player and 130 light infantrymen.[4]

Deployed in an advanced position on the heights near the Authion massif, the *Centuria* had its first combat on 8 June 1793 and proved itself in the defence of the Mangiabò and Perus. On these occasions, Malabaila showed skill and initiative and, thanks to his rank of *maggiore*, also provided leadership for the militia and other advanced companies. On 12 June, during the fighting at Authion, the *Centuria* effectively contributed to the defence of the Testa dell'Authion, where the French were repulsed with heavy losses.

---

3 AST, Ruolini di rivista, Cacciatori Pian, Canale, Pandini, mazzi 1–4.
4 AST, Ruolini di Rivista, Cacciatori Pian, Canale, Pandini mazzo 2.

Estimates of the dead and wounded in the various battles of the War of the Alps can be found in Piedmontese chronicles and documents of the period, but for 8–12 June 1793, the dates of the Battle of Authion, the only reliable source we have for the *Centuria*'s losses are the muster rolls. Those of the first half of 1793, updated until the end of August, allow us to gather some data, albeit incomplete. Casualties are only recorded in the case of those killed in action. From these, it appears that the *1a Compagnia* had only two casualties, killed in the fighting of Perus on 8 June: the 16-year-old Giuseppe Schellino from Monforte and the 20-year-old Domenico Barolo from Portocomaro. There were no combat deaths in the *2a Compagnia*. In addition to the two from the *1a Compagnia*, five others are reported to have died in the Breglio hospital in July and August 1793, possibly as a result of wounds received in battle. After the defeat and heavy losses at the Battle of Authion, the French were hardly inactive, but the muster rolls do not record any other combat losses by Malabaila's soldiers. Harder times were coming, but in the meantime, Malabaila's initiative had proved to be a success and soon others, imitating him, petitioned the King to be allowed to recruit their own companies or *centuria* of volunteer light infantry.[5]

The light infantry of the *Canale* were armed with *sabri* (sabres) carried in sword belts. A belt at the waist held a plain cartridge box, capable of holding 60 rounds, but its inconvenience soon led to its abandonment, and the soldiers of the *Centuria* carried their cartridges in the most varied and imaginative ways.

Since the Turin arsenal did not have weapons of a quality suitable for the specific role of light infantry, the supply of rifles was only partial and was discontinued after a while. The carbines with rifled barrels used by the dragoons and the cavalry had never been very popular in Piedmont in the eighteenth century. When the few grenadiers of the dragoon regiments and the equally few *carabinieri* of the cavalry regiments had attempted to use their 1735 carbines, they had proved disastrous due to their slow loading.[6] On the other hand, rifles could prove invaluable for light infantry in mountain warfare, provided they could be used with the necessary calmness in aiming and firing. However, not all the light infantrymen in the *Centuria* could be issued with the rifled cavalry carbine due to the small number of them available in the Turin arsenal. The rest were issued with *fucili da dragone* without bayonets, which were shorter and easier to handle than infantry *fucili*, and whose accuracy, although not as good as those of the rifled carbines, were sufficient for the type of fighting and the distances involved in Alpine warfare. During an inspection of the *Carabinieri di Canale* on 25 August 1794, it was noted that the *Centuria* had various models of firearms, which were recognised as being in good condition, but it was decided to replace them with 423 identical 1759 pattern *fucili da dragone* with round bronze barrels, 145.7cm long and weighing 3.75kg.[7]

Since *Cacciatori Carabinieri di Canale* had to move easily through mountainous terrain, they were equipped with their own transport. Each company was provided with four mules to carry ammunition, powder, balls and provisions. The unit was rarely equipped with tents, but, at the *centuria* level, the *cappellano* and the *chirurgo maggiore* had their own, which

---

5   AST, Ruolini di Rivista, Cacciatori Pian, Canale, Pandini mazzo 2.
6   Sterrantino, *Le armi da fuoco del vecchio Piemonte*, pp.140–144.
7   AST, OGM, mazzo 73: Rivista d'Ispezione della Centuria Cacciatori Carabinieri di Canale, 15 August 1794.

also served as field chapel and hospital respectively. The two tents, the chest containing medicines and surgical instruments, and the sacred vestments were transported by a pair of additional mules. As far as transport was concerned, this became the standard equipment of mules for all volunteer light infantry companies that were subsequently organised.

Cavaliere Michele Antonio Maria Piano, seeing the success of Malabaila di Canale's initiative, decided to imitate him. On 14 December 1793, he proposed the creation of a *Compagnia Leggera di Cacciatori Volontari* (light company of volunteer chasseurs), which he would command.

Piano was an experienced *capitano luogotenente* in a grenadier company of the *Legione Truppe Leggere* who had been wounded in the Battle of Authion in Val Roia and had quickly recovered.[8] The proposal was immediately accepted by the King. On 21 December 1793, after promoting him to the rank of *capitano*, he issued the order for the formation of the company. The force was to consist of 100 men, made up of the *capitano luogotenente capitano*, *sotto luogotenente*, *sergente di compagnia*, two *sergenti di plotone*, six *caporali*, a *trombettiere* (trumpeter, bugler) and 87 light infantrymen. Recruitment was the responsibility of the company commander, who was also authorised to accept convicted criminals, provided they had not committed an offence that was outside the standards of conduct expected of the army. However, those who were clearly incorrigible were always to be sent back to serve the sentence from which they had been provisionally pardoned. It was implied that exemplary behaviour would merit a royal pardon.[9]

The arming and equipping of the *Piano Compagnia* was provided for in the regulations and separate orders of the same day. The *Corpo Reale d'Artiglieria* had to provide 96 *fucili da dragone* without bayonets, a cartridge box capable of holding 60 cartridges, and a sabre carried in a bandolier of the model adopted by the *Legione Truppe Leggere*.[10] The company began recruiting in the town of Castagnole Lanze, where Piano had been born and lived, and where he had returned to recover from wounds suffered during the 1793 campaign. Satisfied with the company and eager to increase the number of volunteers as much as possible, on 9 July 1794, the King authorised his brother *luogotenente capitano* Giuseppe Piano to raise a second company, thus increasing the corps to a *centuria*. It was now to consist of 307 men, seven of whom were in the *Centuria*'s staff: *aiutante maggiore*, *furiere*, *caporale maggiore*, *armaiolo*, *arciere*, *cappellano* and *chirurgo maggiore*. The two companies were led by three officers each, the *1a Compagnia* by a *capitano comandante*, *luogotenente* and *sotto luogotenente*, the *2a* by a *capitano luogotenente*, *luogotenente* and *sotto luogotenente*. The 147 troopers in each company consisted of two *trabanti*, a *furiere*, a *sergente di compagnia*, two *sergenti di plotone*, six *caporali*, two *caporali sovrannumerari*, a *trombettiere* and 132 light infantrymen.[11]

Michele Piano was more fortunate than Malabaila di Canale, who was never able to provide his company with the hunting horn player it wanted. This was no small problem,

---

8   Lo Faso di Serradifalco, *La difesa di un regno*, pp.473–474.
9   AST, OGM, mazzo 71: Regolamento per la formazione d'una Compagnia Leggera di Cacciatori Volontari, 21 December 1793
10 AST, StM, Vol. 6: Armamento per la Compagnia Leggera di Cacciatori Volontari Piano, 21 December 1793.
11 AST, OGM, mazzo 73: Formazione della 2a Compagnia di Cacciatori Pian, 9 September 1794.

given the fundamental importance of transmitting orders by sound to troops scattered in forward positions and on the move. Michele Piano, who came from the *Legione delle Truppe Leggere*, where there were some trumpeters, managed to persuade one of them to follow him; Carlo Trotti, from Valsesia, who had been a trumpeter in the *Legione* for eight years, became the trumpeter of the *1a Compagnia*. The *2a* also soon had its trumpeter, a certain Giovanni Francesco Ferrero from Savigliano, who enlisted on 2 September 1794.[12]

Loyal to the last to Savoy, Michele Piano rejoined the new King Vittorio Emanuele I (1802–1821) in 1814, as soon as he had recovered Piedmont and returned to Turin. He was assigned the command of the *Battaglione Cacciatori di Nizza*, which he commanded from 1 November 1814 to 10 April 1817.

Luigi Martin, *conte* di Montù Beccaria, was another *capitano* who fought fiercely against the French and who experienced intense personal vicissitudes during the war. His military career was typical of infantry officers in peacetime: he was a *cadetto* in the *Reggimento Piemonte*, then rose through the ranks of the same regiment, becoming a *primo luogotenente* in 1777, a *secondo luogotenente* in 1780 and finally a *capitano* in 1782. On 1 January 1793, he was given command of a militia company in Saluzzo. This led him to propose to the King the creation of a *Compagnia Franca di Cacciatori Volontari* (free company of volunteer light infantrymen). The project was approved and, on 30 January 1794, a regulation was issued detailing the characteristics of the new company.[13]

Martin thus began recruiting 120 men at Revello: *capitano comandante*, *luogotenente*, *sotto luogotenente*, *sergente di compagnia*, two *sergenti di plotone*, four *caporali* and four *caporali sovrannumerari*, two *tamburini* and 104 light infantrymen, to make his company operational when hostilities resumed in 1794. Volunteers were accepted even if charged with desertion or misuse of arms, if they then served throughout the war to redeem themselves. The equipment was similar to that provided to the *Centuria Piano*, but they were armed with ordinary infantry *fucili* of the pattern available at the time. A few months later, on 6 September, Martin was authorised to form a second company, increasing his unit to *centuria* strength. However, the new recruitment never commenced, because, on 17 September 1794, Martin, his *sergente di compagnia* Giovanni Borgogno and 59 light infantrymen were captured by the French in Val Varaita, while they were helping to repel an attack across the Colle dell'Agnello.[14] As Martin was a prisoner of the French, his company was temporarily commanded by Piano. More on Martin and his role in the *Cacciatori Franchi* will be covered later in this book, as he was not able to rejoin the ranks until November 1795.

The last autonomous company of volunteer's light troops, to be established was proposed to the King by a *capitano* of the *Reggimento Sardegna*, Giuseppe Pandini, and approved on 25 July 1794 under the name of *Compagnia Leggera Cacciatori Volontari*.[15] However, the initiative to propose the creation of the new company had been taken by the Austrian *generalleutnant Baron* Michelangelo Colli Marchini, who, noting the exuberance of volunteers

---

12 AST, Ruolini di rivista. Cacciatori Pian, Canale, Pandini mazzo 2.
13 Lo Faso di Serradifalco, *La difesa di un regno*, pp.417–418, and AST, OGM, mazzo 72: Regolamento per la creazione della Compagnia di Cacciatori Martin, 30 January 1794.
14 AST, Ruolini di rivista. Cacciatori Pian, Canale, Pandini [and Martin], mazzo 3.
15 AST, Stabilimenti Militari, Vol. 6: Regolamento per la creazione della Compagnia Leggera di Cacciatori Volontari Pandini, 25 July 1794.

from the Piedmontese infantry regiments in his area, called on Pandini and instructed him to go to Borgo San Dalmazzo to start recruiting to make up the company from the surplus volunteers of the *La Regina, Sardegna, Oneglia, Lombardia, Pinerolo* and *Acqui* regiments. The planned strength was 120 men, and the company was formed with similar personnel to the previous companies. On 17 September 1794, having verified the considerable number of volunteers, the strength of the company was increased to 170 men, but it did not stop at that point because it appears from the muster rolls that on 5 February 1796 the strength of Pandini's company, at that time part of the *Cacciatori Franchi*, was as many as 188 men.[16]

Having finally abandoned the idea of equipping the new light infantry with rifled carbines, it was planned that the Pandini's men would be equipped with bronzed *fucili da dragone*, with the cartridges being kept in the usual black cartridge box worn on the belt. The sabre, carried in a bandolier, completed their armament.

From *Corpo Franco* to *Cacciatori Franchi*

From 1793, with the opening of the Alpine passes, deserters from the French army and Sardinian subjects who had been forced to join the French army after the occupation of Savoie began to arrive from the other side of the Alps. To make the best use of these men, de Vins planned to organise them into a new *centuria* of light infantry, which was called the *Corpo Franco* (Free Corps), recruiting and mixing them regardless of nationality.

The founding regulation of the *Corpo Franco*, compiled by de Vins and issued by the King on 10 March 1793, stipulated that if the massive influx of deserters continued, further *centurie* would be formed. The 326 men envisaged as personnel for the *1ª Centuria* were equally divided into 163 per company. The *1ª* company was to be commanded by a *capitano* and the *2ª* by a *luogotenente capitano*, both with a *luogotenente* and a *sotto luogotenente* as subordinates. As far as nationality was concerned, one of the officers of each company was allowed to be a French expatriate. The composition of the two companies was somewhat different from those of the *cacciatori volontari* companies. They were each composed of a *sergente di compagnia*, a *sergente sovrannumerario*, four *caporali* and one *caporale sovrannumerario*, a *falegname*, two *tamburini* and 150 light infantrymen. The NCO cadres were initially to be provided by the infantry regiments but were later to be replaced by promoted soldiers.[17]

The recruitment of deserters began on 13 March, and they were assembled in the Citadel of Turin, where the six officers were appointed. The *1ª Compagnia* was placed under the command of *capitano* Filippo del Carretto, *cavaliere* of Camerano, the *2a* by *capitano luogotenente* Fidelle de Bonaud, the only French officer. The other four were subjects of Savoy. Filippo del Carretto was an officer of the *Reggimento Aosta* who had been dismissed by the King in 1781 for having married Carlotta de Salinis. Del Carretto had failed to obtain the necessary royal permission and had deserted by attempting to flee to Lombardy with his new wife. As early as 1792, Filippo del Carretto was reinstated in service with the

---

16 AST, Ruolini di rivista. Battaglione Cacciatori Franchi, mazzo 6.
17 AST, OGM, mazzo 70: Costituzione del 1° Corpo Franco, 10 March 1793.

rank of *luogotenente capitano* as an aide to *conte* Gio Batta Felice de Lazzary, the general commander of the troops prepared for the defence of Savoy.[18]

Del Carretto, however, was desperate for a command that would allow him to fight the French and redeem himself in the eyes of the King. He, therefore, seized the opportunity of a command in the *Corpo Franco*, even though it was made up of pardoned deserters and French fugitives.

On 20 March, de Bonaud was authorised to go recruiting to La Giandola, located in Val Roia and headquarters of the fourth army corps, through which deserters from France would pass. In March 1793, with the Alpine passes to the north still blocked by snow and very difficult to cross, Val Roia, located further south and with a somewhat milder climate, was probably the easiest route to cross the Alps.

Despite the difficulties, the flow of volunteers continued. In addition to the French, a considerable number of deserters from the Piedmontese army continued to present themselves for enrolment in the *Corpo Franco*. Thus, on 23 July 1793, the formation of a *2a Centuria* of 326 men was authorised, again in the Citadel of Turin. Meanwhile, the *1a Centuria* left Turin and went to the front, where it immediately saw action.

In the meantime, however, a problem had arisen. The constant quarrels between the French and the subjects of Savoy forced a decision to keep the two nationalities separate. After all, the Kingdom of Sardinia had been attacked and invaded by the French, who were, in a way, an atavistic competitor for the independence of the Savoy states. In the event one French company was not enough to contain them all, and browsing through the muster rolls, there are soldiers of French nationality enrolled in all four companies.

During the winter break, since the two *centurie*, also called the *1°* and *2° Corpo Franco*, now had the strength of a battalion, it was decided to merge them into a single corps, which retained the name of the *Corpo Franco*, and also had a staff that included: an *aiutante maggiore*, a *cappellano*, a *chirurgo maggiore* and a *quartiermastro*. In the lower ranks, the corps staff consisted of a *sergente maggiore*, a *caporale maggiore*, two *armaioli* and two or three *falegnami* in charge of maintaining tents, carriages and carts. Lastly, to drill and train the recruits, who were always housed in the Citadel of Turin where the staff was also located, a *capitano luogotenente*, a *sotto luogotenente*, six senior NCOs and four old soldiers, all experienced but no longer fit for active service, received the recruits in the reserve company, where they trained them to fight.[19]

The orders made the merger of the two *corpi franchi* effective during January 1794 and, on 7 January, the list of officers was formalised. The *maggiore comandante* was Alessandro Borgarelli, *conte* d'Isone. At the beginning of 1793, Borgarelli d'Isone was *capitano* of a *fucilieri* company of the *Reggimento Piemonte*, then of a grenadier one from 12 May. Dismissed for speeches not deemed appropriate to his role, he was later reinstated by the King and was assigned to the *Corpo Franco*. Shortly afterwards, he was promoted to *maggiore comandante* of the *Corpo Franco*. In April 1794 he was wounded during the fighting in Val Roia. On his return, on 10 August of the same year, he was wounded again, in the foot, during the fighting in Val Vermegnana on the Piedmont side of the Colle di Tenda. On 2 April 1796, he

---

18   Merla, *O Bravi Guerrieri!*, pp.114–116.
19   AST, OGM, mazzo 70: Fusione in un unico Corpo del 1° e 2° Corpo Franco. 31 December 1793

was appointed *luogotenente colonnello* of the *2° Reggimento Truppe Leggere* with whom he took part in the last heroic defence between Ceva and Mondovì. He fell into the hands of the French, who released him on 23 June 1796. At the Restoration, he was recalled into service with the rank of *Aiutante Generale*.[20]

Throughout the 1794 campaign, the *Corpo Franco* fought mainly on the southern front and, like the other volunteer light infantry corps, proved combative and determined. The French members of the corps in particular fought to the death, knowing that if they were captured and identified as French, their compatriots in the revolutionary army would undoubtedly execute them.

The officers of the *Corpo Franco* generally suffered losses and wounds in combat and behaved with honour. Moreover, many of them were exposed in advanced positions at the head of companies and platoons, captured by the enemy, and imprisoned for months. But even in a group of heroes, not everyone is always brave. In the *Corpo Franco* there was a case of cowardice in the face of the enemy. On 9 May 1794, *maggiore comandante* Borgarelli d'Isone found it necessary to report the behaviour of one of his officers, *capitano luogotenente* Franz Octavius Lipp, a Swiss national who was in effective command of his company. During the bloody battles of 25–27 April 1794 in Val Roia, Lipp had remained in the entrenchments at the start of the attack on the pretext of being ill. He then left the camp and, after had hastily crossing the Colle di Tenda, went to Cuneo, the headquarters of the reserve company, again claiming to be ill. He was immediately struck off the muster rolls with the justification: 'Removed from the rolls following a letter from the *Regia Segreteria di Guerra* of 9 May 1794 for having kept absent from his corps during the attack of 25 April 1794 and, on the 27th under the pretext of illness, left the camp and went to Tenda and then to Cuneo'.[21]

During the winter break of 1794–1795, it was judged that so many separate companies and *centurie* of volunteer light infantry were proving difficult control. It was therefore decided to merge them into a single corps of 11 companies, the 10 existing ones and one of reserve. Thus, on 7 February 1795, the *Cacciatori Franchi* were born. The 10 active companies were of equal strength and included a *capitano*, a *capitano luogotenente*, a *luogotenente*, a *sotto luogotenente*, three *trabanti*, a *furiere*, a *sergente di compagnia*, two *sergenti di plotone*, two *sergenti sovrannumerari*, six *caporali*, four *caporali sovrannumerari*, two *tamburini*, *garzone chirurgo*, *armaiolo*, *arciere* and 160 light infantrymen, making a well-staffed company of 188 men. The reserve company, of variable strength, and originating from the *Corpo Franco* now included a *capitano tenente*, a *luogotenente*, a *sotto luogotenente*, three *trabanti* and a *furiere*, a *sergente di compagnia*, a *sergente di plotone*, a *sergente sovrannumerario*, four *caporali* (actual and sovrannumerari) and 20 veteran light infantrymen. The control of a corps of about 2,000 men required a corps staff: one officer was assigned for the management of discipline and administration, in the latter task assisted by a *quartiermastro*. The care of the men's souls was entrusted to a *cappellano* appointed from time to time by the general commanding from among those available. From the point of view of health, an important innovation was that each company included a more qualified *garzone chirurgo* instead of the *frater*.

---

20   Lo Faso di Serradifalco, *La difesa di un regno*, pp.237–238.
21   AST, Ruolini di rivista, Cacciatori Franchi, mazzo 1.

The French de Bonaud company was effectively made independent, being managed by its commander in recruitment, administration and discipline.

A key difference between the *Corpo Franco* and the *Cacciatori Franchi* was that the new unit was considered a *corps d'élite*. For this reason, pardoned deserters were now excluded from enrolment. Obviously, this applied only to new recruits because the many pardoned deserters in the companies were to remain there to finish their contracted service. Again, the royal intentions and reality did not always reconcile, and in order to bring the companies up to the planned number of recruits, their commanders often had to turn a blind eye.

Soldiers and NCOs of the *Cacciatori Franchi* were armed with 1759-pattern bronze-plated *fucile da dragone* without bayonet, a sabre on the belt and a strong cartridges box, capable of carrying 60 rounds on their belts. *Caporali* were also equipped with small axes to cut wood for cooking for their squads. Each company's ammunition and other equipment were carried by the seven mules assigned to them.

On 7 April 1795, the amalgamation of the pre-existing companies was complete and the *conte* d'Isone, *maggiore ispettore* (major inspector) of the *Cacciatori Franchi* reviewed the 10 companies and reported to the King. Some points in the report are important for the reconstruction of the corps' history. For example, it had been found that the companies of d'Agliano and Quincinetto, originating from the two *Cacciatori di Canale*, were full of malcontents due to the stern management of the *Cavaliere* di Canale. The companies had been supplied with unsuitable mules, which had to be replaced with more appropriate ones, considering that 'given the nature of the service of these companies and the speed with which they have to transport from one place to another, camp and strike their camp'.

As many of the soldiers were no longer able to continue such arduous service, d'Isone proposed that seven be transferred to the *Battaglione degli Invalidi* (Invalid Battalion) and four, who were able to perform some kind of service, to the *Battaglione di Guarnigione*. Finally, he proposed to discharge another 25, seven with a cash gratuity for their good behaviour, the others without.[22]

The *Cacciatori Franchi* was always at the forefront, often in reckless actions, and suffered a major defeat that severely limited their fighting ability for some time. It was in August 1795 when de Bonaud planned an action aimed at conquering the village of San Martino (now Saint-Martin Vésuble), in the County of Nice. But apart from the immediate psychological effect on the French garrisons in the area and on the morale of the Piedmontese troops in the event of victory, it could not have had any important strategic objectives. After capturing San Martino, the Piedmontese expeditionary corps under de Bonaud would have had no choice but to cross the Alps and return to Piedmont, leaving the area to the French. In fact, it does not seem that the Austro-Piedmontese command intended to send a sufficient number of infantry battalions to permanently occupy San Martino and use the village as a base for later advances. Nevertheless, de Bonaud was so insistent that he succeeded in obtaining de Vins' permission to proceed. Having received it, he involved the following units:

---

22   AST, LUF, mazzo 276, letter dated 7 April 1795.

Three companies of *Cacciatori Franchi* with a total of 12 officers and 478 NCOs and soldiers: de Bonaud's French company, five officers and 197 troops; de Saisi's company, four officers and 183 troops; Quincinetto's company, three officers and 98 troops.

Four companies of *Cacciatori Scelti di Nizza*, totalling 25 officers and 498 NCOs and soldiers: Company della Rocca, seven officers and 111 NCOs and men; Company Cauvin, seven officers and 144 NCOs and men; Company Conte, five officers and 77 NCOs and men and Company Falchi, six officers and 166 NCOs and men.

Company Andorno of the *Corpo dei Guastatori*, four officers and 95 NCOs and men.

About 70 militiamen were to be added to the regular troops, but only to protect the flank of the attack. Even with poor weather conditions along the route to San Martino – heavy rain and even snow – de Bonaud, did not take the sensible decision to stop the mission. Thus, on 1 September 1795, he found himself on the outskirts of the village with no more than a few hundred frozen men with wet powder, unable to fire their weapons. The situation, already critical, was made worse by the fact that the French, alerted to their arrival, were waiting for them with superior forces entrenched in the village. The attack, therefore, ended in disaster, and de Bonaud himself was killed, having received numerous wounds.[23]

A large proportion of the *Cacciatori Franchi* who took part in the action were expatriate French Royalists, serving either in de Bonaud's or de Saisi's companies. In fact, the rosters of the latter company show that almost all the men who belonged to it were French nationals, with a few Savoyards, Nizzardi, Piemontesi, Belgians or Swiss among them.[24] It seems that 86 of these French exiles were captured by the enemy during the action, and we have no evidence of their fate.[25]

The hasty retreat towards Piedmont was risky due to the persistent bad weather conditions and many *Cacciatori Scelti di Nizza* decided to return to their homes. This is reported in the memoirs of *conte* Alessandro Giuseppe Thaon di San Andrea e di Revel, *quartiermastro generale* of the fourth Piedmontese army corps.[26]

The judgement on de Bonaud's unreasonable stubbornness in proceeding with the expedition, first because of bad weather and then because of the knowledge that the garrison of San Martino had been alerted, contrasts with the ideal characteristics of an officer commanding in a partisan war. These rules were largely framed by de Bonaud himself: 'The officers commanding these partisan bands required a great deal of energy, élan and dash, and it was generally recognised this type of service was the most fatiguing and the most dangerous'. The superb 1759 book *Le Partisan* by Jeney gives the qualities of a good chief of light infantrymen:

---

23 B. Pauvert, *L'incursione del cavalier de Bonaud a Saint Martin Vésuble il 1° settembre 1795* (Torino: Acta, 2007), pp.71–99.
24 AST, Ruolini di rivista, Cacciatori Franchi, mazzo 5.
25 Pauvert, *L'incursione del cavalier de Bonaud*, pp.71–99.
26 I. Thaon di Revel, *Mémoires sur la guerre des Alpes et les événement en Piémont pendant la Révolution Française* (Torino: Bocca, 1871), p.285.

1. A lively imagination for plans, and rushes and resources.
2. A penetrating mind, capable of instantly combining all the circumstances of an action.
3. An intrepid heart against all appearances of danger.
4. Steadfast countenance, always assured, and showing no sign of anxiety or indecision.
5. A fortunate memory, to call everyone by his name.
6. An alert, robust and indefatigable temperament, to go through everything, and to give one's soul to everything.
7. An accurate and rapid *coup d'oeil*; that he immediately grasps the fault and the conveniences, the obstacles and the danger of terrain and all the features he traverses.
8. Such sentiments by which he secures the respect, confidence and devotion of the whole corps.[27]

It almost seems as if de Bonaud was searching desperately for success at all costs, even if it meant losing his life or at least losing most of the light infantrymen under his command. In addition to the loss of de Bonaud himself, two other company commanders of the *Cacciatori Franchi, capitani* Saisi and Quincinetto were taken prisoner.[28]

After the heavy losses suffered, the *Cacciatori Franchi,* having partly replenished their ranks with Piedmontese volunteers, still managed to field 23 officers and 498 men for the final defence in the spring of 1796. The position and strength of the companies were as follows: Company Boarino, deployed at Valdieri with three officers and 59 NCOs and men; Company Piano at Limone, with three officers and 98 NCOs and men; Company Buriasco at Bagnasco, with two officers and 77 NCOs and men; Company Francioni at Bagnasco, with four officers and 71 NCOs and men; Company Pandini at Perlo, with three officers and 77 NCOs and men; Company Barret (ex-de Bonaud) at Millesimo, with two officers and 55 NCOs and men; Company d'Agliano near Ceva, two officers and 115 NCOs and men; Company Martin at Cairo, with three officers and 79 NCOs and men; Company Pattono, which had long been in another part of the front, was deployed in the Susa valley, where it was joined in 1796 by the last two companies, all three of which garrisoned the Brunetta Fort.[29]

Shortly before his death, in view of the large number of French volunteers who were still rushing to enlist (at least some of them in de Saisi's company), de Bonaud proposed the creation of a second company of French *Cacciatori Franchi*. This proposal was accepted by the King but was not followed up after the de Bonaud death.

On 12 April 1796, still hoping for Austrian intervention to help the few thousand Piedmontese troops fighting against Bonaparte's army, it was decided to create a twelfth company of *Cacciatori Franchi*, but a few days later, the war ended, and the decision was not followed up. In September 1796, the *Cacciatori Franchi* were disbanded under the terms of

---

27 Louis Michel de Jeney. *Le Partisan ou l'art de faire la petite-guerre avec succès* (La Haye: Constapel, 1759), pp.6–7.
28 Pauvert, *L'incursione del cavalier de Bonaud*, p.79.
29 Pauvert, *L'incursione del cavalier de Bonaud*, p.323.

the Treaty of Cherasco. The officers, NCOs and enlisted men who still wished to continue serving in the Piedmontese army were integrated into the infantry regiments.

The Cacciatori Scelti di Nizza

When the city of Nice and its surrounding territory were abandoned in September 1792, the militia of the County of Nice had followed the Piedmontese army and established themselves in outposts in the Val Roia, where their knowledge of the area had proved invaluable in contributing to the defence. Soon, with the arrival of the first snowfalls, some of the *Nizzardi* militiamen, who were not equipped to spend the winter in the mountains, were allowed to winter in the fortress of Saorgio, while the majority went to Cuneo on the other side of Colle di Tenda.

From Cuneo, a delegation of officers, NCOs and militiamen arrived in Turin on 9 November 1792 to meet the King. They showed him their determination to offer their services in the war against the French who had invaded their homeland. They also resolutely asked Vittorio Amedeo III 'to put them in a position to prove their loyalty, attachment and devotion to his Royal Person and family.'[30] At least, this is what the documents of the time report. We do not know whether the delegation was received by the King himself, but it is very likely that the audience took place. Vittorio Amedeo III was a pleasant man who did not disdain contact with his people, and the loyalty of the *Nizzardi* was an elixir for him. Moreover, the loyalty of the people of the County of Nice was a small consolation for the distress he felt at the embarrassing behaviour of the commanders of the two corps of the army that were supposed to defend Savoy and Nice.

Among the officers who went to Turin was *capitano* Xavier de Saisi (often reported as Saissi, but his signature on a document was Saisi), who commanded units that fiercely opposed the French throughout the hostilities. De Saisi, who was immediately promoted to *maggiore*, was entrusted with an adequate amount of money to provide the NCOs and militiamen everything they needed, even suitable clothing to survive the winter, since they had had to flee their homes in September when the weather was still warm. In order to provide them with some weapons, the members of the delegation were kitted out, then the *Ufficio Generale del Soldo* equipped and procured similar equipment, bayonets and infantry *fucili* for the *Nizzardi* militiamen stationed in the Cuneo area. The King also ordered that companies with 100 men each, including officers and NCOs, should be formed in the province of Cuneo from the Nice militia. These were then to form a battalion to be temporarily attached to the provincial infantry *Reggimento Nizza*. The delegation of militiamen that arrived in Turin was made up of *capitano* de Saisi, five other aristocrats (Giacinto Castagna, *conte* di Gairaud, *vassallo* Andrea Dealbert, *vassallo* Filiberto Boteri, *vassallo* Giuseppe Raimondo Degubernatis di Gorbio and *barone* Galea della Maddalena), six *luogotenenti*, six *sotto luogotenenti*, six sergeants, five *caporali* and nine militiamen.[31]

---

30   AST, LUF, mazzo 271. Letter of 9 November 1792.
31   AST, Ruolini di rivista, Cacciatori Franchi, mazzo 5.

While the *Nizzardi* were concentrated in Cuneo to form the provisional militia battalion established by the King, many others were scattered throughout the Val Roia, and their recruitment was so coveted that on 2 December 1792 even the *Reggimento Chablais* was authorised to send two officers to the fortress of Saorgio to try to recruit some.

There are few records in the Turin State Archives of the events involving these militiamen in 1793 and the first two months of 1794. There are numerous letters sent to Turin by their then commander, militian *luogotenente colonnello* Giovanni Giuseppe Testoris, requesting equipment and aid. Testoris was a militia commander who had not hesitated to leave his notary's office to organise resistance of the militia of Nice to the invaders. As the rank of *luogotenente colonnello* of the militia was purely honorary, on 29 July 1794, Testoris was promoted to the rank of *capitano* of infantry, enabling him to carry out his mission more effectively. As further recognition of his work, when his age and health prevented him from continuing his active service, he was posted as *capitano* to the *Corpo degli Invalidi* with a pension.

In this way, other delicate personal situations were resolved, such as that of *capitano* Andrea Marco Rossetti from the village of Turbia (today, La Turbie), a volunteer from a militia company who had served for months without pay and now, having become an effective infantry *capitano*, received an allowance of £200. Another delicate case that had to be dealt with was that of Pietro Auda of Lantosca (today Lantosque), a militia *luogotenente* who later joined the *Reggimento Nizza* with the same infantry rank. He received £150 to contribute to the costs of caring for his brother, a *capitano* himself in the Nice militia, seriously wounded in the fighting of June 1793 and who later died in the fortress of Saorgio. Finally, another example of *Nizzardi* loyalty is that of *sergente* Giuseppe Brocardi, later promoted to *sotto luogotenente*, who received financial aid for following the retreat from Nice, taking his wife and five children with him.[32]

But the time had come for the *Nizzardi* militia to be organised into a regular unit so that they could make a greater contribution to the war effort. *Luogotenente colonnello* Colli di Felizzano, who was the commander of the *2° Battaglione Cacciatori*, quickly agreed to the proposal of Onorato Maria Foccard, *conte* della Rocca, a skilful commander of the *Nizzardi* militia and a former soldier of the Piedmontese army, having been a *luogotenente* in the *Reggimento Nizza* before a rapid promotion during the war, first to *capitano luogotenente*, then to *capitano*. His promotions were based on his effective command of the Nice militia in various combats, in which he was also wounded. In early 1794, della Rocca was given the task of creating a company of volunteer light infantry recruited from among his volunteers and called the *Cacciatori Scelti di Nizza* (Selected Light Infantry Company of Nice). The project was approved by the King on 26 April 1794, but its execution began just as the French attack from the territory of the Republic of Genoa disrupted the Piedmontese defences of the Val Roia.

With the front line re-established, the company was finally settled. It was to consist of 150 men of all ranks and organised like the previous companies of volunteer light infantry. The *Cacciatori Scelti di Nizza*, as well as colleagues in the ordnance and volunteer light infantry, had the task to 'disturb the enemy and make petty war on him'.[33]

---

32   AST, LUF, mazzo 272: Concessione di gratificazioni regie, 23 October 1793.
33   AST, OGM, mazzo 72: Regolamento per la formazione dei Cacciatori Scelti di Nizza, 26 Apr 1794.

The critical strategic situation on the southern front favoured quick decisions. Taking advantage of the disheartened but numerous *Nizzardi* militia who had followed the Piedmontese even beyond the Colle di Tenda, the company of *Cacciatori Scelti di Nizza* soon became the first of eight, formally divided into two battalions and a staff. The overall strength was numerically comparable to that of a line infantry regiment, but only in terms of numbers because the companies were intended to operate autonomously.

Until the autumn of 1795, the recruitment of *Nizzardi* in the *Cacciatori Scelti di Nizza* remained adequate, although, as we shall see, losses began to be significant, and it became difficult to keep the companies operational due to illness and the injuries sustained in the frequent fierce fighting.

As many officers had also withdrawn beyond the Colle di Tenda alongside the militia, some 30 of them joined the staff and companies of the *Cacciatori Scelti*. Of the many others who remained, some, who were considered more deserving, were placed on a waiting list for assignment to the line infantry as places became available. The others were attached to the *Cacciatori Scelti* to be fully integrated into them when necessary.

Although the companies of the *Cacciatori Scelti di Nizza* had to operate autonomously, there remained a number of tasks for their management that could hardly be performed by the three officers or NCOs in command of the company, which sometimes operated divided into platoons sent to different locations. The administration of the corps, the procurement of uniforms, arms, equipment and food, caring for the sick and wounded, offering spiritual guidance, the collection and storage of the company muster rolls and, finally justice and recruitment were tasks that required dedicated and specialised personnel. The problem was solved by creating one staff for the first four companies and a second for the next four. The two staffs, commanded by a *maggiore*, were organised like the battalion staffs of the line infantry. Following the custom of the Piedmontese light infantry consolidated during the War of the Alps, the two groups of companies of the *Cacciatori Scelti di Nizza* took their names from the commanders of their respective staffs. Thus, at the end of 1795, the first four companies were called 'Ferrere' the second four 'Chevillard'.[34]

Luigi Garetti, *cavaliere* di Ferrere, was a Piedmontese nobleman who, at the beginning of the War of the Alps was appointed *maggiore* of the militia of the Province of Turin. Wanting to fight the French more effectively, he asked to be given an active role and was therefore sent to serve in the *Cacciatori Scelti di Nizza* with the rank of infantry *maggiore* and placed in command of the staff of the first four companies. Appreciated by the commander of the 2° *Cacciatori*, marchese Colli,[35] in March 1796, he was appointed *maggiore* of the *Reggimento Cacciatori*, which had been formed by uniting the *1°* and *2° Cacciatori*.[36]

Giuseppe Vittorio, *cavaliere* di Chevillard, from Nice served in the *Corpo Reale di Marina*, the Savoy navy, at the beginning of the War of the Alps. He had reached the rank of *luogotenente di fregata* (frigate lieutenant). With the navy reduced to a small force, and eager to fight the French for the liberation of the County of Nice, Chevillard was placed in command

---

34 AST, Ruolini di rivista, Cacciatori Scelti di Nizza, mazzo 2.
35 Henceforth, to distinguish the Austrian general Colli from the Piedmontese Colli, we will refer to the former as 'Baron Colli'.
36 Lo Faso di Serradifalco, *La difesa di un regno*, p.364.

of the staff of the second four companies of the *Cacciatori Scelti di Nizza*. He ended the war with the rank of *luogotenente colonnello* of infantry, achieved on 26 March 1796.[37]

Until August 1795, the *Cacciatori Scelti di Nizza* managed to keep their numbers fairly close to their establishment thanks to the continuous flow of volunteers, while bitterly fighting the French in the hope of liberating their county. However, from 2 September, during the overly reckless attack led by *capitano* de Bonaud of the *Cacciatori Franchi Francesi* in which the *Cacciatori Scelti di Nizza* also took part, many were killed or taken prisoner, and many of them, discouraged and close to home, returned to their villages, sometimes only to spend the winter. From that moment, the recruitment of *Nizzardi* slowed down, and the companies had to be brought up to strength with volunteers from other provinces. However, the war was now being fought in Piedmont, with the French trying to cross the Maritime Alps. Faced with the danger of seeing their own lands invaded, the Piedmontese rushed to enlist, and even the *Cacciatori Nizzardi* were able to achieve a reasonable strength. The young people, listening to the veterans' accounts of the partisan war in the village tavern, were inspired by patriotic love and flocked to the defence of Piedmont, thus enabling the fight to continue.

Browsing through the muster rolls for the first half of 1796 for some companies helps to clarify the situation. The della Rocca company in April 1796 had only 94 men, including NCOs and officers, well below the planned number. Of the absentees cited in the same source, it appears that as many as 71 were considered prisoners of the French, 54 of whom had been absent since 2 September 1795, the date of the attempted attack led by de Bonaud. It would have been more accurate to define these men as missing, because there was no certain information about their fate. These could have included those killed, injured and captured or those who, instead of retreating across the Alps, had returned to their homes and remained there. It was hoped that the latter would still return, which was not impossible because, at the beginning of April, the Alps were still covered in snow, preventing them from crossing. In April 1796 Conte's company was also of a reasonable size: 93 men, including NCOs and officers. Besides these, 77 were from Nice, but the others were Piedmontese or of other origins, for example, one from Veneto and one from Liguria in Sanremo.[38]

Thaon di Revel, a reliable source, provides the available data on the location and size of the *Cacciatori Scelti di Nizza* in February 1796, just before the last resistance: two companies, Conte and Galea, were stationed in Limone Piemonte, to defend the exits of the Colle di Tenda. Together, they had 11 officers and 144 NCOs and men. Christini's company was in Bagnasco reduced to a minimum of four officers and 50 able-bodied NCOs and men. Also, in Bagnasco were Falqui's company, with four officers and 62 NCOs and men, and Giletta's company, with four officers and 83 NCOs and men. Domerego's company was in the village of Viola and comprised four officers and 73 NCOs and men. Cauvin's Company was in Mombasile and was the strongest: five officers and 125 NCOs and soldiers. Della Rocca's Company, was very weak, and was stationed in Millesimo with seven officers but only 56 able-bodied NCOs and men. In that February of 1796, which heralded difficult times for the Piedmontese army, the *Cacciatori Scelti di Nizza* was reduced to just over half

---

37 Lo Faso di Serradifalco, *La difesa di un regno*, pp.284–285.
38 AST, Ruolini di rivista, Cacciatori Scelti di Nizza, mazzo 3.

their prescribed strength (39 officers and 643 NCOs and men), and even that was thanks to a significant contribution of Piedmontese volunteers.[39]

At the end of hostilities, the *Cacciatori Scelti* were sent to Garlasco, a Lombard town in the province of Pavia, but then a Savoy possession. Here, they sadly waited to learn their fate. At that time, many Piedmontese deserted, the purpose of their enthusiastic enlistment having ceased. Some *Nizzardi* chose to remain in Piedmont and were discharged, retiring to private life or joining infantry regiments; others returned to their homes and their trade, living under French rule until the Restoration.

Table 5. Summary of the history of the volunteer light infantry during the War of the Alps.

1792	1793	1794	1795	1796
Cacciatori-Carabinieri di Canale (2 Cp, 28 Oct 1792)	Cacciatori-Carabinieri di Canale (2 Cp, 28 Oct 1792)	Cacciatori-Carabinieri di Canale (2 Cp, 28 Oct 1792)	To *Cacciatori Franchi* 10 Cp, 7 Feb 1795)	Cacciatori Franchi (11 Cp)
	Corpo Franco (2 cp 15 Mar 1793. 4 Cp 25 Jul 1793)	Corpo Franco (2 cp 15 Mar 1793. 4 Cp 25 Jul 1793)		
	Cacciatori Pian (1 Cp 14 Dec 1793)	Cacciatori Pian (2 Cp 9 Jul 1794)		
		Cacciatori Martin (1 Cp 30 Jan 1794)		
		Cacciatori Pandini (1 Cp 25 lug 1794)		
		Cacciatori Scelti di Nizza (1 cp 26 Apr 1794, 4 cp 23 May 1794, 8 cp 24 Jul 1794)	8 cp	8 cp
Total 2 Cp	Total 7 cp	Total 17 cp	Total 18 cp	Total 19 cp

Likely inspired by de Vins, the uniforms of most of the new Piedmontese army corps from the winter of 1792–1793 were inspired by those worn at that time by the Austrian army, and colour plate 13 shows a comparison of the two fashions.

The practical Austrian uniforms, characterised by a short white coat without lapels, retained only the tails of the uniforms, which were shortened. A bandolier for a cartridge box and a belt for a sword were worn on the coat, which remained fully buttoned. Most infantrymen wore a leather helmet (*kasket*) with a conspicuous leather front riser, the centre of which was adorned with a small baroque-style brass plate bearing the monogram *FII* of Emperor Francis II. The regiments were distinguished by the colour of the collar, facing, lining and the metal of the buttons. The infantrymen of the regiments recruited in the eastern frontier regions of the Habsburg, Hungarian and other possessions, instead of breeches wore narrow trousers which ended at the ankles, and black leather boots instead

---

39   Thaon di Revel, *Mémoires sur la guerre des Alpes*, p.325.

of shoes. To protect themselves from the weather, soldiers in the Austrian army were issued with a grey overcoat.

Vittorio Amedeo III had a different taste in uniforms. The Piedmontese uniforms imitated the Habsburg uniforms, but without completely abandoning the Piedmontese traditions and blue colour. Lapels were abolished and the tails of the coats were shortened to mid-thigh length. With a few exceptions, the coats were buttoned only at the top to show off the short waistcoat, called a *gilet*. Some corps also preferred to keep their breeches with shoes and knee gaiters, while others adopted the trousers and boots of the Hungarians. They were also given coats, first white and then grey. On the other hand, the soldiers of the regiments who wore the long woollen waistcoats traditionally did not receive overcoats, as they were considered sufficiently covered. However, a limited number of greatcoats were issued to each company to protect soldiers during sentry duty.

The Piedmontese commanders were most imaginative: helmets, busbies and hats were created to replace the classic tricorn hat, which remained in use for all the other corps of the Piedmontese army until the end of the War of the Alps (see colour plates 14 and 15).

The first to adopt the uniform *all'Austriaca* (Austrian-style) in November 1792 were the *Cacciatori di Canale*, whose regulation stipulated that their short blue coat should be distinguished by a light green colour, with white-trimmed collar and facings, white-trimmed turnbacks, and tin buttons. Their *gilets* were also light green, while the trousers were dark blue. The headgear imitated the Austrian *kasket* but was lighter because it was made of felt, and its style was softened by a less conspicuous front riser, adorned with the crowned royal monogram in the centre. On the left side, the helmet was decorated with a blue plume with a red tip.

The two parts of the *Corpo Franco*, the Piedmontese and the French, received their Austrian-style uniform at the beginning of 1793. It was identified by the white buttons loops of the coat, the felt hat with the left side of the brim pinned up, and the blue and red plume. The two nationalities were distinguished by the colour of the collar and facing: yellow for the Savoy subjects, and red for the French Royalists. The other volunteer light infantry companies formed between 1793 and 1794 wore the uniforms shown in colour plate 14 and were distinguished by the colours shown in colour plate 13.

To describe the uniforms of the *Cacciatori Scelti di Nizza*, a few remarks are necessary. In 1794, the unit wore a simple Austrian-style uniform, with carmine-red distinctions (the colour of the aigle in the coat of arms of Nizza) and a tricorn hat. The loyalty shown by the Nizzardi's youth to the dynasty was rewarded by the King in 1795. He gave them a peculiar felt helmet, decorated on the front with a remarkable brass plate with the crowned royal monogram in the centre and a hunting horn in the two lower corners. Above the shield was a brass lion's head with a black fur tail hanging backwards.

In early 1795, the establishment of the *Cacciatori Franchi*, which had its origins in the *Corpo Franco* and into which all the independent light infantry companies named after the commanding *capitano*, except for the *Cacciatori Scelti di Nizza*, were merged, led to the abolition of the previous uniforms. They were replaced by a fully buttoned Austrian-style coat that was distinguished by red lapels and tin buttons. The companies composed of Savoy subjects retained the yellow collar and cuffs of the *Corpo Franco*, while those of the expatriate Frenchmen were pink. A novelty for the Piedmontese army was the headgear, in the form of a fur busby adorned with a blue cockade fixed to the left of the upper edge on which was inserted a plume in the colours assigned to the company to which it belonged. Also of the same colours was the light infantrymen's wavy lace sewn onto the sleeves. The distinctive colours were: d'Isone's company, green with white apex; de Bonaud's company, red and yellow; de Saisi's company, yellow; Buriasco's company, green; Pattono company, blue; d'Agliano's company, blue and red; Quincinetto's company, green and red; Piano's 1° company, white and red; Piano's 2° company, white and blue; Pandini's company, scarlet and the reserve company, black and white.[40]

The short Austrian-style uniforms remained the prerogative of the Piedmontese volunteer light infantrymen up to the rank of *caporale* and were also distributed, apparently without distinction of speciality, to drummers, buglers and hunting horn players. Although we have found no trace of them in the documents, it is likely that these company musicians displayed their speciality distinctions at their *capitano*'s or personal initiative.

The NCOs and officers wore the uniform of their respective corps but retained the long tails of their coats as a privilege. While the NCOs of the *Cacciatori Franchi* wore the busby, nothing was prescribed for the officers, who could, therefore, opt for the tricorne hat.

Arrival of Reinforcements: Light Infantry Companies from Provincial Regiments

In the summer of 1793, the Piedmontese army, which was preparing to retake Savoy via the Moncenisio and Piccolo San Bernardo passes, was short of light infantrymen. So much so that the small company of *Cacciatori di Camoscio*, the militia corps from Valle d'Aosta, were also deployed in Savoy. To increase these small numbers on 30 September 1793, in a hurry and with the regiments already starting to go down from Moncenisio and marching into the Tarantaise, it was decided to use men from the reserve company of the provincial *Reggimento Novara* to form a company of *Cacciatori-Carabinieri*.[41] The *capitano* of the *Reggimento Novara*, Luigi Valperga, *conte* di Barone, who, far from Savoy and having to hurry to the Tarantaise, was entrusted with the command. Barone also commanded the company during the Siege of Toulon where, in December 1793, he fell ill and returned to his homeland, where he was placed on inactive duty.

Initially, the light infantry company from the *Reggimento Novara*'s would consist of 98 men: a *capitano*, a *luogotenente*, a *sotto luogotenente*, *furiere*, two *trabanti*, a *sergente di compagnia*, a *sergente di plotone*, two *sergenti sovrannumerari*, four *caporali*, two *caporali sovrannumerari*, two *tamburini* and 72 light infantrymen. Subsequently, after the unsuccessful invasion, on 11 November 1793, the strength was reduced to 60 men. The light infantrymen of the *Reggimento* wore the normal regimental uniform, with the only distinction being the wavy lace on their sleeves.

To complete the eight company-strong *2° Cacciatori* on 11 November 1793, it was decided to hastily raise a company of light infantrymen in the provincial *Reggimento Maurienne*. This company, too, was also to consist of 60 men, dressed in the normal regimental uniforms

---

40 E. Ricchiardi, *Le uniformi delle truppe leggere dell'esercito del Regno di Sardegna, 1792–1796* (Torino: Acta, 2007), pp.107–126, Fig. 1–10.
41 AST, OGM, Mazzo 88: Costituzione di una compagnia di cacciatori nel Reggimento Novara, 11 November 1793.

distinguished by the wavy lace on their sleeves. Formed in Susa as early as the 16th, the *Maurienne* light infantry company was hastily dispatched to Rivoli to join the *2° Cacciatori* already on their way to Oneglia to be embarked to join the allied troops at the Siege of Toulon.[42]

The creation of the first two companies of light infantry in the provincial regiments created interest in other regiments, so Vittorio Amedeo III, to 'indulge the natural inclination of his subjects in the use of arms', instituted light infantry companies in the other provincial regiments as well. On 14 January 1794 the provincial *Reggimento Mondovì* was the first to form such a company, but, based on experience and the large number of volunteers, the new company had a strength of 100 all ranks, which was better for maintaining a credible and effective force. To reinforce this, from 16 April, each company was allowed to recruit an additional 10–15 men. It was decided that the light infantrymen of the *Reggimento Mondovì* should wear a short Austrian-style coat with the regimental colours, white *gilets* and breeches, light troops' wavy lace on the sleeves and the tricorn hat, but this type of coat was never delivered. As for headgear, it was initially proposed to equip provincial light infantry with a felt helmet, but the innovation was not adopted.[43]

The other provincial regiments quickly followed, and many of them had formed the light infantry companies by March 1794. There were a few exceptions. The *Reggimento Maurienne*, which did not have its own company because it had been permanently incorporated into the *2° Cacciatori,* was authorised in November 1794 to form a second one. But this was not done for the *Reggimento Novara*, whose light infantry company had also gone to *2° Cacciatori*. Finally, the *Reggimento Asti* did not begin forming its light infantry company until 15 April 1796, too late to participate in the war, and so it was disbanded, along with all the others, in August of that year. The only provincial regiment that never had a light infantry company was *Tortona*, due to its persistent difficulty in recruiting in Tortona province.

---

42 AST, LUF, mazzo 272: 11 November 1793. Ordine di marcia per la compagnia cacciatori del Reggimento Maurienne, 11 Novembre 1793

43 AST, OGM, mazzo 71. Costituzione di una compagnia cacciatori nel Reggimento Maurienne, 11 November 1793.

Colour Plate 22.
Luogotenente colonnello and chirurgo maggiore of the Reggimento Guardie (1793–1796).
(Original artwork by Emanuele Manfredi © Helion & Co. 2025)

Colour Plate 23.
Cacciatori volontari of the Piedmontese companies of the *Corpo Franco* (1793–1794).
(Original artwork by Emanuele Manfredi © Helion & Co. 2025)

Colour Plate 24.
Cacciatori volontari (volunteer light troops) and *sergente maggiore* of *Cacciatori Franchi* (1795–1796).
(Original artwork by Emanuele Manfredi © Helion & Co. 2025)

Colour Plate 25.
Cacciatori volontari (volunteer light troops). Left to right: *Cacciatori di Canale*, *Cacciatori Pandini*, and *Cacciatori Martin* (1793–1794). (Original artwork by Emanuele Manfredi © Helion & Co. 2025)

Colour Plate 26.
Cacciatori volontari. Left to right: *Cacciatori di Nizza*, and *Cacciatori Pian* (1793–1794). (Original artwork by Emanuele Manfredi © Helion & Co. 2025)

Colour Plate 27.
Corpo Guastatori: Pionieri and *sergente* (1795–1796).
(Original artwork by Emanuele Manfredi © Helion & Co. 2025)

Colour Plate 28.
Reggimento Granatieri Reali. Getting ready to go into action (1793–1796).
(Original artwork by Emanuele Manfredi © Helion & Co. 2025)

Colour Plate 29.
Reggimento Granatieri Reali. Music Lesson with *musicisti, tamburo maggiore, piffero,* and *tamburini* (1793–1796).
(Original artwork by Emanuele Manfredi © Helion & Co. 2025)

Colour Plate 30.
Artillery lesson. *Capitano* and *cannoniere* of the *Corpo Reale d'Artiglieria* instructing NCOs and grenadiers of the grenadiers' battalion on how to arm an 8-pounder light gun (1793–1796).
(Original artwork by Emanuele Manfredi © Helion & Co. 2025)

Colour Plate 31.
Cacciatori Scelti di Nizza. From left to right: *cacciatore, caporale, caporale maggiore, sergente di plotone, sergente di compagnia,* and *sergente maggiore* (1795–1796).
(Original artwork by Emanuele Manfredi © Helion & Co. 2025)

9

Other Corps

The *Corpo Reale degli Ingegneri*

The *Corpo Reale degli Ingegneri* was made up entirely of officers who had studied scientific subjects such as fortifications and mathematics. They were particularly employed in the design and maintenance of fortifications. During the reign of Vittorio Amedeo III, Spirito Benedetto Nicolis, *conte* di Robilant (1724–1801), a nobleman dedicated to the study of the sciences, held posts in the Royal Arsenal and the Academy of Sciences in Turin. He had developed his knowledge through a long military career with prestigious commissions from the King, such as the exploration of Piedmont and the Valle d'Aosta in search of minerals useful in the manufacture of firearms and artillery pieces. In 1788, at the height of his career, he was promoted to the rank of *luogotenente generale* with the prestigious title of *Primo Ingegnere Militare di Sua Maestà* (His Majesty's First Military Engineer), assuming command of the *Corpo degli Ingegneri Militari*, which he also trained. At the beginning of the War of the Alps, di Robilant proposed to the King that the corps be increased in numbers to adapt it to the defensive needs of fortresses. The number of *ingegneri* (engineers, which was all officers) was thus increased to 46, all with military ranks: a *colonnello*, a *luogotenente colonnello*, two *maggiori*, 10 *capitani*, 11 *luogotenenti capitani*, 10 *luogotenenti*, 10 *sotto luogotenenti* and a *quartiermastro*. The proposal also provided for some of the *ingegneri* to be detached to the frontier fortresses, from which they were also to travel to the surrounding valleys to design and restore the mountain camp fortifications with their artillery emplacements. In the spring of 1793, the *ingegneri* were distributed as follows: in the Valle d'Aosta, six *ingegneri* (a *maggiore*, two *luogotenenti capitani*, one *luogotenente* and two sotto *luogotenenti*); in the Susa valley, four *ingegneri* (one *capitano*, one *capitano luogotenente*, one *luogotenente* and one *sotto luogotenente*); in the Stura valley four *ingegneri* (two *capitani*, two *luogotenenti* and one *sotto luogotenente*); in the County of Nice, three *ingegneri* (one *capitano*, one *capitano luogotenente* and one *luogotenente*).[1]

The *Ingegneri* wore a uniform similar in style to that of infantry officers, with the distinctions of rank and red collar, lapels and cuffs, yellow lining, and gold buttons. Waistcoats and breeches where white (see colour plate 16).

---

1   AST, OGM, mazzo 70: Nota degli Ingegneri comandati nei Dipartimenti, March 1793.

The *Corpo dei Guastatori*

On 23 January 1793, in the context of the suppression of the *Legione degli Accampamenti*, the King issued an order to form a *Corpo dei Guastatori* (Pioneers Corps), which explained that:

> The exigencies of our service require the army should have a *Corpo di Guastatori*, we have looked to the *Legione degli Accampamenti*, in which, as well as a company, there exists a good number of individuals of their own for the formation of this corps, which must be composed of men skilled in earthworks, above all to facilitate the marches of the armies and their passage from one camp to another.[2]

The document does not mention the possible role of the *Guastatori* in the construction or maintenance of mountain defences. However, these specialists were certainly employed for this type of work. They were also used to work on forts and fortifications. On 12 January 1795, for example, the *2° Battaglione* was assigned to work on the fortifications at Cuneo.[3]

The *Guastatori*, or *Pionieri* as they were called elsewhere, were made up of two battalions at the provincial level, under the command of *colonnello* Vittorio Caissotti, *cavaliere di Rubione*, who also commanded the *1° Battaglione*, while the *2°* was under the orders of *luogotenente colonnello* Luigi Mocchia, *conte* di San Michele. Each battalion had its own staff, similar to those of line infantry battalions, and four companies of 113 men each, organised in the same way but with the peculiarity of also having in each one some *armaiolo* and *falegname*, indispensable for the maintenance of the tools and the numerous carriages in their equipment.[4]

Initially, the *Corpo dei Guastatori* was organised in Turin and stationed on the hills overlooking the city to the east, a place where they could practise throughout the winter, until the two battalions were separated – the *1°* to the Susa valley and the *2°* to the southern front. However, as the War of the Alps continued, the location of the battalions was reversed in 1794, with the *2°* in the Susa valley and the *1°* in the south.

Muster rolls show that the *guastatori* companies rarely operated together. Instead, they were deployed individually where they were deemed most needed. From the same sources, we learn that they often did not hesitate to take part in infantry actions. For example, on 7 May 1794, 60 *guastatori* from various companies were captured by French at Bardonecchia, in the Susa Valley, and another 13 on 9 May 1794 in the same place. The two medals for military valour awarded to individuals from the corps attest to this. De Bonaud's 1795 expedition to Val Roia also included a company of *guastatori*, commanded by *capitano* Giovanni Bernardo Andorno, which suffered heavy losses.[5]

On 25 December 1793, in the light of the experience of his first year of war, the *colonnello* pointed out to the secretary of war, who reported to the King, that the *Corpo dei Guastatori* should be strengthened either by creating a third battalion, or by increasing the number

---
2 AST, OGM, mazzo 70: Costituzione del Corpo dei Guastatori (or Pionieri), 23 January 1793.
3 AST, LUF, mazzo 276: letter to assign the 2° Guastatori to Cuneo, 19 January 1795.
4 AST, Ruolini di rivista, Corpo dei Guastatori, mazzi 2–3.
5 AST, Ruolini di rivista, Corpo dei Guastatori, mazzi 2–3.

of companies. However, in the first instance, the commander's request only resulted in the strength of the eight companies being increased by 10 men each, adding four *caporali sovrannumerari* and six *guastatori*, all volunteers. When the need was finally recognised, the establishment of a ninth company was authorised. This was the reserve company, with the usual duties of recruitment and training, consisting of 150 men, of all ranks.

In order to be able to carry out their duties, the corps was supplied with picks, shovels, large and small axes, iron rods for dislodging boulders, ropes and miner's tools for placing explosive charges.[6] The corps was then provided with wagons suitable for transporting tools, earth, baggage and ammunition. There were four-wheeled and two-wheeled carts per battalion. The *colonnello* was to decide whether to request horses or mules to pull the carts. It is very probable, however, that most of the draught animals chosen were mules, which could both pull the carts and be saddled for transport on the mountain trails.

In 1793 the soldiers, up to the rank of *sergente di compagnia*, received, in addition to the sabre of the model previously in use in the *Legione degli Accampamenti*, a short bronze-plated *fucile* of the model designed for the *Granatieri delle Fregate* – the naval infantry corps embarked on the fleet. But shortly afterwards, once the poor quality of these weapons had been revealed, they were replaced with 1752-pattern infantry *fucile* without bayonets.[7]

The first uniform, inspired by that of the *Legione degli Accampamenti*, is not described in any documents but, fortunately, is illustrated in a sketch drawn in 1793 by royal designer Leonardo Marini (colour plate 16). The *guastatore* wore a short blue Austrian-style coat, without lapels, with a blue-sky collar and cuffs, red lining and brass buttons, gold for the NCOs and officials. The *gilet* was white and the breeches blue. On the belt, they wore a small cartridge box of blackened leather, in which they could hold eight cartridges. The sabre, also worn on the belt, was adorned with a sword knot ending in a tassel, made of white and sky-blue woven threads. Their clothing was completed by knee-high black gaiters, buttoned with small brass buttons, and they wore a tricorn hat.

On 14 January 1794, at the specific request of the *guastatori*'s *colonnello*, the breeches and gaiters were replaced with blue trousers and blackened leather boots, probably because of the greater comfort of trousers compared to breeches in mountain warfare, as worn by the *Cacciatori di Canale*, with whom the *guastatori* had collaborated on the southern front. Finally, the clothing was completed by a grey overcoat with sky-blue cuffs, issued to soldiers wearing the short Austrian-style uniform (colour plate 16).

In keeping with tradition, officers and NCOs probably wore the long coat, but without lapels, to match that worn by the corps.

In the last months of 1794, Savoy's *luogotenente colonnello* Giuseppe de Bieux, *conte* di Flumet, acting commander of the corps, asked the Royal Secretariat of War to provide the *Guastatori* with a new, unusual style of uniform approved by di Cravanzana on 19 November. The new uniform was a short Austrian-style coat with a raised blue-sky collar and pointed cuffs of the same colour. On the upper half of the chest, the habit was open and had two lapels fastened at the top with a button, in imitation of the old lapels of the *Legione degli Accampamenti*. The lining was still red. Trousers and boots remained as before. The

---

6   AST, OGM, mazzo 70: letter of 11 March 1793.
7   Sterrantino, *Le armi da fuoco del vecchio Piemonte*, pp.140–144.

fur rucksack was worn with white shoulder straps, which were connected by a chest strap made of the same material and colour. At the waist, above the belt from which the sabre was hung, was a red cloth *casalina* containing the cartridges. Even more characteristic was the headgear, a sort of busby called a *bonetto*, which was issued to NCOs, *tamburini* and *guastatori*. It was made of calfskin, edged with black sheepskin, lined with canvas and with a uniform tassel. Its shape was given by a cylindrical wire frame. In the illustration, the busby is adorned at the front with a moulded brass plate that bears in the centre a Savoy eagle, wings spread, with the modern Savoy coat of arms on its breast, all surmounted by the royal crown (see colour plate 16).[8]

The *Corpo Reale d'Artiglieria*

In the preparation of the defence lines guns were distributed where necessary, and their fields of fire organised for their effective defence. In the mountains, however, it was very rare to be able to deploy artillery of more than 4-pounder calibre. Most of the 8-pounders and all the 16-pounders, therefore, remained in reserve in the corps artillery parks.

Above the inhabited villages, which were at least served by well-maintained dirt roads, it was virtually impossible to move field artillery because 'dragging, even over short distances, was enough to ruin the gun carriage, rendering it incapable of withstanding the torture of firing, and thus making it unsafe and inaccurate.' Pieces heavier than 4-pounders were practically un-transportable by mules because each part weighed more than 18 *rubbos* (about 166kg. One Piedmontese *rubbo* equals 9.225kg). Since a mule could not bear a weight of more than 12 *rubbos* and four mules, with a central load strung between them, would require such wide roads that pulling them would be easier. However, pulling was dangerous because the ropes could easily break, killing or injuring the men and sending the pieces tumbling into the valleys.[9]

Due to the scarcity of howitzers capable of parabolic firing to hit the enemy behind cover, conventional light artillery was the only alternative. Even 4-pounders, which could be dismounted and transported by four sturdy mules, were only suitable for direct and grazing firing. In mountain warfare, the artillery's task was to strike in open sectors, mainly uphill across meadows over which the attacker was forced to advance. The presence of infantry behind drystone walls on the flanks, ready with intense small-arms discharges, could turn the attack into a trap. This, at least, was the theory because the complexity and irregularity of the Alpine terrain, with meadows and rocks, made such a precise arrangement difficult except in rare cases.

The Piedmontese army had, on the basis of past experience, about 20 mountain pieces, which could be transported more easily by mules, and some lighter 2-pounders that could be of some use but were of little value for defence. Three mules were sufficient for the 2-pounders, while the 4-pounder mountain pieces required four: one for the barrel, the

---

8   AST, Ufficio Generale del Soldo, Cpd, mazzo 138, and Ricchiardi, Iconografia militare sabauda.
9   Fiora, artiglieria da montagna, pp.99–118.

second for the gun carriage and wheels, a third for the tools, and the fourth with the initial supply of balls and powder.

The great effort made by the Piedmontese army to equip the redoubts on the heights of the Authion itself, the Milleforche, the Raus and the Ortighera in the summer of 1793, at the time of the victorious Battle at Authion, is surprising, given the difficulty of transporting artillery on mule tracks. It seems that there were no less than 17 pieces on the heights: two howitzers, five 8-pounder field guns, two 4-pounder field guns and eight 4-pounder mountain guns. They were placed in batteries with an adequate supply of projectiles of various types.[10] The fire of this artillery was undoubtedly one of the main factors in the victory. There is also other evidence of the artillerymen's efforts to fire the pieces into the mountains, such as the silver medal awarded to *sergente di plotone* Filippo Pagnone of the *Corpo Reale d'Artiglieria* for commanding a howitzer placed in the Oronaja redoubt in the Valle di Susa on 28 July 1793, that managed to almost destroy the French battery placed in the Malamorte camp.[11]

The downside of mountain warfare was the ease with which positions could be attacked and the guns and gunners endangered. The chronicles of the battles of the War of the Alps often mention artillerymen who kept firing until they were pinned down by the enemy and were not always able to save their pieces.

The sense of duty and valour of the Piedmontese artillerymen, who were as fully convinced as the infantrymen of the need to defend the Kingdom, is testified by the 16 Medals for Military Valour awarded to them by the King.

The men of the Piedmontese artillery wore the classic long-tailed coat, darkened with black collars and cuffs. It was enlivened with a yellow lining and brass metal buttons (see colour plate 17).

The artillerymen received two special single-guard sabres from the King, one for *sergenti* and one for the other ranks. The first had a brass guard surmounted by an eagle's head pommel of the same material. The grip was made of cast brass. The blade was flat, not grooved, with a blunt tip. The weapon came with a wooden scabbard covered with blackened leather and with an iron ferrule inside. The weapon for other ranks was similar, but with a smooth guard, no eagle's head, and surmounted by a brass cap.[12]

Although the *Corpo Reale d'Artiglieria* consisted of four battalions, it only received three flags, one *colonnella* and two *d'ordinanza* (see colour plate 18). A larger number was not planned because the battalions were seldom united, and the companies were scattered in various locations and fortresses.

The *Treno d'Artiglieria* (Artillery Train), in charge of transporting cannons, gun carriages, their spare parts, artillery shells, and sometimes the men's ammunition, was equipped for the 1793 campaign with a structure that the King ordered the *Gran Mastro d'Artiglieria* to implement on 18 December 1792.

A first complex organization was established on 5 March 1793: the corps, consisted of 866 men, 26 of which were officers: a *capitano*, a *capitano luogotenente*, five *luogotenenti*, five *sotto luogotenenti*, an *aiutante maggiore*, a *quartiermastro*, and 12 *marescialli d'alloggio* (*maréchaux*

---

10 Thaon di Revel, *Mémoires sur la guerre des Alpes*, p.51.
11 AST, OGM, mazzo 72, Concessione, 30 January 1794.
12 Lupo, Le lame del Re, pp.359–368.

de logis). NCOs and troops included: a *furiere maggiore*, 12 *sotto marescialli d'alloggio*, 22 *brigadieri* (corporals) and as many *sotto brigadieri*, 750 *palafrenieri* (grooms), 11 *sellai* (saddlers) and 22 *maniscalchi* (farriers). The corps was divided into 10 brigades of 144 horses each plus an eleventh reserve brigade to care for sick horses. Each brigade consisted of 72 pairs of horses and included a *luogotenente*, a *maresciallo d'alloggio*, a *sotto maresciallo d'alloggio*, two *brigadieri*, two *sotto brigadieri*, 72 *palafrenieri*, a *sellaio* (saddler) and two *maniscalchi*.[13]

It was soon realised that the corps needed to be increased in numbers. The King decided the increase during one of his rare appearances in the theatre of operations. Sensitive to the fact that the troops received regular artillery and ammunition support from the fortress of Vinadio, where he was staying, on 12 July 1793, he ordered an increase to the corps. The force now comprised 1,105 men, basically the strength of a regiment, of whom 13 were officers (a *capitano*, a *capitano luogotenente*, seven *luogotenenti*, two *sotto luogotenenti*, an *aiutante maggiore*, a *quartiermastro*), 12 *marescialli d'alloggio*, a *furiere maggiore*, 16 *sotto marescialli d'alloggio*, 32 *brigadieri*, 32 *sotto brigadieri*, 15 *sellai*, 28 *maniscalchi* and 950 *palafrenieri*. The number of horses also increased from 1,530 to 1,830, but the number of brigades remained the same.[14]

The role of the *Treno d'Artiglieria* was crucial in moving artillery to where it was needed. Mixed columns of artillery and train formed a long, rumbling convoy in the eyes of the curious onlookers who saw them pass along the roads amid clouds of dust.

An example of the composition of these columns is the transfer ordered on 28 January 1793 of the artillery detachment with train and wagons between Pinerolo and Saluzzo, just under 40km along a good road through the plains at the foot of the Alps. The convoy had to transfer six 8-pounder field guns, six 4-pounder field guns, and two 4-pounder mountain guns, complete with carriages, limbers, spare wheels, spare carriages for the two mountain guns, spare horse harnesses and various artillery tools. The convoy also carried several barrels of gunpowder, various types and calibres of shots for the guns (858 for the 8-pounder field guns, 1,554 for the 4-pounder field guns, and 279 for the two 4-pounder mountain guns), 22 barrels containing 46,000 *fucili* cartridges, three barrels containing 6,000 pistol cartridges and another three containing spare flints. The whole column was drawn by 103 horses and consisted of the 14 pieces and 16 different wagons (six for ammunition, three caissons, perhaps to transport what was needed for the small-arms, three two-wheeled carts, two four-wheeled wagons, a wagon equipped as a mobile forge, and a large wagon, perhaps to transport the disassembled mountain pieces to be transferred to the mules).

The *Treno d'Artiglieria* detachment that drove the carts was made up by 52 men (a *maresciallo d'alloggio*, a *sotto maresciallo d'alloggio*, three *brigadieri*, two *sotto brigadieri*, 44 *palafrenieri* and a *maniscalco*. In addition to these men, there were 72 *cannonieri* assigned to the firing of the 14 pieces, including five officers (a *maggiore di battaglione*, a *capitano luogotenente*, an *aiutante maggiore*, a *luogotenente*, a *sotto luogotenente*) and a *sergente maggiore*, three *sergenti*, 10 *caporali* and *sotto caporali*, a *tamburino*, an *arciere*, 42 *cannonieri*, a *zappatore* (sapper), a *caporale*, two *maestranze* soldiers (artillery workers), and, finally, a *caporale minatore* and four *minatori* (miners).[15]

---

13 AST, Stabilimenti Militari (StM), vol. 6: Regolamento per il Treno d'Artiglieria, 5 March 1793.
14 AST, StM, vol. 6: Riorganizzazione del Treno d'Artiglieria, 12 July 1793.
15 AST, OGM, mazzo 85: Organizzazione del convoglio del Treno d'Artiglieria, 28 January 1793.

As can be deduced from the composition of the column's command, the *Treno d'Artiglieria* personnel included only one *maresciallo d'alloggio*, with a rank equivalent to warrant officer. Instead, there were five artillery officers, among whom was the *maggiore di battaglione* who commanded the entire convoy as he held the highest rank.

The passage of the convoy must have aroused pride and hope in the commoners and bourgeois who watched it. Artillerymen with their guns were on the march to reinforce the infantry deploying to the Alps.

To distinguish themselves from the artillery, the *Treno d'Artiglieria* personnel wore a coat without lapels, with a red collar, cuffs and lining, the same colour as the waistcoat and breeches, all with yellow metal buttons. The ranks of the *Treno* were those of the cavalry: the *maresciallo d'alloggio* equated to junior officers, while the NCOs were the *sotto marescialli d'alloggio*, equivalent to infantry *sergenti*, the *brigadieri* to *caporali*, and all wore their rank distinctions in gold or yellow lace. The privates, called *palafrenieri*, wore a uniform without distinctions, and all were armed with a sabre carried in a bandolier (see colour plate 17).

Logistics: The *Treno di Provianda* and Private Suppliers

As already mentioned, during the war, Vittorio Amedeo III did not concern himself with uniforms and flags but devoted his weekly meeting with His Majesty's Secretariat of War and the Navy to the much more important issue of supplying the army with everything necessary for its efficiency. However, his actions did not always have an immediate impact due to the difficulty of procuring and delivering supplies, uniform fabrics, tents, weapons and everything needed to support thousands of men deployed in a hostile environment such as the high mountains.

An initial transport organisation between Turin and the decentralised magazines of provisions, ammunition, clothing and various materials was established by signing a service contract with Stefano Tommaso Campana, a private contractor, on 7 February 1793. According to the contract, he was to provide an adequate number of four-wheeled carts and the horses or mules to pull them. Sixty of these carts were to be pulled by four animals and were to be capable of carrying about 1,936kg each. Another 120, pulled by three animals, had to be able to carry about 1,475kg each, and, finally, the last 20, with two wheels and pulled by a single animal, were to carry about 461kg. Campana was also to provide a civilian driver for each wagon, and the service was to begin in mid-April 1793. As this was a transport contract, the contractor was responsible for delivering the items entrusted to him with a written list, signed and countersigned by one of his subordinates.[16]

Once the supplies had been procured, the King's main concern was ensuring the transport service's efficiency. For this reason, when he was near Cuneo, the King listened attentively to the suggestions of the commanding officers who proposed militarising the transports to better control them. He was informed of the shortcomings of the service provided by the private contractor, which included inefficiencies, delays and loss of materials. Vittorio Amedeo III, therefore, decided to issue new regulations providing for the militarisation of

---

16   AST, Cpd, contratto con Stefano Tommaso Campana, mazzo 119.

logistical services, which he did on 12 July 1793 from the fort of Demonte, where he was staying for a few days.

The regulations placed civilian drivers under the command of army officers and NCOs and subjected them to military discipline and law. Campana was still in charge of providing wagons, draft animals and drivers: now there were 440 wagons, of which 400 were drawn by three horses and 40 by one, and there was no mention of four-horse carts.[17] In addition to the wagons supplied by Campana, the train had an unspecified number of mules divided into squads placed where necessary for transportation over mule tracks. The mules and their drivers were also supplied by civilian contractors under different contracts.

Control of the contractors and loads was now entrusted to a new military corps, the *Corpo del Treno di Provianda* (corps of waggoners), and the wagons were divided into four divisions, each of 110 three-horse and 10 one-horse wagons. Each division was, in turn, subdivided into five squads, each of 22 two wagons, of which 20 were three-horse and two were one-horse wagons, the latter possibly being used to transport the personal effects and subsistence supplies for the division's personnel. Each division was commanded by a *luogotenente* who had a clerk to keep track of both the goods and the absences of civilian and military personnel. The 110 civilian conductors were under the command of five *brigadieri* and 10 *sotto brigadieri*. The *Corpo del treno di Provianda*, which supervised the contractors by preventing irregularities and theft, was itself supervised by an inspecting officer.

To guarantee the service, the regulations expressly forbade any officer from diverting the wagons and mules assigned to the *provianda* service, which could under no circumstances be requisitioned for other types of service. The rules were also strict for civil conductors: they could not be absent without permission or deviate their wagons from the planned route. In the first case, they were punished as deserters. In the second, they were subjected to a few days' imprisonment by a *prevosto* at the first failure. Subsequently, they could be subjected to a beating by their colleagues, a punishment also provided for in the case of insubordination. In short, they were treated as soldiers to all intents and purposes.

Since the logistics service was dependent on the supplies organised by the *Ufficio Generale del Soldo*, the latter was obliged to calculate the daily and extraordinary requirements (such as changing a unit's uniforms) for each army corps, calculate the weight and thus the number of wagons and animals needed for transport. There were usually seven planned routes of the wagon trains: from Turin to Susa, or Ivrea and then from Ivrea to Aosta. From Turin to Saluzzo and then on to Cuneo. From Cuneo, then the route continued to either Tenda or Demonte.

Since continuity of service was essential for the subsistence of troops, convoys of wagons had to transport goods between the main depots and those of their assigned army corps, returning immediately for the next load. This type of service was referred to as *traghetto* (ferry service), the routes of which were usually 15 Piedmontese miles per day (approximately 37km; the Piedmontese mile measured 2,466m) on flat roads, a distance that was reduced in the case of rough routes.

The military personnel of the *provianda* received a uniform consisting of a dark blue coat with scarlet lining, white collar and cuffs, 11 white metal buttons sewn on one side of the

---

17   AST, StM, Volume 6: Riorganizzazione del Treno d'Artiglieria, 12 July 1793.

front, and blue waistcoats and breeches. White waistcoats and breeches were allowed in the summer. The tricorn hat was without any lace edging. While the officers were identified by the silver rank distinctions, the *brigadieri* were distinguished by a single silver chevron on the collar and both a single and a slightly spaced double chevron on the lower part of the sleeves near the cuffs. *Sotto brigadieri* kept the chevron at the collar but adorned their sleeves with only the double chevron on their sleeves. The armament provided for *brigadieri* and *sotto brigadieri* was a sabre carried on their belts, but it was probably later decided to also arm them with *fucili* to enable them to protect their loads (see colour plate 1).

The responsibility for covering the route from the army corps depot to the individual units was taken care of by the *furieri*, using the soldiers of the unit and their assigned carts or mules, depending on the type of route.

The Piedmontese *Battaglione di Guarnigione*

In the Piedmontese army, deserving older soldiers were included in the *Corpo degli Invalidi*, which was organised into companies made up of veterans still capable of sedentary service and generally assigned to the comfortable but tedious garrisoning of fortresses. The older veterans, weakened by wounds and disabilities, were allowed, on request, to receive an annual allowance and retire to their homes.

At the beginning of the War of the Alps, de Vins suggested freshening up the operational units of all arms by assigning the oldest and least able soldiers to a *Battaglione di Guarnigione* (garrison battalion), following the practice of the Habsburg army. There were, however, some differences. Of the four Austrian garrison battalions (two each of the *IR5 Erstes Garnison* and *IR6 Zweytes Garrison* regiments) of the army sent to help Piedmont were employed differently. The *IR5* was garrisoned in Turin for the duration of the war, while the *IR6* was employed in Val Roia, where it fought honourably against the French and took part in the Battle of Authion.

The founding regulation of 21 March 1793, stipulated that the new Piedmontese *Battaglione di Guarnigione*, under the command of *colonnello* Carlo Luigi Croce, was to be made up of soldiers who were still capable of effective service, even if they were not capable of mountain warfare. Its mission was that 'when the *Piazza* [fortifications and the Citadel of Turin] for whose defence it is destined, are threatened, it shall show its bravery and loyalty by firm resistance.' In the same document, it was stipulated that the *Battaglione di Guarnigione* would have 740 men distributed between corps staff (*colonnello comandante, aiutante maggiore di battaglione*, two *trabanti*, one *furiere*, one *quartiermastro*, one *cappellano*, one *chirurgo maggiore*, one *tamburino maggiore*, one *armaiolo*, two *falegnami*, one *prevosto* and one *arciere*) and six *fucilieri* companies, each of 121 men and organised in the same way as the infantry companies, with the only exception that in addition to the *tamburino*, they also included fifer.[18]

The uniform consisted of an Austrian-style coat of dark blue cloth, without lapels, with red cuffs, collar and lining, and yellow or gold laces and buttons. The *gilet* was white, with white

---

18 AST, OGM, mazzo 70.

breeches. The overcoat was grey, and the tricorn hat was without lace. The men were equipped with an old *fucile* with a bayonet carried on a belt and a haversack carried on a strap. Two black knee-gaiters completed the uniform. The regulations do not mention this, but it is likely that soldiers from the *granatieri* and *cacciatori* companies were allowed to add a yellow wavy lace as a reminder of their service, and for officers and *sergenti* to wear the long coat decorated with badges of rank and a redingote (a double-breasted coat) instead of an overcoat.

In the summer of 1793, the *Battaglione di Guarnigione* was granted one flag, of which we have no information or drawings, but this was probably a *colonnnella* flag.

Caring for the Sick and Wounded

The *frater* or *garzoni chirurghi* in the companies did what they could to help the wounded with bandages or whatever else was available at that time in the immediate vicinity of the front lines. There was not much they could do, partly because each of them had to be ready to act for a hundred soldiers, who might be scattered in more than one post. After gathering the wounded and injured as far away from the front line as possible, less injured comrades and local peasants would be called in to transport those who were unable to walk on stretchers to the rear. Once there, they were loaded onto carts or mules for transport to the *chirurgo maggiore* tent, which was considered the regimental hospital.

The same was always true for the sick, even in the tragic times when epidemics spread rapidly without the surgeons having the means to combat them. In fact, the *chirurghi maggiori* had only a chest containing equipment and medicines at his disposal and was powerless to deal with epidemics whose origin was unknown and whose cure was yet to come.

A glance at the muster rolls reveals a constant coming and going of sick or wounded from the companies to the regimental hospital and often from this to the *ospedali volanti* (temporary, literally 'flying' hospitals) further back or the main hospitals, known as *ospedali Reali* (Royal hospitals).

Fatal epidemics caused by the living conditions to which young, robust men were exposed remained significant. For example, the *Granatieri Reali*, who defended the Piccolo San Bernardo Pass in the winter and summer of 1793, had their regimental hospital located in the commune of La Thuile where, in July 1793, many men died for dysentery, an easily fatal disease at that time. As abbot F. Fenoil noted in his book *La Terreur sur les Alpes*:

> The conditions for the troops were poor. The cold wind that blows down from the glaciers at night is followed by excessive heat during the day … The soldiers were decimated by an epidemic of dysentery: the whole cantonment was full of the sick, and in the cemetery, four or five people are buried every day. All they had to do was keep themselves very clean, not touch the sick and leave the rest to Providence.[19]

What happened to the *Granatieri Reali* in 1793 is just one example of the tragic situations that must have been much more common than the documents of the time tell us.

---

19   Fenoil, *La Terreur sur les Alpes*, pp.101–106.

A constant flow of sick and wounded between the regimental and *ospedali volanti* and from the latter to the *ospedali reali* in winter was mainly due to illness. In summer, the cause was more likely to be wounds and injuries from combat. Returning to the company after recovery was also problematic. In theory, it was prescribed that soldiers should return in groups accompanied by an NCO or officer. However, this was not realistic for units that had been on the march for days and were engaged on the front line. As a result, individual soldiers were often ordered to return to their unit, but on the way, they decided to desert or visit their families and were then declared deserters. In general, the commanders waited at least a couple of months to declare them deserters, hoping for their return, which often actually happened. Sometimes, after a certain period, a document would arrive signed by a doctor or a priest from the place where the soldiers' families lived, informing them that the soldier had died. Discharged from the hospital but still in a precarious condition and fearing the worst, these men returned to their villages where they hoped for help.

The King and his ministers did everything in their power to provide the best possible care for the sick and wounded. The rules issued on 26 May 1793 to regulate the *ospedali reali*, which were contracted out to private entrepreneurs, were strict:

> The contractor must, at his own expense, maintain a director, a chief apothecary and others as necessary, a sufficient number of secretaries and under-secretaries, one nurse for every 15 patients with a sufficient number of attendants, one or more cooks with their under-cooks and necessary launderers.
>
> Each of these employees will be subordinate to the *direttore generale* (director general).
>
> The *Ufficio Generale del Soldo* will assign a medical inspector and others if the need arises, as well as the necessary surgeons and chaplains.
> The number of nurses to be sent was from 12 to 15.
> The apothecary will be supplied with good medicines in sufficient quantities.
> Secretaries and under-secretaries will keep exact accounts and lists of the patient with exact dates of admission and discharge, recording them by name, surname, father's name, country and war name, company and regiment.
> No sick person will be admitted unless he has a note signed by the *ufficiale del soldo* who controlled his regiment or is sent there from a *ospedale volante*.
> A *guardarmi* (guard of arms) will have a room to keep soldiers' weapons which will be properly registered, including any money they had on them.
> The chief nurse will be responsible for cleaning the rooms, and for night lamps. He will have the rooms aired from time to time as required.
> A nurse will be present every night.
> The cook will have to cook the food for the patients in a different place from the food for the staff and prepare rations for the patients and staff.
> The contractor must provide beds etc. and everything necessary, including sufficient bed sheets for changing.[20]

---

20 AST, Cpd, mazzo 122: Capitoli per l'impresa degli Spedali, 26 May 1793.

These were very strict clauses that were often not adhered to and which required inspections and controls, with the aggravating factor that, as the inspectors' reports state, sometimes the spaces necessary for the proper management of the hospital during the winter months were often occupied by troops stationed there for the winter. Malpractice and inefficiency, at a time when there were no adequate medicines to control epidemics, inevitably led to the dangerous spread of infectious diseases, both among the patients and the staff.

On 8 January 1793, the *chirurgo generale*, head of the sanitary organisation, at the request of the *chirurghi maggiori* of various regiments of infantry, cavalry and dragoons, petitioned the King to allow them a military uniform, 'like that used by the troops of the other powers and especially by the Austrian'. The pattern drawing of the uniform given them has not so far been found, but fortunately a figure from the period reveals it. The *chirurgo maggiore* wore a uniform coat of plain light blue cloth, with black cuffs and collar and gold buttons. The lining of the coat was red, the same colour as the waistcoat and breeches. The only distinction of the *chirurgo maggiore* was the single line of gold lace on the waistcoat and pockets edged with lace, with a second chevron on the inside (see colour plate 16). Shortly afterwards, to give the *chirurghi maggiori* proper formal authority, they were given the rank distinctions of a *sotto luogotenente* of infantry. *Chirurgo generale* Rejneri was given those of a *capitano luogotenente*. The *garzoni chirurghi* received a similar uniform but without any distinctions.

Royal Pardons for Deserters

If a soldier deserted during the war, he knew he had ample opportunity to get away with it. There were no identity documents with photographs, nor were any civil registry office; the registration of births, deaths and marriages was left to the parishes. Even the addition of a few essential details such as general information, patronymic, place of residence and dates of birth and enlistment, sometimes accompanied by a brief description of physical features such as hair colour and little else, recorded in the muster rolls during the War of the Alps, was of little use. This was partly because the volunteer could give false information, as there was no way of verifying his identity. However, as the war went on, the need for men to replenish the companies made it easy for the recruiter, knowing that there were few means of verification, to turn a blind eye.

Each regiment sent out recruiting *sergenti* and *caporali* to encourage men to enlist. In the case of the reconstituted *Reggimento Maurienne*, for example, recruiters preferred to go to the Valle d'Aosta or the high Alps of Chisone and Susa which were essentially French speaking, but they did not hesitate to recruit anyone who turned up.

The commanders, who should have immediately denounced as deserters those soldiers who missed the monthly inspection carried out by the paymaster, sometimes waited several months to do so. The reasons could have been many and varied: knowledge of the individual involved and his inclination to visit his family, who were often in areas a few days' march from the camp; uncertainty about the reasons for his absence at the first monthly review after combat, where even limited repositioning of the company had been necessary; when it had been impossible to find out from his comrades whether he had been killed, seriously wounded or taken prisoner by the enemy; or whether he had fled the unit in a panic.

The muster rolls show that this indecision and long delay in declaring desertion was the norm, especially for units that were often deployed behind enemy lines for guerrilla actions, such as the *Cacciatori Franchi* or the *Cacciatori Scelti di Nizza*.

After some time, a deserter could present himself to another corps, even giving his true name, and, given the impossibility of checks by the recruiter, be enlisted. The aim of the recruiters was to replenish the companies, and that of the deserter was to collect the enlistment bonus. If a diligent *ufficiale del soldo* discovered the offence, the consequences of the re-enlisted deserter were minimal. He was easily pardoned and sent back to his original corps, provided he continued to behave properly for the rest of the war.

Particularly serious was desertion while on guard duty or in combat. This crime, which was not always correctly recorded in the muster rolls, was easy to detect because, for accounting reasons, the *ufficiale del soldo* used to record what items of the uniform and weapons the deserter had removed. The fact that the deserter has taken his *fucile* and *sabro* with him was a clear indication that he was attempting to evade armed service.

The rosters also tell us that desertions occurred quite often in a small group. Mass desertions are almost never documented but could occur, especially in the autumn as the sum of several contiguous small groups, when fighting had ceased, and soldiers did not feel up to the rigours of winter and a subsequent campaign.

In the case of provincial soldiers, the municipalities were responsible for ensuring that the quota of men to be supplied was met, and they kept records. The return of the deserter to his community could not be kept secret in the family for long. Although it does not appear that he was often denounced, the need for a fellow countryman to replace him in the regiment must have been a serious social problem.

Officers who fled in the face of the enemy out of cowardice or who applied to the King for a leave of absence for reasons of age, health or family were certainly discharged.

Desertion, an endemic phenomenon in all eighteenth-century armies, was dealt with a bit more effectively than in previous wars because of leave cards. The exact period of absence had to be indicated on the leave card, and the place where the soldier lived and the name of his parents had to be entered on a leave certificate. Personal data that could sometimes help track down the deserter.

If discharged, the soldier had to keep the *foglio di congedo* (leave pass) with himself at all times, on pain of arrest.[21]

In more serious cases, the punishment for desertion was very severe and could go as far as the death penalty, especially if the deserter was an NCO. The gallows, however, was rarely used in the Kingdom of Sardinia, where it was much more common to pardon deserters who, depending on the nature of their desertion, were sent to serve long sentences in the Citadel of Alessandria or, during the War of the Alps, to serve in the *Corpo Franco*.

---

21 For an in-depth study of the Piedmontese army leave sheets, see E. Ricchiardi, 'Congedi militari sabaudi. Parte prima 1685–1802', *Armi Antiche*, 2010, pp.61–106. <https://www.academia.edu/93075994/Congedi_militari_sabaudi_Parte_prima_1692_1802>, accessed 19 November 2024.

Military leave pass granted on 8 September 1796 by the *Reggimento Maurienne* to *granatiere* Claude Alex of *1° Compagnia*, from St Jean d'Arve in Maurienne. Alex, whose company was part of the *7° Granatieri*, fought the entire War of the Alps, being honourably discharged. For his conduct on 19 August and 7 September 1793 during the fighting in Savoy, he was decorated with the Silver Medal for Military Valour. (Private collection)

The Frustration of the Cavalry

There were eight mounted regiments in the Piedmontese army, four of dragoons – *Dragoni del Re, di Piemonte, della Regina* and *del Chiablese* – and four of cavalry – *Savoia Cavalleria, Piemonte Reale, Aosta* and *Cavalleggeri del Re* (although the latter was not actually light cavalry). The regiments were reorganised on 16 August 1792 into two campaign squadrons and two for garrison duty, which also trained recruits. Each squadron was composed of two companies. These were weak regiments, with a total of 397 men, of whom only 250 were the actual available fighting strength of the campaign squadrons, and of these, only 218 were mounted.

The regimental staff consisted of the *colonnello comandante*, an *aiutante maggiore*, a *furiere maggiore*, a *quartiermastro*, an *armaiolo*, a *chirurgo maggiore*, a *prevosto* and an *arciere*. The two garrison squadrons consisted of a total of 147 men, of whom 61 were mounted, so each of the four companies could only deploy about 15 mounted men of all ranks.[22]

After the French attack, while the infantry and artillery regiments were brought up to full strength and new specialities were formed, little attention was paid to the cavalry, which was considered unsuitable for Alpine warfare.

At the beginning of the war, there were a few campaign squadrons in Savoy and Nice, but they soon proved to be of little use as they retreated with the rest of the corps into the narrow Alpine valleys towards the Piccolo San Bernardo Pass, Moncenisio Pass or the Colle di Tenda. This led to the decision to dismount the regiments. The first to be dismounted were the dragoons, who were then equipped with packs, shoes and gaiters.[23] After a while, the cavalry was also dismounted and was given the same foot equipment. So, about 1,000 horses had to be retired to suitable stables.

During an inspection on 8 March 1794, the commander of the *Dragoni del Re*, who had been on duty in the rear of the Val Roia front for two months, had to ask for the replacement of the regiments' shoes, with which they had made long marches, 'because they were worn out from rigours of the campaign.'[24]

Some cavalrymen or dragoons were fortunate enough to be able to make themselves useful by riding the mail horses of the stations set up for the rapid delivery of correspondence between the army corps and the capital. This activity was so important that in addition to them, the *Dragoni Guardacaccia* from the Household's troops were also employed and, from 1794, two squadrons of the *Dragoni di Sardegna*, the island's gendarmerie, were sent to Piedmont to help in the task. Even some of the few hundred dragoons of the Austrian auxiliary corps were turned into postmen, probably to ensure communication between de Vins and his Austrian troops.

In April 1796, the Piedmontese cavalry finally had the satisfaction of charging the French. On 21 April, in order to protect the retreat of the small Piedmontese army corps, which for days had been trying to slow down the overwhelming French forces under Bonaparte, the two campaign squadrons of the *Dragoni del Re*, evidently remounted, attacked and disrupted the vanguards of the much larger French cavalry force advancing towards the retreating Piedmontese columns. The French cavalry regiments, not all of which were engaged, were the *1er régiment de hussards*, the *20e dragons*, and the *22e* and *24e chasseurs à cheval*. In what became known in the annals of the Italian cavalry as the *Carica del Brichetto* (Charge of the Brichetto), the commander of the French cavalry, *général de division* Henri Christian Michel de Stengel (1744–1796), was severely wounded in the arm and head and died on 28 April from his wounds.

In recognition of the determination and courage it took for the *Dragoni del Re* to attack the vanguards of the French cavalry with two weak squadrons, Vittorio Amedeo III awarded a Gold Medal for Military Valour that was pinned on each of the two *Dragoni del Re* guidons.

The cavalry wore a blue coat without lapels, while the dragoons wore lapels. The distinctive colours of the eight regiments were as summarised in colour plate 20. On their shoulders,

---

22   AST, OGM, mazzo 69: Riorganizzazione dei reggimenti di cavalleria e dragoni, 16 August 1792.
23   AST, OGM, mazzo 71: Appiedamento dei reggimenti di dragoni, 17 August 1793.
24   AST, OGM, mazzo 71: Lettera del comandante dei Dragoni del Re per chiedere scarpe nuove, 8 March 1794.

the troopers wore a triple fish-scale epaulette of white or yellow metal, and in addition, all mounted corps wore chamois waistcoats and breeches.

The rank distinctions of the officers were like those of the infantry, while those of the *marescialli d'alloggio* were distinctive: they wore a uniform of finer cloth with gold buttons and an all-blue sash around the waist. Their epaulettes were also distinctive: metallic and with three rows of fish scales, like those of the troops, but the right one ended in a fringe and the left one was adorned with a small piece of molleton cloth, about 14mm long, held in place by a line of lace, all gold or silver.

The only NCOs in the mounted regiments were the *brigadieri*, who wore the troop uniform but were distinguished by gold or silver buttons. Their cuffs were edged with a single row of lace with a second double row below, and their collar with a single row of lace, all of the same colour of metal as the buttons.

Lastly, the *Cavalleggeri* and the *Dragoni del Re* troopers, belonging to the King's regiments, had their coat enhanced with white frogs that ended in a tassel, while those of the *marescialli d'alloggio* and the officers were embroidered in silver. The *brigadieri* wore silver tassels mixed with silk of the same colour.

Each mounted regiment had four standards, one per squadron. The first of these was a *colonnella*'s, while the other three were *ordinanza*'s. In addition to the richly embroidered Savoyard and regimental symbols, the branch of service was distinguished by its form. The three cavalry regiments carried waved square *stendardi* (cavalry standards), about a metre across. The four regiments of dragoons carried ensigns with two points at the fly, called *cornette* (guidons). Finally, the ensigns of the *Cavalleggeri del Re* were single pointed at the fly, and were called *fiamme* (cornets) (see colour plate 20). All the ensigns had a sleeve of the same fabric as the fabric on the field, on a blue-coloured tournament staff, surmounted by a gilded brass finial engraved with the great arms of the Kingdom of Sardinia. Below the finial were tied a blue cravat and a cord with a tassel at each end.[25]

---

25 Ricchiardi, *Bandiere e stendardi*, pp.233–254.

10

The Loyalty and Vicissitudes of a Small Navy

Savoy's small *Corpo Reale di Marina* (the navy) of 1792 was largely concentrated in the port of Villafranca, near Nice, the only important harbour of the Savoy mainland territories. The city of Nice was less than a dozen kilometres from the River Var, which marked the border with France. Until 1789, no threat to the County of Nice by the neighbouring kingdom of Bourbon France, closely related to the house of Savoy, seemed possible. On the contrary, the French naval force anchored in the port of Toulon could come to the rescue. But suddenly, the revolution of 1789 changed everything, and Vittorio Amedeo III, surprised by the events like all the European powers, only belatedly took measures to increase the garrison to defend the County. The fleet anchored off Villafranca, was subjected to increasing risks, which materialised in the defeat of 1792. Of course, if the powerful British Mediterranean fleet had already been present in that tragic September, things might been different, but British ships did not arrive in the area until later, and the capture of Nice was facilitated by the delay with which the British fleet commanded by Vice Admiral Lord Hood (1724–1816), commander-in-chief of the Mediterranean squadron, arrived in the Mediterranean to oppose the French.[1]

In any case, the small Savoyard fleet could not have made a significant contribution to the defence of Nice, as it consisted only of small vessels, some of which had mixed propulsion; both oars and sails. The sole purpose of the Savoy fleet was to defend the coast of Sardinia against pirate raids, and so only small sailing vessels capable of manoeuvres between headlands and in shallow waters, and others that retained some oar propulsion, were needed in the absence of wind on the island's rugged coastline. The effectiveness of the island's maritime defence is also confirmed by the fact that the half-galleys were able to capture small Barbary sailing ships that were taken into service and renamed as the galiots, *Sibilla* and *Serpente*, as well as other smaller ones. In addition to the smaller vessels in September 1792, the two old and inefficient frigates, the *San Vittorio* (32) and the decommissioned *San Carlo* (50), were at anchor in the harbour of Villafranca. The *San Vittorio* was commanded by *capitano* John Ross, a former British naval officer who had engaged in the Savoyard navy as a volunteer *guardiamarina* (midshipman) in 1765. Ross served Savoy for 30 years, rising to the rank of *capitano*, and commanding the *San Vittorio* and later, as we shall see, the *Alceste*. He was also the last British officer to serve in the Savoyard navy.[2]

---

1   See B. Ireland, *The Fall of Toulon. The last opportunity to defeat the French Revolution* (London: Orion, 2005).
2   A. Antonicelli, 'From Galleys to Square Riggers: The Modernization of the Navy of the Kingdom of Sardinia', *The Mariner's Mirror*, 2016, pp.153–173.

The two larger ships were joined by two corvettes, the *Carolina* and the *Augusta*. While the French did not bother with the useless *San Carlo* and captured the two corvettes, Ross hastily assembled officers and sailors from his crew on 28 September 1792 and, with men from other ships, escaped capture and managed to set sail, reaching the refuge of the Tuscan port of Livorno a few days later. He took with him no fewer than 381 men, 20 of them officers, including the commander of the *Regia Marina*, Pietro Francesco Davier, *cavaliere di Foncenex*. The *San Vittorio* then managed to reach the port of Genoa, where the authorities allowed it to dock but forced most of the crew to disembark and disarmed the ship. The frigate was thus interned, and Ross was unable to refit her and return to sea until the following year. There were inconveniences due to the boredom of routine activities and living away from families. Indeed, muster rolls show that by November 1793, 51 sailors had deserted, either by disembarking clandestinely in Genoa or by failing to return from leave granted to them.[3]

Before embarking on the *San Vittorio*, de Foncenex had ordered the *Battaglione di Marina* to join the retreating army and concentrate in the fortress of Saorgio. The battalion was the infantry unit that garrisoned the forts and docks of Nice but whose soldiers were only very rarely embarked. In fact, for service afloat, the battalion was joined by the *Granatieri delle Fregate* (Frigate Grenadiers) company, made up of veterans who performed the function of marines, but without their own officers, as they when they were aboard, they had to be under the exclusive command of navy officers.

The *Battaglione di Marina* was made up of a battalion staff and four *fucilieri* companies and was basically comparable in rank and structure to a line infantry battalion. The main difference was the absence of light infantrymen in the companies and of a grenadier company. Formed in 1792, the *Battaglione di Marina* had somehow linked to the *Granatieri delle Fregate* company, which had existed since 1775, but was in fact independent, because the latter's 71 soldiers serving in 1792 were not listed in the battalion's muster rolls. However, the *Battaglione di Marina*'s purpose was only to provide the men necessary to maintain the *Granatieri delle Fregate* company up to strength. The battalion also received auxiliary gunners who, who alongside the gunners of the *Corpo Reale d'Artiglieria*, were to contribute to the artillery fire of the forts protecting Villafranca.

The French, in their eagerness to pursue the retreating Piedmontese army towards the Val Roja to achieve its total defeat, did not possess the means to hold prisoners. As a result, many sailors and *Granatieri delle Fregate* managed to escape and reach the Piedmontese lines, a few kilometres from Nice, where they were sent to reinforce the garrison of the fort of Saorgio. From there, on 10 January 1793, 128 sailors were reviewed in Turin, given new uniforms, rearmed and temporarily sent back to Saorgio.[4] Other *Granatieri delle Fregate* and sailors who managed to escape from captivity made their own way to Genoa on 20 December 1792, joining what remained of the crew of the *San Vittorio*.[5] This shows that the Savoyard navy, composed mainly of *Nizzardi* and *Onegliesi*, demanded to serve and had no intention of giving up the defence of the Kingdom of Sardinia against French attacks.

---

3   AST, Ruolini di rivista, Compagnie di Marina, mazzo 56 and Thaon di Revel, Mémoires sur la guerre des Alpes, p.10.
4   AST, OGM, mazzo 70: Ordine di inviare i marinai a Saorgio, 10 January 1793.
5   AST, LUF, mazzo 271: Ordine di inviare a Genova marinai e granatieri delle fregate, 20 December 1793.

Some of the captured navy officers were released on parole by the French on 20 February 1793, promising not to serve on active duty for some time. Among them were the two governors of the castle of Villafranca and the fort of Montalbano, *luogotenente colonnello cavaliere* Luigi De May, the first of three De Mays who fought in the war, and *colonnello* Carlo Maria, *vassallo* Cacciardi. The latter, left without orders by the commander of the County of Nice, *luogotenente generale* de Courten, surrendered without a fight and, for this, was prosecuted but received only a light sentence.[6]

The command of the *Battaglione di Marina* was entrusted to *luogotenente colonnello conte* Francesco Ignazio Vitale, who was promoted to *colonnello* shortly afterwards. It is here that we find the second De May, *capitano luogotenente* Carlo Luigi. Coming from the *Reggimento Saluzzo*, Carlo Luigi was promoted to *capitano* in the *Battaglione di Marina*, then remained there when the battalion became the *Reggimento Oneglia* and served throughout the course of the war, reaching the rank of *maggiore di battaglione*.[7]

After the loss of Nice, the ineffectiveness of the *Battaglione di Marina* having clearly been established, the corps began its transformation into an infantry regiment, first with the name of *Nouvelle Marine* (21 January 1793), then, when the second battalion was formed, as *Reggimento Oneglia* (8 February 1793). Oneglia, now firmly established in the national ordnance infantry, no longer had any relationship with the navy and was employed throughout the war in the fourth army corps.[8]

Since it was impossible to use the frigate *San Vittorio*, which would certainly have been lost if it had faced the French fleet, the King authorised the arming of four feluccas for commerce warfare and to protect the Savoy's coast between Oneglia and Loano from raids by French light vessels. The feluccas were manned by the available Savoyard navy ratings commanded by four navy officers, including the *luogotenente di bordo cavaliere* Gaetano De May, the third De May who was involved in naval affairs during the War of the Alps, and the *primo luogotenente di bordo cavaliere* Baudolino Mattone di Benevello. The King then authorised the fitting out of a dozen small sailing vessels, most of them commanded and manned by people from Oneglia. There were also three members of the noble family Nizzarda Mattone di Benevello who participated with honour in the War of the Alps, demonstrating the loyalty of the nobility Nizzarda to the cause. In addition to the brave *cavaliere* Baudolino, *conte* Alberto was appointed on 17 November 1793 as *sotto luogotenente* of the militia of Cuneo, then *luogotenente* of infantry in the *Reggimento Vercelli*, and later went on to command one of the two grenadier companies of that regiment, which was included in 4° *Granatieri*. On 7 June 1795, Alberto was promoted to *luogotenente* of a *fucilieri* company and thus returned to the *Reggimento Vercelli*. Finally, on 20 May 1794, the *cavaliere* Simone, joined the *Cacciatori Carabinieri di Canale* as a provisional *sotto luogotenente*, but soon had to be sent on leave because, due to his age, he was no longer able to take part in the kind of warfare undertaken by the volunteer light infantry corps.

---

6   Scharfroth M. F. Les troupes suisses au service du Royaume de Sardaigne. *Armi Antiche* (Torino, 1968: 133-147), p.138.
7   Lo Faso di Serradifalco, *La difesa di un regno*, p.324.
8   AST, OGM, mazzo 70: Il Battaglione di Marina diventa reggimento Nouvelle Marine, 21 January 1793. AST, StM Vol 6: Nouvelle Marine cambia nome in Oneglia, 8 February 1793.

On 25 July 1793, the rearming of the *San Vittorio* began, with the preliminary idea of sending to Genoa sailors who had temporarily served in the seas around Oneglia and Loano, where they were to be replaced by 45–50 of the militia from Nice or Villafranca then in Oneglia, who had volunteered for naval service.[9]

The action of the Savoyard light flotilla sailing along the coast of Liguria continued for a long time. As late as 9 November 1795, Baudolino Mattone di Benevello was in command of the brig *La Concezione*, which was part of that fleet.[10]

The rearming of the *San Vittorio*, probably opposed by the Genoese authorities who had always been hostile to Savoy, did not take place quickly, but the frigate was able to leave Genoa and set sail for her fate by the early autumn of 1793. At the end of September, it joined British, Spanish and Ragusan ships ferrying the *2° Battaglione* of the *Reggimento Piemonte* and the *2°* of *de Courten* from Sardinia to Toulon, where they were to join the Savoyard expeditionary at corps at the siege.

Their arrival in the roadstead of Toulon, crowded with British, Neapolitan and Spanish frigates far more powerful than the old *San Vittorio*, must have made the men who served it realise its limitations.

The siege lasted just under four months (27 August–19 December 1793) and during the evacuation of the various expeditionary corps, the *San Vittorio* was set on fire and rendered unserviceable, but the Piedmontese willingly replaced it with capture of the French frigate *Alceste* (*Magicienne* class), armed with a main battery of twenty-six 12-pounder long guns, and with six 6-pounder guns on the quarterdeck and forecastle.[11]

During the following months, *Alceste*, commanded by Ross, was attached to the British Mediterranean fleet. On 6 June 1794, Ross received orders to set sail to deliver orders to the British squadron blockading Toulon. On 8 June 1794, while sailing towards Toulon, the *Alceste* saw a large squadron that Ross believed was the British fleet. Instead, it was a French squadron that had sortied out of Toulon three days earlier. Not believing that French ships could have evaded the British blockade, Ross hoisted British colours and approached quickly, only realising his mistake when he spotted the French tricolour hoisted on the nearest frigate, which opened fire. After a four-hour engagement, the *Alceste* had to surrender and so rejoined the French fleet, only to be captured by the British in 1799.[12]

The distinctive colour of the uniforms of the Navy uniforms was crimson, the colour of the eagle above three green hills rising above the waves in the coat of arms of Nice. The officer's uniforms used that colour on collar and cuffs. They wore a blue coat without lapels, with a white lining, and grey breeches and waistcoat. The rank distinctions were of gold lace, which also edged on the front of both coat and waistcoat and its pocket flaps. Finally, the ship's officers wore gold triple fish scale epaulettes with fringes, and a tricorn hat edged with gold lace and buttons of the same the same metal holding the cockade (see colour plate 21).

The ratings wore a uniform of a pattern almost certainly adopted in January 1793. It consisted of a short dark blue Austrian-style coat without lapels, with a crimson collar,

---

9   AST, LUF, mazzo 272: Ordini per riarmare la fregata San Vittorio internata a Genova, 25 June 1793.
10 AST, LUF, mazzo 277: Lettera per assegnare al Brigantino La Concezione un marinaio, 9 November 1795.
11 Sardinian Fifth Rate frigate 'Alceste' (1793), <https://threedecks.org/index.php?display_type=show_ship&id=2965>, accessed 15 January 2025.
12 Antonicelli, *From galleys to square riggers*, note 86.

cuffs and lining, and brass or gold buttons according to rank. Underneath, they wore a dark blue *gilet,* and the uniform was completed with wide blue trousers. They were armed with a *coltellaccio* (cutlass), carried hanging from a leather sword belt with a brass plate on the front showing the crowned royal monogram. The headgear was the new felt helmet already adopted by the *Cacciatori Carabinieri di Canale*. It was decorated at the front with a half-moon-shaped brass plate with the royal monogram placed above two crossed anchors (see colour plate 21).

The *Battaglione di Marina* wore the uniform of the line infantry, with a coat with the same rank distinctions and with crimson collar, cuffs and lapels, and white lining. The waistcoat and breeches were white. Finally, the *Granatieri delle Fregate* dressed in the same uniform as the *Battaglione di Marina*, but serving embarked, wore grey waistcoats and breeches.

The uniform of these grenadiers was enriched by an elegant helmet with a visor and decorated with two crossed anchors surmounted by the royal crown, Finally the helmet had a brass crest with black feathers. They wore the characteristic distinctive yellow or gold wavy lace of the grenadiers on their cuffs. The *Granatieri delle Fregate* also wore a blackened leather cartridge box for eight cartridges on their belt, decorated with a round front plate possibly adorned with the royal monogram. They were armed with a *fucile* with a bronzed barrel and a *coltellaccio*. Sailors had the same weaponry but without a bayonet. The *coltellacio* was long-bladed with a brass hilt and double guard. The wooden handle was lined with blackened leather, held in place by brass wire. The blade was straight, flat, smooth, and 676mm long, held in a blackened leather scabbard, with an internal iron tip protector (see colour plate 21).[13]

From the winter of 1795, with the French occupation of Liguria and the loss of Oneglia, the fleet of commerce raiders based there could no longer operate. Some sailors retreated to Piedmont and were sent to reinforce the garrison at the fort of Ceva, others reached Sardinia, which was still in the possession of the Savoy family, where they joined the half galleys and small sailing ships that were based there, maintaining the operational continuity of the Savoyard navy and flying the Savoy ensign for all the Napoleonic era.

From the end of December 1814, with the acquisition of the entire territory of the former Republic of Genoa, the port of Genoa became the main base of the fleet, and from that time, the Savoyard navy began to grow in importance.

---

13 Lupo, *Le lame del re*, pp.312–317.

11

The War (1792–1793): Recovery from Setback and the Start of the Fighting

1792

On 22 September, the *Armée du Midi*, some 8,000 strong under the command of *lieutenant général* Anne-Pierre Montesquiou-Fezensac began the invasion of Savoy.[1] Although the Piedmontese army corps in defence of Savoy was almost as large, its units were scattered over a vast territory because of the need to defend all the possible routes from France as well as the capital Chambéry. In Savoy, the Piedmontese army at that time had 12 ordnance infantry battalions (*1° Guardie, 2° Savoie, 1°* and *2° Monferrato, 1°* and *2° Aosta, 1°* and *2° La Marina, 1°* and *2° Rochmondet* and *1°* and *2° Sardegna*), two provincial battalions of the *Legione degli Accampamenti*, seven provincial infantry battalions (*1°* and *2° Genevois, 1°* and *2° Maurienne, 1°* and *2° Susa, 2° Casale*), a battalion of the *Legione Truppe Leggere*, six cavalry squadrons (*1°* and *3° Dragoni della Regina*, all four squadrons of *Cavalleggeri del Re*) and finally an artillery company.[2] The number of battalions may seem high, but, as we have seen, these were units not yet ready for war, reduced to the bare minimum, with the *2° battailons* of the infantry, as well as the dragoons and cavalry regiments all practically non-existent. Understrength and unaggressive units, uncertainly led by inexperienced commanders, suddenly found themselves under attack by politicised and very aggressive troops, who fought with a vehemence hitherto unknown. The result was panic, and the regiments tried to cross the Alps as quickly as possible and find refuge in Piedmont and the Valle d'Aosta. Some of the more solidly commanded infantry regiments, such as the *Reggimento Aosta*, acted as an effective rearguard during the retreat to the Piccolo San Bernardo, while the panic-stricken *Reggimento Sardegna* fled, to the point that the regiment's three senior officers were subsequently discharged and stripped of their ranks. Among them was Giuseppe Magliano, a *colonnello* who had commanded the *Sardegna* since 1789, who redeemed himself by regaining his rank and a royal pardon by enlisting as a simple volunteer in the *3° Granatieri*, distinguishing himself in the 1793 fighting.[3] The

---

1 Ilari et al, *La guerra delle Alpi*, p.29.
2 Ilari et al, *La guerra delle Alpi*, p.26.
3 Lo Faso di Serradifalco, *La difesa di un regno*, p.407.

retreat through difficult mountain valleys proved the irrelevance of the cavalry, who lost almost all their horses.

Having reached the Piccolo San Bernardo, the regiments, leaving a few troops behind, descended into the Valle d'Aosta to take up defensive positions between La Thuile, Morgex, Courmayeur and Arvier. This was just in time because the first heavy snow began to fall in the Alps on 11 October. Other units, garrisoned in Carouge, a municipality near Geneva, asked the Genevan authorities for permission to reach the Valle d'Aosta via Valais and the Passo del Gran San Bernardo. In this way, the Swiss of *1°* and *2° Rochmondet* and one company of the *Legione Truppe Leggere* managed to return safely.[4] To show himself to the troops who were now defending the Valle d'Aosta, the *duca* del Monferrato left his usual residence in the city of Aosta on 25 October and soon reached the Petit St Bernard Pass, where the defenders were entrenched.[5]

More fortunate was the part of the Piedmontese army corps garrisoning the Maurienne; *1°* and *2° La Marina* and *2° Casale* remained cohesive, effectively resisting the French and managing to establish themselves on the Passo del Moncenisio, where they were joined by *1° and 2° Asti*, hurrying from Susa.[6] As the snow level rose, militia and some regulars were left behind on the now impassable Passo del Moncenisio, while the battalions overwintered further down.

The army corps set up in 1792 to defend Nice was mainly concentrated in the city and consisted not only of most of the *Corpo Reale di Marina* (*Corpo degli Equipaggi* (Crew Corps), *Battaglione di Marina* and the *Granatieri delle Fregate* company), but also of nine ordnance infantry battalions (*1° Piemonte* – the *2°* was garrisoned in Sardinia – *1°* and *2° de Courten*, a battalion of *Christ*, *1°* and *2° La Regina*, *1°* and *2° Lombardia* and a battalion of *Saluzzo*), four provincial infantry battalions (*1°* and *2° Nizza*, *1°* and *2° Mondovì*) two companies of the *Legione degli Accampamenti* and two of artillery, to which was added three mounted squadrons (one of the *Dragoni di Piemonte* and two of the *Aosta Cavalleria*).[7]

Retreating precipitously to the mountains of Val Roia, the Piedmontese army corps nevertheless managed, by pivoting between the fort of Saorgio and the mountains on the right of the Roia torrent, to halt the French advance and hold the position with the help of thousands of *Nizzardi* militiamen.

From Nice, some of the navy personnel managed to save themselves on the frigate *San Vittorio*. Many others managed to escape from captivity and reach Saorgio or Genoa. The *Battaglione di Marina*, ordered to leave Villafranca to follow the retreating army, also managed to reach Saorgio. On 22 October, *luogotenente colonnello* Alessandro Giuseppe Thaon, *conte* of Revel and Sant'Andrea, was sent by the King to assume the role of *quartiermastro generale* of the Val Roia corps. With ambitions of revenge but without reinforcements, Sant'Andrea, after a few actions between Sospello and the Braus, had to give up when the first snows arrived and simply held the positions and outposts throughout the winter.[8]

---

4   Pinelli, *Storia Militare del Piemonte*, p.94.
5   E. Cais di Pierlas, *Storia del Reggimento di Susa e suo ingresso a Nizza in avanguardia austriaca* (Torino: Gerbone, 1900), p.27.
6   Pinelli, *Storia Militare del Piemonte*, pp.91–92.
7   Ilari et al, *La guerra delle Alpi*, pp.62–63.
8   Thaon di Revel, *Mémoires sur la guerre des Alpes*, p.14–17.

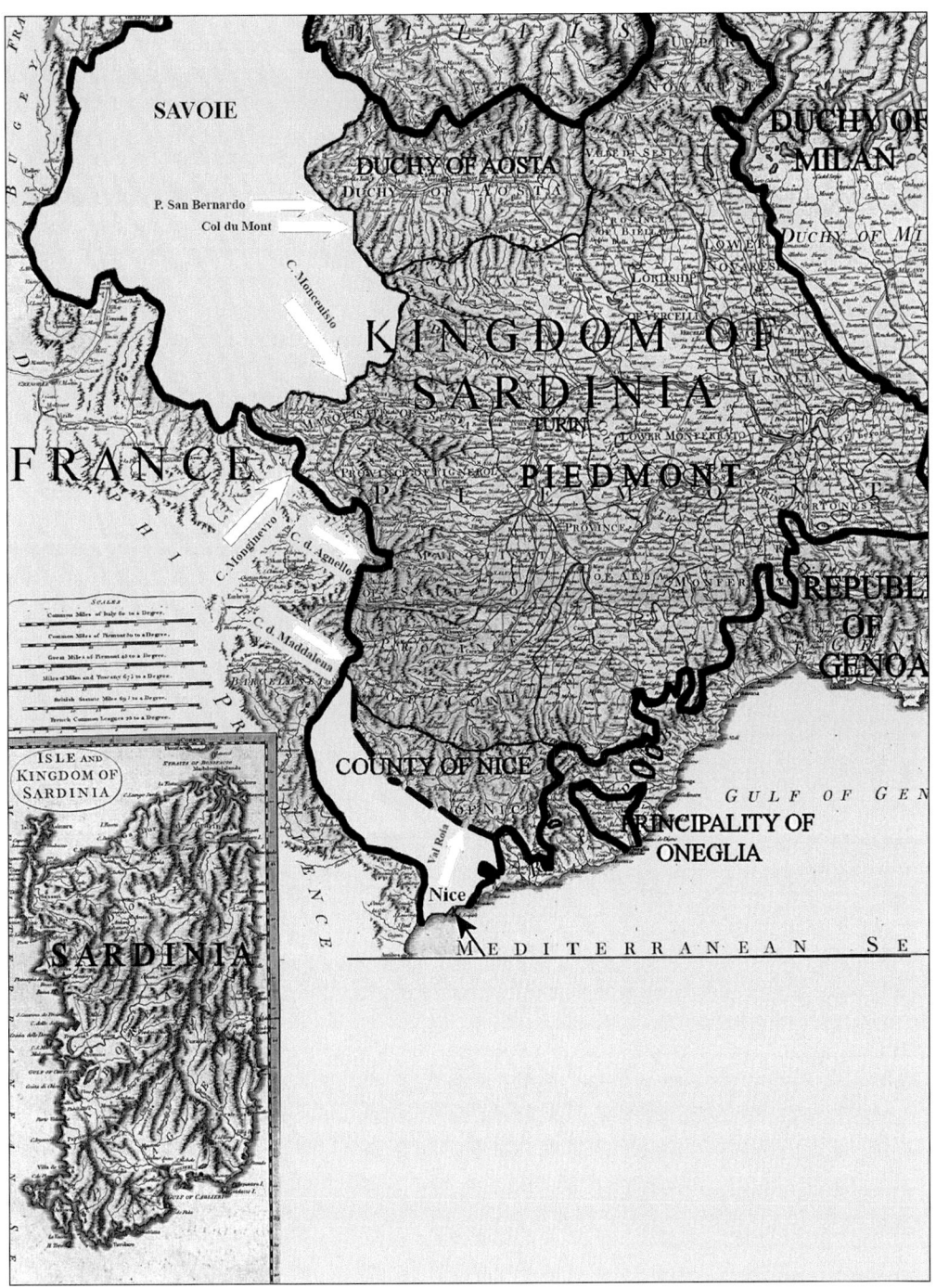

December 1792, the defensive lines. (A. Antonicelli (2016, Fig. 1), with permission. Modified by the Author.)

1793

After a screen of militia and regulars had garrisoned the Alpine passes, which were already well protected by the snow, the King, with the arrival of the campaigning season, summoned his advisers and Baron de Vins to decide on the best line of defence. Based on the experience of previous wars, it was thought that the maximum French effort would be made across the Colle dell'Agnello in order to invade Piedmont through the Val Varaita, emerging onto the plain at Saluzzo. It was a more difficult proposition for the enemy to attempt an invasion via Colle della Maddalena, defended at the bottom by the fort of Demonte and then by the fortifications of Cuneo. It was, therefore, decided to send an army corps composed of the regiments considered to be most reliable and the Austrian auxiliary corps to those valleys. The arrival of the enemy from the Valle d'Aosta, Susa and Val Roia could not be ignored. It soon became clear that the Piedmontese army did not have sufficient forces to defend all the passes and attempt a counterattack. For these reasons, Vittorio Amedeo III's requests to Austria for a much larger army corps became increasingly urgent, but in vain.

The movements of the revolutionary army towards the Low Countries convinced the British government to take part in the war. Thus, was born the First Coalition, which was joined by Russia (25 March 1793), Piedmont (25 April), Naples (12 July), quietly by Austria (31 August), and the Grand Duchy of Tuscany (28 October). The alliance, however, brought the Kingdom of Sardinia nothing but the presence in the Mediterranean of the pugnacious British fleet commanded by Vice Admiral Lord Hood, but no troops that could have helped the Austro-Piedmontese army or that could have contributed to the liberation of Nice. On the contrary, Piedmont was asked to provide ground troops for the Siege of Toulon, which it had to divert from the Alpine defences and almost completely denude Sardinia, now well protected by the British fleet.[9]

The Deployment of 9 June

Mobilisation was carried out in stages. First, the *1°* battalions of the line infantry regiments were made operational and sent to the battlefront. While the *2°* battalions were also being made operational, priority was given to outfitting the grenadier and light companies in order to send them as quickly as possible to the newly formed independent battalions of these two specialities. At the beginning of March, the *2°* battalions were nearly fully manned and trained while at the same time being deployed on public order duties. Shortly afterwards, however, they were also sent towards the Alps. Sometimes, due to the urgency of reinforcing the corps, if the first of the two battalions' *centurie* were ready, it was despatched without waiting for the second.

Four army corps thus quickly took shape as they reached their assigned locations, and by early June 1793 were constituted as follows.[10] The first corps, with about 6,000 men, was nominally under the command of Benedetto Maurizio, *duca* del Monferrato, but the actual

---

9   Ilari et al, *La guerra delle Alpi*, p.84.
10 Ilari et al, *La guerra delle Alpi*, pp.46-49.

command was exercised by *brigadiere generale* Giuseppe Bertone, *cavaliere* di Sambuy, who was also the commander of the regiment made up of the *2° and 10° Battaglione Granatieri*. The headquarters of this army corps was located in Aosta, and it was responsible for the defence of the extreme right of the Alpine arc separating Piedmont from France. It was deployed in the Valle d'Aosta, from Val Veny to the Col du Mont. This corps was made up of two battalions of *Granatieri Reali*, four national ordnance battalions (*1° and 2° Monferrato, 1° and 2° La Marina*), four provincial battalions (*1° Mondovì, 1° Genevois, 1° and 2° Torino*), and three Swiss (one *de Courten*, two *Rochmondet*). The cavalry consisted of the *Cavalleggeri del Re* regiment and the artillery of four companies with 14 artillery pieces.

The second corps defended the approaches to Piedmont through the Moncenisio and Monginevro passes. It was commanded by *luogotenente generale* Vittorio Amedeo Sallier de la Tour, *marchese* of Cordon (1726-1800), who remained in command because he was well established at court, despite having been one of those responsible for the disastrous retreat from Savoy the previous year.[11] Technically unskilled, he drew on the experience of his brother, *capitano* Joseph Amadeus Sallier, *conte* de la Tour (1737–1820).[12] This army corps consisted of some 4,300 men and relied on the powerful system of forts in the Susa and Chisone valleys. It included the *2° Battaglione Cacciatori*, four battalions of grenadiers (*2°, 6°, 7° and 10°*), five battalions of national ordnance infantry, four provincial (*1° and 2° Susa, 1° and 2° Maurienne*) and one of foreign infantry (*1° Chablais*). Some 200 dragoons and three companies of *cannonieri* with 14 artillery pieces completed this corps, with headquarters located in Susa.

The third corps defended the Po, Varaita, Maira, Stura and Gesso valleys and the Agnello (2748m) and Maddalena (1996m) passes. At the beginning of the war, it was considered the most important of the four corps, and, in June 1793, many of the Piedmontese army's battalions and most of the Austrian expeditionary corps, totalling about 11,000 men, were concentrated in this area. The headquarters of the third corps was placed in the central position of Casteldelfino and entrusted to the Austrian *feldmarschall-leutnant* Strassoldo. Under him were the Austrian *generalmajor* Provera and the Savoyard *principe* Carlo Emanuele di Savoia-Carignano (1770-1800). The Waldensian valleys (Luserna and San Martino) were left to the five local militia companies.

To the defence of the Po, Varaita and Maira valleys were assigned about 3,000 Austrians (*Strassoldo* grenadier battalion, *1° and 2° IR44 Belgioioso, 1° and 2° IR48 Caprara*), 1,600 Piedmontese (*1° Piemonte, 5° Granatieri, 2° Mondovì, 1° Granatieri Reali*), 400 Swiss grenadiers (from the *Peyer-Im-Hoff, Bachmann* and *Zimmerman* new regiments), a battalion of *Freikorps Gyulai* (815) and two artillery companies with eight pieces. The headquarters were in Casteldelfino.

The defence of the Stura valley was entrusted to Strassoldo with about 4,000 Piedmontese soldiers in nine infantry battalions (*1° and 2° Guardie, 1° Savoie, 1° and 2° Aosta, 1° and 2° Ivrea, 1° and 2° Asti* and about 2,000 *fucilieri* from the Swiss *Peyer-Im-Hoff, Zimmerman* and *Bachman* regiments). The headquarters was in the fortress of Demonte.[13] However, the experiences of previous wars had shown the French that these valleys were not an easy

---

11 Lo Faso di Serradifalco, *La difesa di un regno*, p.523.
12 Lo Faso di Serradifalco, *La difesa di un regno*, p.522.
13 Ilari et al, *La guerra delle Alpi*, p.84.

target, as the fierce battles of 1743–1744 in the Varaita and Maira valleys had illustrated, and so they made only weak attacks there. Then, in the autumn of 1793, important parts of the third corps were transferred to the fourth army corps, where the French were making their main effort to break through. This direction of attack was unusual and had only been attempted on a small scale in previous wars.

Finally, the fourth corps was under the nominal command of Benedetto Maurizio, *duca* del Chablais, who had as his deputy *maggior generale* Carlo Francesco Thaon, *conte* di Revel Sant'Andrea. The latter was the real commander of this corps, since the Duke rarely went to the Val Roia. This corps, which was concentrated for the defence of the County of Nice and, it was hoped, the recovery of the city, quickly became the most important, outnumbering the third corps. It initially consisted of 22 battalions, with an effective strength of just over 9,000 men. There were eight Piedmontese battalions of the national ordnance (*1° and 2° Saluzzo, 1° Oneglia, 1° Sardegna, 1° and 2° La Regina, 1° and 2° Lombardia*), six provincial infantry battalions (*1° and 2° Nizza, 1° and 2° Vercelli, 1° and 2° Tortona*) and one battalion of the Swiss *Christ* Regiment. Later, four more provincial battalions seem to have been added (*1° and 2° Casale, 1° and 2° Acqui*), increasing the force accordingly. The elite infantry was represented by the *1° Cacciatori* and four *Granatieri* battalions (*1°, 4°, 8° and 9°*). Some brand-new companies of *Cacciatori Volontari* had also arrived in the area, the *Cacciatori Carabinieri di Canale* and the *1° and 2° Corpo Franco*, the latter including French expatriates. Finally, several hundred valuable militia from Nice, who knew the Val Roia intimately, manned the forward posts and acted as guides for the other units. A report dated 16 June 1793 shows that 17 artillery pieces (two howitzers, five 8-pounders, two 4-pounder field pieces and the same number of mountain artillery pieces) were placed in the Val Roia.[14]

A month later, on 4 July, the situation of the fourth corps after the Battle of Authion, reported in an administrative document summarising the number of rations needed that day, was already different from that of the previous month due to the constant movement of battalions sent where necessary, and did not take into account, and perhaps it was impossible to do so in such a short time, the losses suffered in the fierce fighting of the previous month. The document reports a total of 16,937 men in the fourth corps, distributed as follows:

> Seven ordnance infantry battalions. *1° and 2° Saluzzo* (1024 men), *1° La Regina* (509), *1° Sardegna* (519), *1° and 2° Lombardia* (1016), *1° Oneglia* (509).
> Eleven provincial infantry battalions. *1° and 2° Nizza* (984), *1° and 2° Vercelli* (984), *1° and 2°* Casale (984), battalion of *Tortona* (495), *1° and 2° Susa* (984), *1° and 2° Acqui* (984).
> A battailon of *Legione Truppe Leggere* (508).
> One battalion of Swiss ordnance infantry *Reggimento Christ* (509).
> Four grenadiers battailons, one of which Austrian (2088).
> Light troops: a battalion of *1° Battaglione Cacciatori* (480), *Cacciatori Carabinieri di Canale* (342), *Corpo Franco* (326).
> Two Austrian infantry regiments. A battalion of *IR6 Zweytes Garnison Regiment* (1200), a battalion of *IR44 Belgioioso* Regiment (1160).

---

14 Thaon di Revel, *Mémoires sur la guerre des Alpes*, p.51.

Artillery (582).
Milizia Nizzarda (750).
Provianda squads separate from the regiments (281).
Quartier Generale of the corps (36).

Of course, as usual, these are theoretical figures – at least 25 percent would have to be subtracted from these figures to give the actual strength at the battlefront. This would be about 12,700 men, figures quite different from the previous ones.[15]

As for the number of artillery pieces in the fourth corps at the time, Thaon di Revel reports that there were two howitzers, five 8-pounders, two 4-pounder field pieces, eight mountain pieces, some 4- and some 3-pounders, making a total of 17.[16]

As early as April 1793, the French began to test the strength of the enemy's defences in the upper central part of the Val Roia. At the same time, the Piedmontese fourth army corps, supported by a few Austrian battalions, counter-attacked, and the *Milizia Nizzarda* and the volunteer light infantry corps kept control of the position in the face of the revolutionary battalions.

The Battle of Authion

On 8 June 1793, a French force of about 20,000 men, under the command of *général de division* Gaspard de Brunet (1737–1793) launched the decisive attack that was to end with the Austro-Piedmontese retreat. The aim was to allow his army, part of the *Armée d'Italie* commanded by *général d'armée* François Cristophe Kellermann (1735–1820), to break through into the plain. The French were opposed by the Austro-Piedmontese, who were numerically much smaller but well entrenched. They theoretically numbered about 12,000 men, divided into 4,000 on the right wing (nine battalions, 400 militiamen and 12 artillery pieces) and another 8,000 on the left of the Roia river (16 battalions, 1,200 militiamen and seven artillery pieces).

Between 8 and 12 June 1793, relying on the fortified field defences, the fourth corps managed to repel the furious French attacks, suffering considerable losses but maintaining a large part of the defensive line.

At the end of the five days of fighting, there was great uncertainty about the extent of French losses; de Brunet, perhaps to play down the failure, admitted to 1,200 men out of action, while other sources put the figure at 2,000 or more. The Piedmontese losses are better documented. The most accepted version indicates the loss of 92 officers (19 of which killed in action or later from wounds received, 14 prisoners of war, 56 wounded and three absent without leave, possibly deserters) and 1,205 NCOs and soldiers (115 dead, 499 prisoners or missing and 591 wounded). However, some of the prisoners and missing were later able to rejoin their units, reducing the final casualty figure.[17] Among the missing officers,

---

15 AST, IdA, mazzo 4: Forza dell'Armata del Contado di Nizza, 4 July 1793.
16 Thaon di Revel, *Mémoires sur la guerre des Alpes*, p.51.
17 C. De Antonio, 'Authion', *Memorie Storico Militari*, 1911, pp.367–526.

there were few cases of cowardice in the face of the enemy, but an insignificant percentage compared to their large numbers.[18]

The impact of the victory had an important effect on the morale of the Piedmontese army, whose officers and soldiers realised that the disasters of 1792 would not be repeated. Unfortunately, de Vins' inertia, perhaps encouraged by Vienna, did not permit the success to be exploited, with no attempt to reconquer other parts of the County of Nice, dampening the enthusiasm of Vittorio Amedeo III's soldiers and fuelling the discontent of the Piedmontese officers, who were better informed than their subordinates.

Disputes between commanders soon led to mutual distrust and a complete lack of unity of command between the Austrian and Piedmontese armies. This prevented the necessary joint action from being taken, when it would have been vital. But at least the few thousand Austrian soldiers actually on the Savoy side were of some help. The battalion of *IR44 Belgioioso*, certainly not one of the most famous of the Austrian army, and even the senior soldiers of the *IR6 Zweytes* garrison regiment, from whom no heroic deeds could be expected, held out well against the French attacks, sheltered as they were by dry stone walls and flanked by battalions of the far more aggressive Piedmontese army.

Many officers of the Val Roia corps received decorations, honours and promotions. Only eight Silver Medals were awarded to the troops, showing that Vittorio Amedeo III applied the regulations to the letter and awarded them only in cases of exceptional, proven bravery.[19]

For the failed series of attacks between 8 and 12 June 1793, de Brunet was tried on trumped-up charges and imprisoned in Paris, where he was guillotined on 17 November 1793. His superior, Kellermann, risked the same fate on different charges but escaped. This was the punishment for failure in France at that time.

The Siege of Toulon

In the late spring of 1793, with the resumption of fighting and the success in repelling the French at Authion, Vittorio Amedeo III began to hope for the possibility of recovering Savoy and Nice. His hopes were fuelled by the news from France, where the populations of several French regions and cities were declaring themselves Royalists and beginning to rebel against the harassment of the supporters of the Revolution and the fact that more and more men were forced to take up arms to pursue their aims of imposing revolutionary values on the whole of Europe. The other European powers began to realise that they had to act, especially Britain, which had the world's largest and most powerful fleet but a limited army.

Be that as it may, when the Royal Navy finally arrived in the Mediterranean, one of its first actions was to force the French fleet back into harbour, notably that of Toulon, forcing them to abandon their naval expansionist plans. It was impossible for Lord Hood, commander in the Mediterranean, to ignore the cries for help from the Royalists in the cities of Marseille

---

18   See for a detailed description of the battle of Authion by officers of the Kingdom of Sardinia or later: Pinelli, *Storia Militare del Piemonte*, pp.177–212, Thaon di Revel, *Mémoires sur la guerre des Alpes*, p.55. Ilari et al, *La guerra delle Alpi*, pp.107–119. De Antonio, 'Authion', is particularly detailed, with plenty of documents and maps.
19   De Antonio, 'Authion', pp.425–426.

and Toulon. A decision on intervention in Toulon became urgent when the revolutionary army managed to occupy and sack Marseille. The citizens of Toulon, who had given asylum to Marseillaise fleeing the reprisals of the Revolutionary army, put pressure on Hood, who finally decided to intervene. However, to put his decision into practice, he consulted his allies and urged them to create the land army he lacked. He obtained contingents from Spain and the Kingdom of Naples but received only vague assurances from Austria, which ultimately did not send any contingents.

On 19 July 1793, the people of Toulon saw the British fleet appear on the horizon, and a boat was detached carrying Lieutenant Edward Cook to negotiate and receive the requests of the Toulonnais, who were now starving due to the blockade of the city. By this time, the situation was deteriorating rapidly as confusion reigned in the city, in the port and in the harbour, where citizens and French sailors from the fleet moored offshore were in danger of clashing. Negotiations between British officers and the leaders of the city went on for a long time until, on 24 August, a British delegate presented a statement from Hood proposing to accept the city as an ally of the legitimate King of France. There was no time to hesitate, for Robespierre had seized full power in Paris on 28 July and launched the *Terreur*. Finally, on 27 August, the British ships of the line entered Toulon harbour, followed the next day by the Spanish. At that moment, Hood declared that he was taking possession of Toulon in the name of Louis XVII of France, heir to the throne, and at the same time urged the King of Sardinia to send a contingent. To this request Vittorio Amedeo III gave a positive response, in the hope that the conquest of part of Provence would then result in the liberation of Nice.

Maggiore Thaon di Revel, who was personally very much in favour of a positive response, was appointed by the King as commissioner to the allies in Toulon, promoting him at the same time to *luogotenente colonnello*. Thus, he arrived in Toulon to represent the interests of the Kingdom of Sardinia and was ordered to send regular reports directly to his monarch.[20]

Once diplomatic relations had been established, the Piedmontese contingent had to be formed. The King of Sardinia found it difficult to move valuable battalions from the defence of the Alps, but he was aware of the need to restore the credibility of his army after the disasters of 1792. In a meeting with his advisors and de Vins, it was decided to send three elite battalions detached from the front and two others taken from the garrison troops of Sardinia, who had not yet fired a shot but would certainly follow the example of their more experienced colleagues.

On 17 September 1793, the *4° Granatieri* and the *1° Cacciatori*, with a total strength of about 800 men, left for Oneglia, where they were to prepare for embarkation.[21] Thaon di Revel reports that these first two battalions were embarked on the frigate *San Vittorio* and some merchant ships and arrived in Toulon on 27 September.[22]

Later, the *2° Piemonte* and the *2° de Courten* Swiss, were brought from Sardinia. Finally, in November, the *2° Cacciatori* also arrived in Toulon to complete the small Piedmontese expeditionary force. The highest-ranking Piedmontese officer was Swiss *brigadiere generale* Francesco Antonio Buellier, commander of the *2° de Courten*, but the actual commander

---

20   Thaon di Revel, *Mémoires sur la guerre des Alpes*, p.138.
21   AST, IdA, mazzo 6: Il 4° Granatieri e il 1° Cacciatori vanno a Oneglia per imbarcare per Tolone, 17 September 1793.
22   Thaon di Revel, *Mémoires sur la guerre des Alpes*, pp.141–142.

of the expeditionary corps was *luogotenente colonnello* Ignace Thaon, *cavaliere* di Revel (1760-1835), by virtue of the prerogatives granted him by Vittorio Amedeo III.

A considerable force was thus concentrated in Toulon, but not enough to counter the first French attacks of the revolutionary army, which were about to become fierce. The force at Hood's disposal consisted of 3,350 British, 7,150 Spanish, 6,650 Neapolitans and 2,470 Piedmontese (*4° Granatieri* 500, *1°* and *2° Cacciatori* 1000, *2° Piemonte* 520, *2° de Courten* 450) and 1,600 French Royalists, probably from the city's *Garde nationale*, making a total of 21,220 men. However, as usual, these numbers were only theoretical since they were reduced by various services, indispositions, casualties, etc. The actual fighters were fewer in number, and, in any case, the troops did not arrive at the same time, so the multi-national expeditionary corps did not reach this size until the end of November.

The fighting for the forts surrounding Toulon immediately became fierce, as had been strongly ordered from Paris. The soldiers of the Piedmontese army, especially those of the three elite battalions, were highly valued in the constant fighting and almost always operated in close contact with the British.

Part of the French success was due to the concentrated and well-directed fire of the artillery pieces in the manner devised by Napoleon Bonaparte, then a young artillery officer, and much of it was due to the ever-increasing size of the French army corps engaged in the liberation of Toulon. It became increasingly difficult for Hood to hold his positions, and the joint command of the expeditionary corps began to consider the possibility of redeploying troops and abandoning the siege. This decision was strongly opposed by Thaon di Revel, who was fully aware that such a defeat would make the reconquest of Nice impossible. However, as the enemy's constant attacks and artillery fire became unsustainable, Hood was forced to give in, and Thaon di Revel resigned himself to the inevitable. It was decided that the British would set fire to the 13 French ships anchored near the arsenal (nine 74-gun ships and four frigates), the stores and the arsenal itself and the Spanish would do the same to the French ships anchored in the harbour. The evacuation of the expeditionary force would take place from 17 December 1793.[23]

As soon as the news reached the Royalists in Toulon and the evacuees from Marseille, they were horrified by the massacres they feared would take place and clamoured to be evacuated as well. The embarkation took place in great confusion, not least because it was carried out at night. The Royalists, seeing officers and soldiers of the Allied armies rushing out to sea to join the boats that would take them to the ships, did everything they could to follow them, and some of them drowned in the attempt.

Fortunately, several fishing boats and rowing boats were moored in Toulon, and a significant number of Royalists were able to save themselves by following the fleets as they put out to sea.

Thaon di Revel reports that the Piedmont veterans' steadiness and discipline were commendable on this occasion as well. Most of them were embarked in ships of the British fleet and other civilian vessels. Under these circumstances, the only frigate of the *Regia Marina*, the *San Vittorio*, which was no longer being able to sail, was set on fire. As compensation, Piedmontese officers and sailors took possession of the French frigate *Alceste*, which,

---

23   Ilari et al, *La guerra delle Alpi*, pp.98–99.

having raised the Savoy naval flag, sailed for Oneglia carrying as many men as possible. The others reached the same port on British ships.[24]

The Attempted Recovery of Savoy

In 1793 was decided by the King to invade Savoy using the first corps via the Piccolo San Bernardo and the second via the Moncenisio Passes. The theoretical strength of the two corps at that time was about 14,400 men. The 8,000 men under the command of the *duca del Monferrato*, assisted by the experienced Austrian *generalmajor* Eugen Gillis Wilhelm d'Argentou (1743–1819) from the staff of de Vins, were to provide the invasion force.[25]

Shortly before the start of the invasion, the medical situation of the Piedmontese troops massing in La Thuile was discussed. On 8 July 1793:

> Conditions were bad for the troops. The cold wind that blew down from the glaciers at night was followed by excessive heat during the day. The thermometer was at 30 [°C], the highest it had been this century. The soldiers were decimated by an epidemic of dysentery: the whole cantonment is full of sick people. The Prince was in good health, although he was staying in the parish church, next to the cemetery, where four or five people were buried every day. Not to touch the sick and to leave the rest to Providence.[26]

Their condition contributed to the delays and indecision as to the date of the start of the attack, which would only begin on 15 August 1793. Finally, the decision was made to begin the operation, and the first corps began to roll through the Piccolo San Bernardo. The King and the Prince were also comforted by the news brought to them by some Savoyard nobles that the population of the region was against the French occupation and would rebel *en masse* at the news of the arrival of the battalions, some of which were partly made up of Savoyards.[27]

At the same time, the second army corps emerged from the Moncenisio towards the Maurienne with a paper strength of about 4,000 men commanded by *luogotenente generale* Sallier de la Tour de Cordon with his brother *capitano* Joseph Amadeus Sallier de la Tour, while another 2,400 were left at Ulzio under the command of *Brigadiere Generale barone* Pio Chino to guard Monginevro.[28]

The Savoyards' rebellion did not take place, mainly due to the forced enlistment of many men by the French and the lack of weapons to equip the rebels. In fact, neither the Prince, nor de Vins, had even thought of having an adequate number of *fucili* and equipment for the militiamen transported to Savoy.

---

24 Much of the narrative of the Siege of Toulon as seen from the Savoyard side was taken from Thaon di Revel, *Mémoires sur la guerre des Alpes*, Chapter VII.
25 Ilari et al, *La guerra delle Alpi*, p.126.
26 Fenoil, *La Terreur sur les Alpes*, pp.12–16.
27 P. Guichonnet, *Le Monts en feu. La guerre en Faucigny, 1793* (Annecy: Academie Salésienne, 1995), p.235.
28 Ilari et al, *La guerra delle Alpi*, p.126.

The French managed to counter the two Piedmontese corps with the same number of men, and the expedition, despite the bravery deployed by the troops, was reduced to a useless waste of enthusiasm, and human and material resources. Between 28 September and 6 October, the Piedmontese had to withdraw from Savoy before the snows came, and they did not fully recover it until 1815.

The Surprising Valais Route

In order to protect the Piedmontese advance on the right flank in the Tarantaise from Faucigny, it was considered necessary to send some troops into the Vallée de l'Arve to incite the inhabitants to revolt and block the French. The solution proposed by the Savoy aristocrats, who were experts in the area, was to bypass the Mont Blanc massif by sending a column of mules, with the tacit consent of the Valais authorities, via Martigny to Chamonix, on the other side of the massif via the Col de La Forclaz (1,527m), now crossed by a convenient road, but then only accessible by mule track.

A small corps of about 200 men, all young and enthusiastic volunteers, was assigned to the enterprise: 120 from the *Genevois* and 81 from the *Maurienne* regiments. They were led by volunteer officers who were a mixture of Savoyards with some French Royalists.

The small corps was placed under the command of Savoyard officer Joseph Emmanuel Guiges de Revel, former *maggiore* of the *Chablais* Regiment. Prepared in Aosta, the force arrived at Saint Remy, the last town in the Valle d'Aosta, and set off across the Gran San Bernardo Pass towards Martigny around midnight on 9 August 1793.

The long column consisted of 180 mules carrying arms and provisions for four days. The soldiers carried only their bayonets at the request of the authorities of the Canton of Valais, leaving their *fucili* on the mules. Otherwise, they wore the uniform of their regiment and were fully equipped with 50 cartridges, packs and bayonets, the latter concealed under their waistcoats.

On 12 August, these strong mountaineers reached Vallorcine, the first village in Savoy, where they opened the crates to take out their *fucili* and repelled a small detachment of French troops, taking two prisoners. In Vallorcine, the community welcomed them with the ringing of church bells and cries of 'Vive le Roy!'. On the 13th, they arrived in Chamonix, at the foot of the other side of Mont Blanc, where their welcome was less enthusiastic, and it was considered necessary to set up armed patrols at night to protect the rest of the column. In the morning, however, many villagers from Chamonix and the surrounding area decided to follow the column, which reached Servoz on the 14th, descending to the Sallanches plain in the Vallée de l'Arve on the 15th, where they were given a festive welcome and surrounded by villagers hoping the column would bring arms and ammunition to fight the French. It seems that no one had thought of this, and the impossibility of arming the villagers against the French was one of the causes of the expedition's failure. Another cause was the uncertainty of command because the column received conflicting orders from de Vins, still in Turin, and from d'Argentou, who only sent orders from Tarantaise rather than sufficient arms and reinforcements.

Vehemently attacked by the French and Savoyards recruited into the French *Garde nationale*, the column and the almost unarmed militiamen resisted bravely for several days, but in the end, the mission that had given so much hope to the Royalists of Faucigny failed.[29]

Attacking to Liberate Nice?

In early August, news arrived, partly through a growing number of French deserters, that the enemy was evacuating Nice, presumably to send reinforcements to rebellious Toulon and to prevent feared British aid to the insurgents. The news was greeted with joy by the Piedmontese. The *duca* d'Aosta, who was in favour of taking advantage of events, and went with his entourage to inspect the advanced areas of the front. It was perhaps he who suggested the raids that took place on 4 and 16 August to disrupt and identify the enemy's strength and position. An attack on Lantosca was carried out from 6 to 10 September by a large force (about 20,000 men), but some misunderstandings caused it to fail because of the delay in the intervention of the Aosta corps in the Val Vesubia. This was the result of the difficulty of crossing the Alpine peaks that separate the Stura di Demonte valley from the Vesubia and Tinea valleys.

Other attacks took place, again planned while the French were occupied at Toulon, towards Giletta (14 and 18 October 1793) and Utelles (21 October–21 November 1793), but they too failed to achieve their objectives.

The failures increased the climate of suspicion, with the Piedmontese authorities openly accusing de Vins of deliberately holding back the attacks. The King, demoralised and pressed on all sides, defended him but did not have the strength to intervene decisively. This situation would weigh heavily on next year's operations.

Once the snows fell, the battalions withdrew to Piedmont for the winter and *generale* Sant'Andrea decided to have the front garrisoned by the *Milizia Nizzarda* and 3,200 regulars, quartered in barracks, isolated houses and villages.

At the end of the year, the deployments were almost the same as those of the previous winter, and the Piedmontese were able to hold off the French everywhere, but to break through in 1794, the enemy radically changed their strategy.[30]

---

29 The detailed chronicle these events is in Guichonnet, *Le monts en feu*, pp.261–290.
30 Ilari et al, *La guerra delle Alpi*, pp.133–141.

12

1794: Resistance at All Costs!

In January 1794, the War Council chaired by the King decided on the distribution of the various corps stationed on the frontier. A new factor was that fearing a French attack from the south, the corps defending Val Roia had to detach part of its troops for the vital garrisons of Mondovì and Ceva. The division into four army corps was also changed, with the first, second and third grouped into a so-called Army of the Alps, recklessly placed under the high command of *capitano generale duca* d'Aosta.

The Army of the Alps was divided into four commands. The 10,000 men assigned to the defence of the Valle d'Aosta, nominally captained by the *duca* del Monferrato, were under the command of the Swiss *maggior generale* Georges Benoit Rochmondet, *colonnello proprietario* (colonel-proprietor) of the Bernese Swiss regiment of the same name. The 3,000 men defending the Chisone and Susa valleys and the Moncenisio and Monginevro passes were under the command of *maggior generale* Pio Chino. The 2,000 men deployed in defence of the Maira, Varaita and Grana valleys were under the command of *Generalmajor* Giovanni Provera. Finally, 7,000 men nominally under command of *capitano generale* Carlo Emanuele di Savoia-Carignano were placed to garrison the Stura valley and the fort of Demonte.

The fourth corps, placed under the command of the useless de Vins, now called the 'Austro-Sardinian Army', detached around 12,000 men for the defence of the Val Roia, under the command of *luogotenente generale* Baron Colli and *luogotenente generale* Giuseppe Antonio Dellera, *barone* di Corteanzo (1720–1801). Dellera, commander of the *Legione Truppe Leggere*, was highly appreciated by the troops because he cared for their welfare and shared their hardships.

In addition, under the command of Austrian *Generalmajor* Eugen Gillis Wilhelm Graf Mercy d'Argentau (1743–1819) was the corps detached for the defence of Ceva and Oneglia, the latter commanded by *brigadiere generale* Luigi Costa della Trinità, *marchese* di Montafia.[1]

The 12,000 men defending the Val Roia were divided into two corps, the first facing the route from Nice to the Colle di Tenda, the second to defend the ridge that separated the mountainous left flank of the Val Roia from any advance from Liguria and the Valle del Tanarello. The composition of the two corps is summarised in a detailed situation report

---

1 Luigi Costa della Trinità, *marchese* di Montafia was promoted to *maggior generale* in November 1794 for his conduct when in command of the *Reggimento Regiment* during the Battle of Authion. Lo Faso di Serradifalco, *La difesa di un regno*, p.307.

drawn up by the War Office on 17 April 1794 to assess the supplies needed. In defence of Val Roia and Val Vesubia were deployed 13 battalions:

> Four of national ordnance (*1°* and *2° Monferrato* (850 men), *1°* and *2° Oneglia* (600)
> Four of provincial ordnance (*1°* and *2° Torino* (850), *1° Asti* (400), *2° Mondovì* (250)
> Two of Swiss ordnance (*1°* and *2° Peyer-Im-Hoff*, 800)
> The *5° Granatieri* (300)
> The *1° Cacciatori* (500)
> A battalion of the *IR6 Zweytes Garnison Regiment* (1,040)
> The *Cacciatori Carabinieri di Canale* (230).

To this theoretical total of 5,820 men must be added 38 companies of *Milizia Nizzarda*, a force of 1,800 men, plus 700 artillerymen with pieces and ammunition carried by 100 men from the *Treno d'Artiglieria*. Thirteen cavalrymen, probably for despatches, completed the corps. However, a further 2,513 men were arriving by forced march: *1°* and *2° Saluzzo* (800), *2° Cacciatori* (300), *8°* and *9° Granatieri* (600). They were deployed on the ridge towards Liguria as soon as they arrived.

Before these last arrivals, the report of 17 April indicates that 11 battalions were deployed on the ridge from Tanarda to Tanarello to face any enemy originating from Liguria: Five of provincial ordnance: *1°* and *2° Pinerolo* (800 men), *1°* and *2° Nizza* (400), *2° Tortona* (250), *1°* and *2° Granatieri Reali* (600), *1° Cacciatori* (250), the complete *Corpo Franco* (400), *1°* and *2°* Austrian *Belgioioso* regiment (1,400) to which were added three companies of *Milizie Nizzarde* (250 men).

For the necessary transport and the artillery train of this mass of men and artillery, there were 200 horses for the *Treno d'Artiglieria* and 13 for the horsemen. The *treno dei muli* (mule train) was then made up as follows: 250 muleteers with 800 mules for regimental transport, 200 muleteers with 450 mules for the transport of provisions, and 50 muleteers with 150 mules for the transport of mountain artillery. The total number of draft animals was 1,863.[2]

Situation of the Revolutionary Army

The year 1794 seemed likely to be a very difficult one for Vittorio Amedeo III and his generals. In France, power had passed into the hands of the *Comité de salut public*, ending the sad period of the *Terreur*, and military planning was now managed by the capable Lazare Carnot (1753–1823). Thanks to Carnot, by early 1794, the French Revolutionary army was strong enough to take the offensive on all fronts. Combining the line troops' experience and the volunteers' enthusiasm, the army conceived by Carnot was on its way to becoming a formidable war machine, with a balanced army of 800,000 men – an incredible number by the standards of the time – thanks to mass conscription. Command was now entrusted to young, eager officers drawn from the ranks. They were motivated by the possibility of

---

2   AST, IdA, mazzo 10: Stato della consumazione giornaliera del Corpo d'Armata del Contado di Nizza, 17 April 1794.

rapid advancement in the event of success and the fear of severe, even extreme, punishment in the event of failure. This was the opposite of what had traditionally happened to the commanders of other European armies, who came from the nobility and remained in command into old age.

In addition to the officers, there was also the novelty of the *Comité représentants en mission* with the various army corps, who monitored the work of the commanders and energetically carried out the task of increasing the combativeness and revolutionary impetus of the battalions.[3]

Carnot's reorganisation enabled the French to deploy two armies with a total strength of 98,000 men against the Kingdom of Sardinia, of whom about 70,000 were on the front line, facing about 36,000 Austro-Piedmontese. A virtually unstoppable force. Even if all the 20–25,000 Austrian soldiers in Lombardy had been deployed together with the Piedmontese in the Alps, victory against such as enemy could not have been assured.

The army deployed by the French in the lower County of Nice and the neighbouring valleys, the *Armée du Var*, named after the river that formed the border between Nice and Provence, had a nominal strength of around 58,000 men, of whom 40,000 were in the front line.

The French plans for 1794 provided for the conquest of the Piccolo San Bernardo and Moncenisio passes to threaten Aosta and Turin on the front of the Chisone, Susa and Aosta Valleys where the *Armée des Alpes* operated, with a vigorous attack to fix in place the defending Piedmontese battalions. To the south, however, almost completely neglecting the intermediate valleys, which were only attacked with diversions, a new offensive was launched on the Val Roia, aiming to occupy the Colle di Tenda pass and reach Cuneo, thus debouching onto the plain. Finally, they would occupy Oneglia and the passes of the Maritime Alps, the Colle di Nava (934m) and the Colle San Bernardino (957m) to open the road towards Ceva and Acqui.[4] But things did not go to plan!

Surprise Attack?

While the French were drawing up the attack plans of their *Armée du Var*, the Piedmontese followed the movements of the ever-growing French regiments through espionage and the spontaneous reports of loyal *Nizzardi*. Dellera had guessed that *général de division* André Massena (1758–1817) planned to surprise them on the flank by advancing towards the Alps from Dolceacqua and on Ormea after occupying the Nava and San Bernardino passes, weakly defended by the 2,000 or so men under the command of the hesitant Austrian *Generalmajor* Argenteau. Dellera proposed to withdraw the garrison regiments to the Val Roia, stationing them on the ridges of the Maritime Alps around the Colle di Tenda and to send an Austro-Piedmontese army corps towards Dolceacqua and the surrounding heights to block, or at least slow down, the French advance towards Liguria.

---

3   G. Lefebvre & A. Mathiez, *La Rivoluzione Francese* (Torino: Einaudi, 1960), vol.2, p.116.
4   Ilari et al, *La guerra delle Alpi*, pp.147-149.

Dellera's proposal, presented to the King, was discussed and rejected by Turin's Council of War, although it was warmly supported by the more experienced generals, such as Thaon di Sant'Andrea, and only partially by the doubtful and indecisive Vittorio Amedeo III. The contrary opinion of de Vins, concerned about defending Lombardy, together with that of the accommodating and inexperienced First Secretary of War, *marchese* Fontana di Cravanzana, led to the decision to reject the plan. Meanwhile, Dellera, who was receiving constant information about the advance of French regiments towards Menton and Liguria, repeated his proposal to the King, but his insistence was angrily rejected in writing by Cravanzana in unpleasant tones. Dellera was also worried by the news that the command of these troops was entrusted to the brave Massena, himself originally a Savoy subject born in Nice, who, therefore, had a good knowledge of the territory. Under him as artillery commander was the little-known Napoleon Bonaparte, but whom the Piedmontese had seen in action during the Siege of Toulon.

Nevertheless, several measures were taken. Some Piedmontese battalions were sent as reinforcements to Val Roia, but they were insufficient and far from the minimum necessary. Also, about 4,000 Austrians were sent to the upper Val Tanaro and Val Bormida, not to protect the southernmost side of the Piedmontese deployment but rather to cover the advance of the Austrian army corps coming from Lombardy, whose sole objective was to prevent the French from reaching the road to Milan. The Austrians, as usual, allowed the French offensive to clash with the insufficient Piedmontese forces and the few Austrian battalions that had arrived in Piedmont the previous year.

The Conquest of Val Roia and Colle di Tenda (April–May 1794)

The operation considered a priority for the *Armée du Var* was that against Oneglia. The aim of the manoeuvre was to occupy the last remaining seaport on the Kingdom of Sardinia's mainland, rendering it unusable for the Piedmontese, and to use it as a base for the supplies needed for the advance of the ground troops. Landing at Oneglia, a Savoy possession, would have made the transit of troops through the territory of the still-neutral Republic of Genoa unnecessary. This concern, as we shall see in a moment, did not prevent the ruthless revolutionary army from trampling on Genoa's neutrality.

However, it was decided to give Massena only part of the *Armée du Var*. He had 'only' 20,000 men at his disposal: 31 battalions, 17 heavy and 20 light artillery pieces, some of which had been abandoned by the Piedmontese troops in their hasty retreat from Nice in 1792. An overwhelming force compared to the 2,000 men the Piedmontese were able to deploy to defend the city.

Having failed to take Oneglia by sea due to the presence of the British fleet, on 2 April Massena and Bonaparte proposed to take Oneglia by land, as planned, thus violating the sovereignty of the Republic of Genoa.[5]

On 5 April, Massena's army left Menton and entered Genoese territory at Ventimiglia. On 7 April, it reached the Ligurian villages of Pigna, Triora and Taggia, the first two were

---

5 Ilari et al, *La guerra delle Alpi*, pp.149–150.

at the foot of the Maritime Alps and were bases for attacking towards the left flank of the Val Roia, the third on the Ligurian coast, with Massena himself in command, was a day's march from Oneglia.

On 8 April, while Massena moved toward Oneglia, the French attached the Val Roia, advancing towards Briga to fix the Piedmontese. They were blocked by the fire of the powerful artillery of the fort of Saorgio and by the resistance of the *2° Mondovì*.

When news of Massena's movements to attack Val Roia on the flank reached Turin, it threw the court and the Austro-Sardinian command into panic, not before time. *Baron* Colli, who had been given command of the defences on the southern front on 5 April, Argenteau and Provera hurriedly left their comfortable Turin apartments and, it is to be hoped, regretted having opposed Dellera's proposal so strongly. In the meantime, Dellera, the only one on the spot, took the preliminary steps, spurred on by constant news of the French movements. He first diverted as many troops as he could from the defence of the lower Val Roia and reinforced the line of the ridges of the Maritime Alps at an altitude of between 1,600 and 2,200m that overlooked the French bases of Pigna and Triora. The manoeuvres of the two opposing armies were still hampered by the snow because in the Maritime Alps, the snow melts quickly due to the influence of the Mediterranean, but for the same reason, falls in abundance.[6]

Dellera's problem, and that of *Baron* Colli as soon as he arrived, was that they did not have enough troops to defend the Val Roia from all the attacks at the same time, and so he urged the battalions that were on the march or still in their winter quarters to speed up or move to cross the Colle di Tenda.

On 24 April, 15 battalions were deployed to defend the left flank of the Austro-Piedmontese defences: *1°* and *2° Guardie*, *1° Piemonte*, a battalion of *Saluzzo*, *1°* and *2° Belgioioso*, *1° Cacciatori*, *1°* and *2° Granatieri Reali*, *2° Asti*, *1°* and *2° Tortona*, *1°* and *2° Pinerolo*, and *2° Nizza*. These units were numerically inferior to the French. The approximately 6,000 Austro-Piedmontese were able to counter the attack of about 8,500 French, who had to march uphill, but the defensive line was too long (about 15 kilometres), so the French could easily gain local superiority where necessary.[7]

The Piedmontese began to realise that French superiority would prevail. On 27 April, *Baron* Colli began to order the most systematic retreat possible towards the Colle di Tenda and some of the units on the long ridge between the Val Roia and Liguria retreated towards the Colle di Tenda, across peaks and passes still covered in snow. In his orders, *Baron* Colli did not forget the small garrison of 160 men at the fort of Saorgio. He gave orders to the commander, *colonnello* Giuseppe Maria Muffat di Saint Amour de Chanaz, to evacuate the garrison on the morning of the 28th, after spiking the guns. Saint Amour, however, thought it wiser to evacuate on the night of the 27th, anticipating the abandonment of the fort a few hours early. For this minor breach of orders, which had no real effect on the progress of operations, he was accused of high treason, taken to the Citadel of Turin, tried and sentenced to death by firing squad. The sentence was very harsh and certainly unjust.[8]

---

6   Ilari et al, *La guerra delle Alpi*, p.151.
7   Ilari et al, *La guerra delle Alpi*, pp.153–154.
8   AST, LUF, mazzo 274: Sentenza colonnello Muffat Comandante del Forte di Saorgio, 3 June 1794.

It was carried out on 3 June 1794 near the Citadel. The serious events of the Val Roia thus had their scapegoat.

On 11 April, Massena, with Bonaparte's close support, disappointed by the poor results he had achieved so far and by the lively resistance of the Piedmontese who demonstrated their resilience, planned an action towards the Colle di Nava, to threaten the Piedmontese defences from the rear. The manoeuvre, carried out with less than a division, was successful thanks to a scarcity of Piedmontese troops, who were heavily engaged elsewhere, and to the surprising immobility of Argentau's corps. On 16 April, the French, under the direct command of Massena, occupied the virtually undefended Colle di Nava, to descend towards Ormea in the Valle del Tanaro, whose garrison was easy prey as it consisted of only a hundred or so old soldiers of the *Corpo degli Invalidi*, and on the 17th they reached Garessio. Other French units went up the Val Neva towards Colle San Bernardino, a line defended by the *Lombardia* regiment alone, which withdrew from the field. It is likely that *colonnello* Angelo Nicolao Oreglia di Farigliano, who commanded the *Lombardia* regiment for the entire duration of the war, had received the news that Argentau had left Garessio to the French without a fight and was retreating along the Tanaro valley towards Bagnasco and Ceva, leaving the Piedmontese flank to its fate.[9]

The Abandonment of Val Roia, 28–29 April. Under the heavy pressure of the furious French attack from Nice and Liguria, with the sudden surrender of the fort of Saorgio, and lastly with the French arrival in Ormea and Garessio, the Piedmontese were forced to retreat towards the Colle di Tenda and reorganise at Borgo San Dalmazzo, a village near the fortified town of Cuneo, where field defences were set up.

The Role of the Rearguard

Baron Colli had maintained a rearguard corps around the village of Tenda, at the top of the Val Roia, to give the commissariat in charge time to evacuate the magazines on the pass so that they would not fall prey to the French, and to attempt to hold the pass itself.

The role of the *commissariato di guerra* (war commissariat) and the personnel of the *Corpo del Treno di Provianda*, the latter assisted by private contractors, was crucial. The *commissario di guerra* in charge at Val Roia reached Tenda on 28 April and analysed the situation, reporting to the War Intendant in Turin on the latest events. On that day, the *commissario* had already managed to move most of the stores from Val Roia to the village of Tenda and had requisitioned mules and carriages to ensure their rapid further transport over the Alps. The artillery train with its carriages and mules had also managed to bring out the artillery still in the possession of the Piedmontese to the village and was heading for the pass on the hastily repaired and snow-cleared road. In his letter, the *commissario* also informed Turin that he hoped to have time to evacuate but had planned to set fire to the stores if attacked before evacuating them. In the meantime, Tenda and the road were defended by the rearguard troops, which included the ever-heroic *Granatieri Reali*, under the strong and skilful command of Bellegarde.

---

9   Ilari et al, *La guerra delle Alpi*, p.154.

Fortunately, it did not have to come to such extremes as the French had allowed themselves a pause before beginning a new advance. The *commissario* at Tenda was also concerned with bread and other provisions to supply the retreating troops and provide what was necessary for first aid to the wounded. A few days later, when the danger of enemy movements resumed, the same *commissario* had to hastily transfer the stores to Limone Piemonte, the first village after the Col and from there to safety between Borgo San Dalmazzo and Cuneo, at the other foot of the Alps.[10]

On 4 May, in a second letter, the *commissario di guerra* informed Turin that he had saved everything that could be saved. It was an epic achievement. During the confusion of the retreat, he had managed to save the stores of an entire army corps, finding wagons and mules wherever possible, even bringing them from beyond the Alps. It was an important factor in the continuation of the war and in preventing the French from re-equipping at the expense of the Piedmontese army and one that underlines, if proof were needed, that in war, it is not only the fighting units that matter.

The strategic imperative of the Piedmontese command was to preserve regiments as much as possible from being routed while maintaining their fighting capacity. This aim was well known to the Piedmontese generals, who, over the centuries, had always had to fight against potentially superior forces. In fact, while more powerful or even overwhelming armies, such as the French of 1794, were able to compensate for losses and return to the attack in a relatively short time, a small army such as the Piedmontese could not do the same. Winning a battle with too many casualties was risky in the long term. The Piedmontese success in preserving units is confirmed by the fact that despite the poor Austrian aid, which was so limited, the 30–35,000 Piedmontese soldiers on the line managed to hold out until April 1796.

The French Offensive Toward the Colle di Tenda and Val Vermegnana (7–10 May)

On the evening of 6 May preparations were made to evacuate the rearguard that had saved the storehouses. This was made up of three provincial infantry battalions from the *Nizza* and *Asti* regiments placed on the mountainous left of the Roia, while in the village of Tenda (816m), at the start of the climb to the pass of the same name, were placed the two battalions of the *Granatieri Reali*, under the command of Bellegarde, to which the *Freikorps Gyulai* had just been attached.

To the south-east of the Colle di Tenda, on the heights overlooking Carnino in the Tanarello valley, the *5° Granatieri* (grenadier companies from *Aosta*, *de Courten* and *Mondovì* regiments) guarded against the feared French ascent from Ponte di Nava, along the valley, which did not take place, perhaps because of too much snow. At the bridge over the Roia closest to the town of Tenda, the *Guastatori* commanded by their *luogotenente colonnello* Giuseppe Bieux, *conte* di Flumet, had been placed to protect a battery of four pieces.

---

10   AST, IdA, mazzo 10: Lettera al Contadore Generale in Torino, 30 April 1794.

On 10 May, the usual fierce French attack finally led to the abandonment of what remained of the Val Roia and the Colle di Tenda position. The Piedmontese, still led by Bellegarde and his pugnacious *Granatieri Reali*, halted the enemy advance by establishing themselves further down, between Vernante, Roccavione and Robilante, in the Val Vermegnana, to block the road towards nearby Borgo San Dalmazzo where the other troops retreating from the Val Roia and *Baron* Colli's command were located.[11]

Political Problems in Paris

Between May and July 1794, the French attempted to overrun the Piedmontese defences in the Stura, Maira and Varaita valleys with the aim of investing the fort of Demonte and Cuneo. Their success was only partial.

Between the second half of July and the beginning of August, the political situation in France forced them to go onto the defensive, and so, on 8 August, the Revolutionary forces ceased their attacks and withdrew but retained control of the Colle di Tenda and on some localities in the upper Val Vermegnana. The news of the French retreat was received with perhaps too much enthusiasm by both the command and the population, and with relief by the troops, who now had some time to recuperate, reorganise and re-equip.

The pause, however, was short-lived, for in September the French, encouraged by the improving political situation in Paris, resumed their attacks, which were easily repulsed mainly by light companies of the line infantry regiments, the *Corpo Franco* and the *Cacciatori Scelti di Nizza*.[12]

The French Occupy the Piccolo San Bernardo, Moncenisio and Monginevro Passes

Taking advantage of their great numerical superiority between March and May 1794, the French not only attacked the defences of the Val Roia but also set out to conquer the other Alpine passes. Their aim was to take them and, if possible, advance towards the plain. Led by *général de division* Thomas Alexandre Davy Dumas, 30,000 French troops attacked the 12,000 Piedmontese, nominally under the command of the *duca* del Monferrato, who were defending the Alpine passes from the Val d'Aosta to Monviso.

At the beginning of April 1794, a few battalions were concentrated in the defence of the Val d'Aosta. High up, defending the still heavily snow-covered Piccolo San Bernardo, was the Swiss *Reggimento Rochmondet*, under the command of *luogotenente colonnello* Jean Rodolphe Stettler (1749–1809), who later that year was promoted to *colonnello* and gave it his name and commanded it until 1798. At that time, the *colonnello comandante* was Georges Benoît de Rochmondet (1728–1795), but he was in Aosta, commanding the corps of the Valle d'Aosta, while the *duca* del Monferrato was still in the comfort of Turin.

---

11   Ilari et al, *La guerra delle Alpi*, pp.164–165.
12   Lo Faso di Serradifalco, *La difesa di un regno*, pp.95–100.

The attack began on 20 April, and on the 23rd Stettler had to clear the pass by retreating towards La Thuile, joining the line infantry regiments *La Marina*, *Saluzzo*, and *Vercelli* and *3° Granatieri* below. After receiving the news of the retreat on 25 April, the *duca* del Monferrato reached Aosta in forced stages. As soon as he arrived, he had to deal with a serious disagreement between the Piedmontese officers and Rochmondet because the news had spread that the Piccolo San Bernardo had been taken due to the treachery of the Swiss officer who commanded a redoubt that was essential to the defence. Panic-stricken, the Prince planned to abandon Aosta and move the defences a little further down the valley while maintaining an advanced post with artillery on the bridge at Villeneuve, at the entrance to Valdigne. A little later, perhaps after listening to more experienced officers, the Prince wisely authorised the defence of Rocca Tagliata in the commune of Arvier, a place where the Valdigne narrows to a gorge only a few meters wide, crossed by the Dora Baltea and easily defensible. Thus, the defence of La Thuile and Morgex was abandoned, the latter easily passable via the Col San Carlo (1,951m) whose road was certainly accessible. The position of Rocca Tagliata could also be bypassed by the French by going over the Col du Mont, and then descending through the Valgrisenche, but the pass was only crossed by a path. As a result, while the Rocca Tagliata road was never attacked, the Col du Mont, garrisoned during the winter months by the local *Cacciatori di Camoscio*, changed hands several times, but the Piedmontese positions towards Arvier were never attacked. In the summer, the French retreated from La Thuile and between 10 and 16 June 1794, the Piedmontese, having heard the news, advanced as far as Morgex and, crossing the Col San Carlo, reached the seventeenth-century entrenchments known as the 'Principe Tommaso entrenchments', located in the valley, not far from La Thuile. They fortified them with two batteries of six pieces each. The village was then reoccupied and the advanced guard reached as far as Pont Serrand, on the road up to Piccolo San Bernard. On 16 June, the Piedmontese troops, led by *colonnello* Giuseppe Thaon of Revel di Sant'Andrea, commander of the *Reggimento Susa* and supported by four 8-pounders and two howitzers attempted to capture the Piccolo San Bernardo Pass, but without success.[13]

Between 3 and 10 May 1794, the French appeared at the Monginevro Pass, which was weakly defended by the Piedmontese. In this attempt, the French succeeded in descending into the upper Susa valley, occupying Cesana and Oulx, easily driving the few defenders away, but the French were stopped below at Chiomonte. Their action did not lead to any concrete results since the real objective was the conquest of the Moncenisio Pass, whose road led directly to Susa and which, moreover, was effectively defended by the well-equipped and garrisoned Forte della Brunetta.

Having diverted the attention of the Piedmontese with their manoeuvre in the upper Susa valley, on 12 May, the French attacked the Piedmontese redoubts placed in defence of the Moncenisio Pass, where two line infantry battalions, one from *Reale Alemanno*, the other from *Reggimento Ivrea*, supported by artillery were placed. After a long resistance, the two redoubts had to be evacuated, and the defences resisted lower down to defend the road leading from Moncenisio to Susa, but the manoeuvre failed because the French, apparently led by pro-French locals, managed to descend towards Novalesa. They threatened the

---

13   Ilari et al, *La guerra delle Alpi*, pp.161–168.

Piedmontese units from behind, who, after suffering losses, took refuge under the protection of the artillery of the fort of Brunetta on the orders of *maggior generale* Chino, in charge of the defences of the Susa valley.[14]

Thus, by mid-May, all the Alpine passes had come under the control of the French Revolutionary army, which, fortunately, made only weak attacks on the entire front during the summer months, partly due to the renewed bloody power struggles in Paris, which culminated in the execution of Robespierre (28 July 1794). However, with the political situation in Paris restored, the French army, which needed to rest the units badly mauled by the fierce Piedmontese defence, was satisfied with the progress it had already made and did not attempt to break out onto the plains for that year. In the Susa valley, the French had taken control of the upper valley and had established themselves at Salbertrand, Bardonecchia, Cesana and Chiomonte, without, however, attempting to besiege the forts of Exilles (upper Susa valley), Fenestrelle (upper Chisone valley), which were placed to defend the road that descended from Monginevro, limiting themselves near the latter to placing the vanguard at Quattro Denti mountain, close to Chiomonte. Finally, a purely symbolic French outpost was set up on the Assietta Pass, which was uninhabitable in winter.[15]

The Part Played by the Austrian Army, May–December 1794

At the end of August 1794, a small Austrian army corps of 12 infantry battalions and six cavalry squadrons finally entered Liguria, having violated Genoese neutrality on the pretext that a similar violation by Massena had resulted in only weak complaints. The objective of the corps was to march on Savona and occupy it. The Austrian intention was not to support the Piedmontese army in the defence of the routes to Ceva but to prevent the French from entering the Po valley along the Colle di Cadibona–Carcare–Cairo Montenotte–Dego route and then, follow the Val Bormida, near Acqui Terme. The British Minister in Turin, Viscount John Hampden Trevor (1748–1834), who had travelled to Alessandria to obtain more precise information on Austrian movements, received news of the inconclusive Battle of Dego (21 September 1794) and wrote to the *primo segretario agli Esteri* (First Foreign Secretary), *conte* Giuseppe Francesco Girolamo Perret d'Hauteville, in Turin, urging him to try to persuade the Austrian Emperor to support the defence of Piedmont from the Alpine region with many more troops. Trevor realised that without the bulwark of the Piedmontese army, the likelihood of Lombardy falling into French hands was high and not at all in British interests. Unfortunately, despite high-level contacts, Austria did not change its plans, and, moreover, the British had no ground troops to send to help Vittorio Amedeo III.[16] The Emperor of Austria even sent de Vins, who had been recalled to his homeland months earlier and relieved of his command at the King's express request, to command the Austro-Piedmontese army. Unfortunately, the character of the good Vittorio Amedeo III

14　Ilari et al, *La guerra delle Alpi*, pp.165–166.
15　AST, Cpd, mazzo 136: Contratto per le forniture alle Truppe Piemontesi della Valle di Susa, 19 December 1794.
16　Lo Faso di Serradifalco, *La difesa di un regno*, p.102.

was not up to the standards of his ancestors Vittorio Amedeo II and Carlo Emanuele III, who would not have tolerated such a serious outrage.

This continuing behaviour on the part of Austria and its generals led to total mistrust between the Piedmontese and Austrian high officials, generating resentment to the detriment of the common defence.

Looking at the map, it is clear that Austria intended to defend the Val Bormida, which meant that their lines of retreat diverged from those of the Piedmontese, the former towards Acqui Terme, the latter towards Ceva and Mondovì. This was well understood by Massena, who, as early as 1794, tried to defeat the two armies separately. The Austrians, however, did not learn the lesson, and in 1796, Napoleon Bonaparte carried out a very similar manoeuvre with complete success, causing the Piedmontese army to collapse, and he then continued to conquer Milan.

The Indecisive First Battle of Dego, 21 September

In August, the Austrian army of Lombardy, under the command of *Feldzeugmeister* Olivier Remigius Graf von Wallis, now convinced that the French were no longer a threat to the Piedmontese, began to move its corps towards Liguria, asking the Piedmontese army to join it. This did not convince the Austrian general, *Baron* Colli, however, and in fact, the French reappeared in the Alps in September with the aim of fixing his Austro-Piedmontese corps at the foot of the Alps. Had *Baron* Colli, rightly made cautious and suspicious by two years of his Austrian colleagues' non-collaboration, listened to Wallis, the demonstrations by the French in September 1794 might have turned into a decisive advance, with disastrous consequences for the outcome of the war.

Wallis's plan was to make a final breakthrough into Liguria to drive out the French and maintain control. *Baron* Colli, however, while hoping for Austrian success, did not believe that he could neglect the defence of the Alps, through which he could easily be bypassed.[17] *Baron* Colli explained his doubts in a letter to Thaon di Revel dated 30 August 1794 from Borgo San Dalmazzo, in which he wrote:

> I took advantage of the enemy's planned retreat for a moment and pushed them hard. We killed some of them and took a hundred prisoners, which will serve to pay part of the debt we owe them. The enemy is entrenched at the Col [of Tenda], which for me is like the Pillars of Hercules, which I cannot cross alone. They tell me that the cavalry has returned to Tende, with reinforcements and 30 cannons. The storm has not completely dissipated.[18]

Meanwhile, between 18 and 19 September the Austrians were already abandoning Liguria, retreating under the pressure from Massena.

---

17   Ilari et al, *La guerra delle Alpi*, pp.183–189.
18   Thaon di Revel, *Mémoires sur la guerre des Alpes*, pp.221–222.

The French commander had started to move from Liguria with a corps of 15,000 men to pursue them. However, he was stopped in Dego, a small town where the Val Bormida widens into a plateau about two kilometres wide, where Wallis's troops could be deployed to face the enemy. The outcome of what later became known as the First Battle of Dego was inconclusive, and both opposing armies had to pull back and reorganise, with Wallis retreating to Acqui and Massena to his original bases.[19]

The Positions of *Baron* Colli's Army Corps in October 1794

Fortunately, and inexplicably for the troops, who lacked the political information necessary to interpret the situation, between 9 and 10 September, the French began to abandon their positions at Roccavione, Robilante and Vernante in the higher Val Vermegnana, retreating towards the Colle di Tenda. In their retreat, they were pursued by the *Cacciatori Scelti di Nizza*, a company of the *Corpo Franco* commanded by *luogotenente capitano* Angelo, *cavaliere* de Vinea, and other companies of volunteer light troops, followed a few hours later by three grenadier battalions. The French rearguard engaged the Piedmontese troops to protect their comrades' retreat, and in the clashes of 11 September de Vinea was killed.

After reaching Limone Piemonte, the last village before the pass, the Piedmontese advance came to a halt, as precise orders prevented them from going any further to avoid running the risk of encountering the bulk of the French forces, who were well equipped with numerous artillery pieces. The French thus remained the masters of the Colle di Tenda.

In the second half of September, to fix the Piedmontese troops in the Alpine valleys and to prevent them from intervening towards Liguria, the French attacked the heads of several valleys but without advancing further.[20]

For what was considered the final defence of the southern sector by a beaten but still fighting army, some 18,000 men were available to defend the Gesso, Vermegnana, Stura, Maira, Varaita and Po valleys under the effective command of *Baron* Colli. This consisted of:

- 25 line infantry battalions: 1° and 2° *Guardie*, 1° and 2° *Monferrato*, 2° *Pinerolo*, 1° and 2° *Sardegna*, 1° and 2° *Peyer-Im-Hoff*, 1° and 2° *Oneglia*, 1° and 2° *Savoia*, 1° *Asti*, 1° and 2° *de Courten*, 1° and 2° *Christ*, 1° and 2° *Torino*, 1° and 2° *Casale*, 1° and 2° *Nizza*, and the Austrian 2° *Belgioioso*.
- Six grenadier battalions (*1° and 2° Granatieri Reali, 1°, 9° and 11° Granatieri*, and the Austrian grenadier battalion *Strassoldo*).
- The light troops were represented by the *1° and 2° Battaglione Cacciatori*, four companies of the *Corpo Franco*, four companies of *Cacciatori Scelti di Nizza* and all the companies and centuries of volunteer light troops (*Canale, Piano, Pandini, Martin*).

---

19 Lo Faso di Serradifalco, *La difesa di un regno*, pp.100–101. Wallis described the Dego battle in a conversation with Thaon di Revel: Thaon di Revel, *Mémoires sur la guerre des Alpes*, pp.223–224.
20 Lo Faso di Serradifalco, *La difesa di un regno*, pp.97–100.

The position, fortress and field artilleries were served by about 1,500 artillerymen, with an adequate artillery train.

Finally, the entire *Cavalleggeri del Re* and *Aosta Cavalleria* regiments were stationed around Cuneo.[21]

Baron Colli was also in command of a secondary corps stationed at Mondovì and Ceva. In Mondovì and its surroundings, there were about 6,865 men, of whom 491 were militia manning the advanced posts. The regular troops were as follows:

Six and a half battalions of line infantry: *1° Piemonte, 1° Maurienne, 1° Pinerolo, 2° Asti, 1° and 2° Mondovì* and part of the Austrian *1° Belgioioso*.
Four grenadier battalions: *2°, 4°, 5° and 8° Granatieri*.
The light troops were represented by the three *Cacciatori* companies of the *Asti, Acqui* and *Oneglia* regiments.
Two companies of *Guastatori*.
The artillery included 165 artillerymen and 69 men of the *Treno d'Artiglieria*.
Finally, on the plain overlooking Mondovì were quartered the Austrian *Stabsdragoner* and the *Dragoni La Regina* regiments.

The corps stationed at Ceva, which was to act as a link between the Piedmontese corps and the Austrian army of Lombardy and to defend Tanaro valley, consisted of 7,759 men, including 271 local militia to which were added 280 militia and 81 sailors withdrawn from Oneglia. The regular troops of this corps were:

Seven line infantry battalions: *2° Piemonte, 1° and 2° Aosta, 1° and 2° Acqui, 1° and 2° Lombardia*.
1° and 4° *Battaglione* of *Legione truppe Leggere*.
The Piedmontese artillery was represented by 190 men, including gunners and train.

The Austrian units included in this corps were a 514-man unit of the *1° Belgioioso*, the *Freikorps Gyulai*, the *IR48 Schimidfeld* (formerly *Caprara*) and 51 artillerymen.[22]

---

21 AST, IdA, mazzo 10: Stato della consumazione giornaliera del Corpo d'Armata comandato dal *Luogotenente Generale Barone* Colli, 21 July 1794.
22 AST, IdA, mazzo 11: Stato della forza delle Truppe presidiate nel Mondovì, 10 October 1794.

13

1795–1796: Last Hopes

1795, the Austro-Piedmontese Army at the Opening of Hostilities

As the winter wore on, the various corps of the Piedmontese army somehow managed to regain their maximum strength. This was reported to be a total of around 53,400 men, with 113 artillery pieces, served by 1,569 gunners and 664 men of the *Treno d'Artiglieria*. The estimate of the actual number of men available, as given in the official documents, seems to be too optimistic and deliberately exaggerated. As usual, to gain a more realistic idea of the actual strength, it is necessary to deduct about 25 percent, to account for men who were not available for various reasons, which would bring the actual strength on 10 March 1795 to just over 40,000 men.

The army were spread over a very wide front, but more units had to be concentrated in Mondovì and Ceva to cope with the arrivals from Liguria. On 10 March 1795, the army was therefore divided into five army corps, which are described in detail below.

Valle d'Aosta army corps, 5,220 infantrymen and 320 cavalrymen:

> 14 line infantry battalions, *1° and 2° Saluzzo*, *1° and 2° La Marina*, *1° and 2° Stettler*, *1° and 2° Vercelli*, *1° and 2° Novara*, *1° and 2° Susa*, *3° Granatieri*, *2° Legione Truppe Leggere*.
> One dragoon regiment: *Dragoni di Piemonte*.
> 26 artillery pieces served by 352 gunners, probably also assigned to the artillery of the fort of Bard.
> Susa army corps:
> 5,450 infantrymen: 16 battalions: *1° and 2° La Regina*, *1° and 2° Bachmann*, *1° Zimmerman*, *1° and 2° Genevois* with its *Cacciatori* company, *1° and 2° Maurienne*, *1° and 2° Ivrea* with its *Cacciatori* company, *2° Guastatori*, *2°, 6°, 7° and 10° Granatieri*,
> 12 artillery pieces served by 94 gunners.

Army corps of the Pellice and Germanasca valleys:

> 1,850 infantry men: *1° and 2° Nizza* with its *cacciatori* company, reserve companies of the *Lombardia*, *Morienne*, *Nizza* and *Pinerolo* regiments.
> 480 cavalry men, *Dragoni del Re*, two squadrons of *Dragoni di Sardegna*
> 27 artillery pieces served by 114 gunners.

The number of guns in this corps was unusually large, and it probably acted as a central reserve and training unit. Placed in the quietest part of the front line, several battalions which had been badly shaken in the fighting of 1794 and needed more time to recover were assigned to this corps.

Saluzzo valleys corps (Po, Maira, Varaita and Stura valleys):

> 3,550 infantrymen. Nine battalions: 1° and 2° *Savoia*, 1° and 2° *Oneglia*, 1° and 2° *Torino*, 1° and 2° *Casale*, 1° *Cacciatori*.
> French *Corpo Franco* (de Bonaud company).
> 16 artillery pieces served by 192 gunners.

This part of the front line was also considered quiet and manned by units that, having been badly shaken in 1794, needed to be reorganised.

Grande Armata (Germanasca and Stura valleys, Mondovì and Ceva):

> 17,400 infantry men: *1° and 2° Guardie, 1° and 2° Monferrato, 1° and 2° Piemonte, 1° and 2° Aosta, 1° and 2° Lombardia, 1° and 2° Reale Alemanno, 1° and 2° Christ (previously Grigione), 1° and 2° Streng (previously de Courten), 1° and 2° Peyer Im Hoff, 1° and 2° Mondovì, 1° and 2° Asti, 1° and 2° Pinerolo, 1° and 2° Tortona, 1° and 2° Acqui, 1° and 2° Granatieri Reali, 1°, 4°, 5°, 8°, 9° and 11° Granatieri, 1° and 4°* battalions, *3a* and *4a Cacciatori* companies and *3a* and *4a Granatieri* companies of the *Legione Truppe Leggere*, the *cacciatori* companies of the *Acqui* and *Oneglia* regiments, *2° Battaglione Cacciatori*, two companies of *Cacciatori Carabinieri di Canale*, four companies of *Corpo Franco*, one company of *Cacciatori Volontari Piano*, one company of *Cacciatori Volontari Martin*, one company of *Cacciatori Volontari Pandini*, seven companies of *Cacciatori Scelti di Nizza*, *1° Guastatori*.
> 1,600 cavalry: *Cavalleggeri del Re, Piemonte Reale Cavalleria, Savoia Cavalleria, Aosta Cavalleria, Dragoni del Chablais*.
> 32 artillery pieces. In total, the *Grande Armata* had 817 gunners who also served in the various fortifications.

The Austrian auxiliary corps, attached to the *Grande Armata* was made up of:

> *1° and 2° IR48 Schmidfeld* (previously *Caprara*).
> *1° and 2° IR44 Belgioioso Regiment*.
> *2° battailon* of the *IR6 ZweytesGarrison Regiment*.
> Grenadier Battalion *Strassoldo*.
> *Freikorps Gyulai*.
> *Stabsdragoner*.[1]

---

1   AST, Materie Militari, Imprese Militari, mazzo 12 di addizione (this binder [mazzo] contains detailed reports from 1795 on the state of affairs and the disposition of the units of the Piedmontese army and the Austrian auxiliary corps.) and AST, LUF, mazzo 276, situazione, 12 April 1795.

This was the situation at the beginning of 1795, but as they returned to the line from their garrisons, there were continuous transfers of battalions from one corps to another according to the needs of the moment. In addition, during the year, all volunteer light companies were merged into the new light infantry corps called *Cacciatori Franchi*. Only the eight companies of *Cacciatori Scelti di Nizza* were left independent. To complete the picture, the four battalions of the *Legione Truppe Leggere* were split in two to form the *1° and 2° Reggimento Truppe Leggere*.

June 1795, the Piedmontese Advance.

In order to cooperate with de Vins' advance along the Bormida valley and the Austrian operations in Liguria, units of *Baron* Colli's army corps advanced through the mountains on both sides of the Tanaro valley to reconquer it. The aim was to push the French back towards the sea and to take possession of the Melogno and San Bernardino passes in order to threaten the left flank of the French position in the Riviera. On 27 June, *maggior generale* Montafia's division moved out and succeeded in driving up to the summit of Mount Spinarda (1,357m), a key high point for the defence of the Melogno Pass (1,028m), and where the French had entrenched themselves. At the same time, the Piedmontese vanguard attacked the defences of Colle San Bernardino (957m) but without attempting to conquer it. Shortly afterwards (2–14 July), *Baron* Colli seemed to wake up, and the Piedmontese divisions of his corps were able to come down fighting from the mountains on the left of the Tanaro valley, occupying Garessio, screened by a few companies of the *Cacciatori Franchi* who had entered it a few hours earlier, immediately after the French had evacuated it. To continue the manoeuvre by threatening the French left flank, the Piedmontese further descended the slopes of the left of the Tanarello valley, weakly attacking Viozene and Carnino, but without going so far as to capture them. Thus, when the lines stabilised on 14 July, the French still maintained possession of Ormea, Colle di Nava and the Tanarello valley on this side of the Maritime Alps.[2]

In August, to completely drive the French out of the northern side of the Maritime Alps, de Vins ordered *Baron* Colli to drive the French out of Ormea and the Tanarello valley, and bring his left to the Col di Nava. But, as usual, *Baron* Colli found excuses not to obey, leaving the enemy a gateway on this side of the Maritime Alps, which they exploited at the end of the year. In fact, in October 1795, a French division was still occupying Ormea and the Colle di Nava through which it secured supplies from the Riviera. The division also had advanced posts at the Colle di Termini, Viozene and Carnino, in the upper Tanarello valley, through which, when snow permitted, it could maintain open communications with the French troops defending the Colle di Tenda.[3]

As can be seen, the continuing disagreement between *Baron* Colli and de Vins, both Austrian generals, prevented the French left from being expelled from the Piedmontese territories they still occupied in the Tanaro valley.

---

2 Ilari et al, *La guerra delle Alpi*, pp.208–221.
3 Ilari et al, *La guerra delle Alpi*, p.223.

In August, *Baron* Colli decided that his corps should attack the French in the Val Roia and try to regain the County of Nice, bypassing the strong French positions on the Colle di Tenda and the entrenched camp located in the village of the same name. The plan was to act in conjunction with the advance of the Austrian main corps commanded by de Vins along the Ligurian Riviera towards the city of Nice. Perhaps the plan could have succeeded, given the crisis the enemy was going through at the time, with supplies and reinforcements in short supply. However, the two Austrian generals were not on good terms and could not agree on the plan. For *Baron* Colli, the affair ended with a sterile and ineffective attack on the French positions on the Colle di Tenda.

Also in August, Ignazio Thaon di Revel, *quartiermastro generale* of the Susa Valley army corps, planned to recapture the Moncenisio Pass but the attack was unsuccessful.

Although *Baron* Colli was still afraid of a French advance through the Alpine passes, especially from the Colle di Tenda, which was heavily garrisoned by the enemy, he had to move some of his troops to support de Vins' Austrian troops, which were moving towards Liguria on their right flank. A situation report entitled 'State of the positions and strength of the Austro-Sardinian Army commanded by His Excellency Lieutenant General Baron Colli. Bagnasco, le 9 Juillet 1795' gives us the details of the deployment of the Austro-Piedmontese forces available for the defence of Ceva and the Tanaro Valley.[4]

In the department of Ceva, commanded by the *Maggior Generale* Montafia, which included both the garrison of Ceva and the troops camping between Cima della Spinarda and Colle del Melogno:

> The garrison of the fort and the City of Ceva consisted of *2° Piemonte* and the remnants of *Corpo degli Equipaggi di Marina*, a total of 557 men, of whom 416 were in the ranks, and ready to fight.
>
> Around the camp of Spinarda as a reserve were the following units, with a strength of 7,453 men, of whom 5,146 in the ranks: *1°* and *2° Stettler* with its *cacciatori* company, *1°* and *2° Acqui* with its *cacciatori* company, *1°* and *8° Granatieri*, *1°* and *2° Legione Truppe Leggere*, three companies of *Cacciatori Scelti di Nizza* (commanded by *capitani* Giletta, Christini and Domerego), the *Cacciatori* company of the *Oneglia* regiment, one company of the *1° Guastatori*, *1°* and *2° IR44 Belgioioso*, one company of the *Freikorps Gyulai* and 53 artillerymen.

In the department of Mondovì, under the nominal command of the *Principe* di Carignano and effective command of *luogotenente generale* Dellera, on the left of the Tanaro valley, with a strength of 9270 men, of whom 7,197 were in the ranks, there were the following units:

> *2°, 4°, 5°, 9°, 10°* and *11° Granatieri*.
> *1°* and *2° Granatieri Reali* and its *cacciatori* company.
> *2°* battalion of the *2° Reggimento Truppe Leggere*, with its *granatiere* and *cacciatori* companies.

---

4   AST, Materie Militari, Imprese Militari, mazzo 12 d'addizione.

1° Piemonte, *1°* and *2° Mondovì* with its *cacciatori* company, *1°* and *2° Torino*
Three companies of *Cacciatori Franchi* (commanded by *capitani* Pandini, Ambroise, Buriasco).
One company of the *1° Guastatori*
A detachment of Austrian *Stabsdragoner*.
248 gunners.

Loano: de Vins' Defeat, July–November 1795

In July, de Vins managed to advance his corps towards the Riviera by occupying the heights between Bardineto and Loano in Liguria and sending two battalions to Pietra Ligure and Finale Ligure, towns on the coast, to test the state of the French defences between Zuccarello and Toirano. The Piedmontese battalions were present during this advance. They could have taken part by attacking the French on the left flank but did not intervene due to the lack of precise orders from *Baron* Colli.[5]

There were several clashes between the French and the Austrians in October, but neither side was victorious. Meanwhile, on 22 November, de Vins, convinced that operations would be suspended for the winter because of the advancing bad weather, left the army corps to winter elsewhere, passing interim command to *Feldzeugmeister* Wallis. On 22 November, perhaps not accidentally, while de Vins was en route, the French attacked the positions of the Austrian army, to which six battalions of the *Piedmonte*, *Monferrato* and *La Marina* regiments had been attached. On the 24th, the battle was disastrously lost, and the corps, commanded by Wallis between 25 and 30 November, had to leave Liguria and retreat to its original positions.[6]

Piedmontese Resistance and the Retreat to Ceva, 22–28 November 1795

On 22 November, the French, concentrated against the Austrians, had left the front held by the Piedmontese quiet, only keeping them on the alert with small patrol actions. It seems, however, that *Baron* Colli was unaware of the fighting between the French and the Austrians, even though the echoes of gunfire and cannonades could not have failed to reach him. He assumed that it was only a rearguard action by the French to protect their retreat to winter quarters, as de Vins had mistakenly predicted. It is curious that *Baron* Colli, who disliked de Vins so much, accepted his judgement. On the 23rd, everything changed. The French division of *général de division* Jean Mathieu Philippe Sérurier (1742–1819), which occupied Ormea, the Colle di Nava and the Tanarello Valley, from which *Baron* Colli had decided not to expel him, attacked vehemently with a strength of about 9,000 men. The French advance had two main axes – the first was towards the Colle San Bernardino, located on the right of the Tanaro Valley, the second was towards the Bric Mindino (1,881m), located on the left

---

5   Lo Faso di Serradifalco, *La difesa di un regno*, pp.122–128.
6   Ilari et al, *La guerra delle Alpi*, pp.226–229.

of the same valley, at the height of Garessio. The primary attack was blocked by about 500 Piedmontese well deployed in the main positions and under the command of the resolute Colli di Felizzano with his *2° Cacciatori*, effectively assisted by the *cacciatori* company of the *Oneglia* regiment, 73 *Guastatori* and 11 gunners, assigned to two artillery pieces.

The second attack was more successful, however, because a battalion of the Austrian *Belgioioso* regiment had abandoned the position during the first assault. Fortunately, the spontaneous redeployment of the *4°, 5°, 8°, 9°* and *11° Granatieri* slowed down the French attack, despite the loss of some artillery pieces.

In the meantime, however, news of the precipitous retreat of Wallis's Austrian army corps had reached *Baron* Colli and convinced him to order a retreat himself to the Ceva camp, not least because the victorious French opposed to Wallis had been able to reinforce the *général de division* Sérurier troops in Ormea with another 8,000 men. During the retreat, however, the Piedmontese, who were constantly slowing down the French, were able to preserve the fighting capacity of its army corps.[7]

Ceva, a Safe Refuge? 28 November–31 December 1795

The entrenched camp of Ceva must have been of little value when the Piedmontese army abandoned it the following year after little resistance. The fort of Ceva was also of little strategic value, neglected by the French, who overran it without fighting. On 30 November 1795, *Baron* Colli, fearing that the French would try to bypass Ceva from the north and thus put an end to the duel with the Piedmontese army that had been giving them a hard time for three years, hoped for the help of the Austrian army, which, however, was moving away towards Acqui, and as usually interested only in defending Lombardy. What *Baron* Colli did not know, however, was that the French were also exhausted by the cold and a lack of supplies and were eager for a break. For these reasons, they retreated to Garessio, keeping control of the Melogno, San Bernardino, Colla di San Giacomo (796m), and Colle di Cadibona (746m) passes. The possession of the passes and the occupation of the upper Tanaro valley would allow them to resume operations from various directions the following spring.[8]

Reassured by the news that reached him from the French lines, *Baron* Colli began to hope that he would be able to hold the positions of Ceva and Mondovì, and thus save Piedmont from defeat. However, it was essential that his army corps maintain contact with the Austrian army to resume joint operations the following spring. To this end, he placed detachments at Bagnasco, in Val Tanaro, on the Mombarcaro-Cosseria line and took other precautions to ensure his defence.

During this last winter of the war, the bickering between the Austrian generals did not cease. Wallis accused de Vins of abandoning him. The only good news was that de Vins finally wrote to Vittorio Amedeo III that he had been granted a leave of absence from the Emperor of Austria and had retired for good.

---

7 Ilari et al, *La guerra delle Alpi*, pp.229–230.
8 Ilari et al, *La guerra delle Alpi*, pp.230–233.

1796: The Last Bloody Fighting

In February, 13,489 men were assigned to the defence of Ceva and the Tanaro valley, but only 7,904 of them were actually available, as many were on leave or in hospital, or were new recruits who had not yet arrived. During the winter, the most uncomfortable forward positions were manned by the *Cacciatori Franchi,* the *Cacciatori Scelti di Nizza,* and the Croats of *Freikorps Gyulai,* while the grenadiers, who had been sorely tested in 1795, were partly placed in the second line to rest and be reinforced.

In and around the Tanaro valley there were: four companies of *Cacciatori Franchi,* five companies of *Cacciatori Scelti di Nizza,* the *2° Reggimento Truppe Leggere,* with its own grenadier and *cacciatori* companies, two companies of the *Torino* regiment, and a hundred Croats of the *Freikorps Gyulai.*

In order to maintain contact with Wallis's Austrians who had retired to winter at Acqui, and to guard the passages from the Colle di Cadibona, *Baron* Colli had placed detachments in various advanced positions: a company of *Cacciatori Franchi* with 100 Croatians from *Freikorps Gyulai,* a company of *Cacciatori Scelti di Nizza,* together with the *cacciatori* company of the *Acqui* regiment and a hundred Croats, *2° Cacciatori* along with 30 Croats, *1° Tortona* and *1° Acqui,* and finally, serving with Wallis's corps, *1°* and *2° Vercelli* and *2° Acqui.*

These forward posts were also wintering bases near the front line, and the troops were housed in villages. The plans, of course, assumed that at the first sign of French movement, the units scattered over a relatively large area would be able to concentrate as necessary.

To defend the entrenched camp of Ceva, up to the village of Pedaggera, the following units were assigned:

> *1°* and *2° Reale Alemanno, 1°* and *2° Genevois, 1°* and *3° Stettler, 1°* and *2° Chablais, 1° Oneglia.*
> *2°, 8°* and *9° Granatieri.*
> Two weak battalions were assigned to winter in the fort of Ceva: *2° Savoia* and *2° Stettler,* which had a total only 470 men under arms at the time.

The defence, as can be seen, was entrusted to many weak units scattered over a vast territory that could not hope to withstand for long the disruptive French attacks whose commanders, as usual, could decide where to concentrate their forces.

Baron Colli was also concerned about having a reserve and could only place 11 weak battalions between Mondovì and Morozzo, nine of which were grenadiers, totalling 5,038 men, of which 2,191 were available at that time: *1°* and *2° Granatieri Reali* with their own *cacciatori* company, a few battalions of *Granatieri* and, finally, the *1°* and *2° Mondovi* with their own *cacciatori* company. This was all that was available after 42 months of war, with the rest of the army committed to the defence of the Alpine range.[9]

---

9   Thaon di Revel, *Mémoires sur la guerre des Alpes,* pp.323–326.

Napoleon Bonaparte in Command

As if the situation were not desperate enough, *général de division* Napoleon Bonaparte, whose abilities were still in their infancy, was sent to command the *Armée d'Italie*. His military genius, his bursting desire to excel, and his ability to inspire his troops with his speeches would give the Piedmontese army and even the more opinionated Austrian generals their coup de grace.

Bonaparte arrived in Nice on 27 March 1796. Known militarily only for his important contribution as artillery commander during the Siege of Toulon, he had been given the command on the strength of his political merits. The army he took command of was not in the best of condition, mainly due to a lack of food, adequate clothing, and delays in the payment of wages that had made the soldiers he commanded particularly undisciplined. After solving the most urgent problems, he immediately set about implementing the plan he had already discussed with Massena when he was only the artillery commander of his corps: quickly separate the two enemy armies, force the Austrians to retreat, knowing that this would take them further and further away from the Piedmontese, defeat them separately by concentrating the *Armée d'Italie* on the latter, then turn with unusual speed towards the Austrian army, defeat it and conquer Lombardy. In both cases, the 24,000 men he had at his disposal would be facing armies of half his size, giving him a local superiority he would not have had if the two opposing armies had been allowed to unite. He might still have won, but he would have been left with an exhausted and reduced army, unable to begin the advance to conquer Milan immediately. Finally, Bonaparte's plans took into account all the possible variants of the proposed scenario, allowing him to take advantage of any favourable situation the enemy gave him.[10]

Having repulsed the Austrians who were advancing towards Voltri on 10 April, the French attacked towards Montenotte (present-day Cairo Montenotte) on 12 April and Millesimo on 13–14 April, defeating the Austrian troops stationed there. The French then advanced towards Dego where they again defeated the Austrians on 14–15 April. Having defeated the Austrians, the French advanced towards Ceva to attack and defeat *Baron* Colli's small Piedmontese corps. The small, fortified town was occupied by Bonaparte between 16 and 17 April, while Sérurier's division from Ormea also advanced along the Tanaro valley to rejoin the main force.

From the Colle di Cadibona, on reaching Carcare, the valley split in two. To the right, following the course of the Bormida, after about six kilometres, an hour's fast march, one reached Montenotte, after another seven kilometres, a little more than another hour's march, one reached the plain of Dego, by which one reached the plain of Acqui (today Acqui Terme). In the other direction, after about four kilometres, there was the hill overlooked by the ruins of the castle of Cosseria, and after only another four kilometres the village of Millesimo. Without considering the very short distances between the places where the French fought between 12 and 14 April, such a series of close victories might seem almost miraculous. In reality, it was a series of coordinated attacks, carried out one after the other, certainly all victorious, and they perhaps should be better considered as one great battle lasting four

---

10 Lo Faso di Serradifalco, *La difesa di un regno*, p.140.

days from 12 April (Montenotte) to the 15th (Dego). As early as the 16th, the French troops should have been able to invest Ceva, only 15 kilometres away from Millesimo, but they did not reach it until the 17th, exhausted by the continuous fighting and by the losses they had suffered, including the significant casualties inflicted on them by the heroic defenders of the castle of Cosseria on the 13th and 14th, and the need to consolidate the victory at Dego on 15 April, where the Austrians had been severely defeated.

Be that as it may, Bonaparte's troops moved quickly towards Ceva, only a few hours' march from Millesimo, which Sérurier's division was also approaching, only slightly slowed down by the skirmishes of the few Piedmontese troops opposing it.

In the meantime, *Baron* Colli was trying to make the best possible use of the few thousand Piedmontese soldiers under his command, still hoping for Austrian help, which did not come.

The Unfortunate Sacrifice at Cosseria, 13–14 April 1796

Filippo del Carretto, who had only a few days before taken command of the *3° Granatieri*, was said to have had a force of some 20 officers and 548 grenadiers at Cosseria (the grenadier companies from the *Monferrato*, *La Marina* and *Susa* regiments). He hardly had that many. More realistically, deducting 25 percent, del Carretto had at his disposal a total of around 430 Piedmontese grenadiers. Unfortunately, it is not possible to verify the force's real strength when it entered the ruined castle of Cosseria, as the defeat led to the loss of the muster rolls, making an accurate reconstruction impossible. In any case, Filippo del Carretto, together with as many men of the *Freikorps Gyulai* as he could gather, decided to barricade the castle to slow down the French advance, hoping to gain time for the arrival of help that might have improved the situation of the Austrian and Piedmontese armies. But help did not come, and he was one of the victims of the siege. The castle of Cosseria was already ruined and difficult to hold, and the defenders, who had no artillery, had only a few dozen cartridges per man. Del Carretto was aware of the military situation and could only hope for help. However, knowing the area perfectly well, he knew that the position of Cosseria was crucial for the Austro-Piedmontese and decided to try to hold it. He knew that the defence would not last long with limited ammunition, but he played for all he had.

The various sources testify to the courage and determination of the fierce defenders of Cosseria who, sheltered by the crumbling walls, were able to fire into the mass of the far more numerous French attackers. On 14 April, it was all over. Most sources put the loss of the Austro-Piedmontese to around 150 men, while estimates of French losses range between 1,000 and 1,500 men killed or wounded.[11]

---

11 A detailed description of the siege of Cosseria can be found in G. Amoretti, *Cosseria 1796, guerra, popolazione, territorio* (Torino: Omega Edizioni, 1996), pp.9–34. Maltese Enrico, 'Cosseria (13 aprile 1796)', *Memorie Storico Militari*, 1909, pp.282–319.

Between Ceva and Mondovì

As soon as the news of the defeats suffered between Millesimo and Dego reached *Baron* Colli, he decided to concentrate his meagre troops and abandoned the defence of Ceva, leaving one battalion to garrison the fort of Ceva and six battalions to defend the field fortification of Pedaggera (*2° Cacciatori*, a battalion of *2° Truppe Leggere, 1° and 2° Acqui, 1° and 2° Genevois*). The latter locality was attacked by the French on the 16th, who quickly took advantage of their successes. It was furiously defended at first but evacuated the next day, allowing the French to occupy Ceva on the 17th, leaving the fort's garrison undisturbed as Bonaparte considered it useless to waste time capturing it. In the meantime, *Baron* Colli set up a defensive line on the left bank of the Corsaglia stream, which was fast-flowing at the time, preventing an easy crossing, but which was in any case only 30–60 metres wide and crossed by several bridges and an aqueduct, which the Piedmontese only partially demolished. The position was not defensible for long, however, as the stream could easily be bypassed from the north. But it was the only credible obstacle that the Piedmontese could exploit to gain a few days in the fading hope of seeing the Austrians appear.

The centre of the Piedmontese defences was in the village of San Michele di Mondovì, located on the left bank of the torrent behind which were the heights of the Bicocca (564m), also garrisoned. San Michele was only about 10 kilometres from Ceva, a distance that could be covered in a few hours.

On the 19th, with their usual speed, and after only one day's rest, the French began to invest San Michele, which the Piedmontese fiercely defended, but having easily crossed the Corsaglia, the French forced the defenders to concentrate on the heights of Bicocca, from where a Piedmontese counterattack succeeded in retaking San Michele, allowing the defenders to evacuate during the night of 20 April the area and retreat towards Mondovì.

The last possible line of defence was to stand on the left bank of the Ellero stream, which ran roughly parallel to the Corsaglia for about six kilometres and with the town of Mondovì, weakly defended by an ancient castle, on its left. Once the stores were evacuated, the Ellero line was also abandoned, and the remaining Piedmontese units, without precise orders, followed the instincts of their officers and withdrew towards Fossano, while senior commanders wished to defend Cuneo or the weaker Cherasco to the bitter end, but by now, after 44 months of resistance, it was all over.

The Charge of the *Dragoni del Re* and the Surrender of Mondovì

On 21 April, the Piedmontese cavalry, finally back in the saddle, had its moment of glory. Two squadrons of the *Dragoni del Re* charged the vanguard of the French cavalry that was rashly rushing to harass the Piedmontese retreat on Fossano. At Carassone, the two squadrons (*1°* and *3°*), temporarily halted their advance and surprised the small escort of the French cavalry commander, *général de division* Stengel, who was mortally wounded and died shortly afterwards near Mondovì.[12]

---

12 The, *Brichetto* charge is described in detail in E. De Rossi, 'La cavalleria nella giornata di Mondovì, 21 aprile 1796', *Memorie Storico Militari*, 1909, pp.35–46. R. Puletti, *Caricat! tre secoli di Storia dell'Arma di Cavalleria* (Bologna: Capitol, 1973), pp.68–71. Lo Faso di Serradifalco, *La difesa di un regno*, p.149.

All that remained was the weak garrison of Mondovì, which, in the general confusion, seems not to have received the order to retreat and which surrendered to the French. It consisted of the two line infantry regiments *Guardie* and *Stettler*, which were reduced to a total of about 700 men.[13]

The Armistice of Cherasco and its Implications

The armistice signed by the representatives of Vittorio Amedeo III at Cherasco on 27 April 1796 was sanctioned by the peace between the French Republic and the Kingdom of Sardinia, signed in Paris in May of the same year. The terms of the peace included the cession of Nice and Savoy to France and French control over all Piedmontese territory south of the Tanaro and Stura rivers. There were also plans to significantly reduce the army, dismantle the fortresses at Brunetta and Exilles, and maintain the occupation. Savoy was also to leave the way clear for French troops to fight against the Austrians in the rest of Italy.[14] The Piedmontese army ceased to be in a state of war on 1 June 1796 and was quickly reduced to a total of between 30–35,000 men.

Vittorio Amedeo III, aged and embittered by the defeat and the harsh conditions imposed by the victors, died, probably of a broken heart, on 16 October 1796.

What followed is a different tale – the role of the Piedmontese army during the Napoleonic Wars.

---

13 Pinelli, *Storia Militare del Piemonte*, p.661.
14 AST, Materie Militari, Imprese Militari, mazzo 12 d'addizione, n° 3: Sospensione d'ostilità conclusa a Cherasco, 28 April 1796.

Bibliography

Archival Sources

Archivio di Stato di Torino (AST)
Materie Militari, Imprese militari, mazzo 12 d'addizione
Livre des orders du Régiment Rochmondet, mazzo 74
Ordini Generali e Misti, mazzi 64, 69–75, 85, 88
Regia Segreteria di Guerra e Marina. Lettere all'Ufficio Generale del Soldo, mazzi 271–274 and 276–277
Regia Segreteria di Guerra e Marina, Miscellanea I, mazzo 1
Ruolini di Rivista (Muster rolls): Battaglione Cacciatori Franchi mazzi 1, 5–6. Cacciatori Scelti di Nizza mazzi 2–3. Compagnie Canale, Pian Pandini [and Martin] mazzi 1–3
Compagnie di Marina mazzo 56. Guastatori [Pionieri] mazzi 2–3
Granatieri Reali mazzo 1. Reggimento Maurienne mazzi 4–5
Stabilimenti Militari, vol.4–6
Ufficio Generale del Soldo, Contratto provviste diverse, mazzi 113, 119, 122, 136, 335
Ufficio Generale del Soldo, Intendenza Generale d'Armata 1792-1796), mazzi 4, 6, 10 and 11
Ufficio Generale del Soldo, Relazioni a Sua Maestà, mazzi 19–23
AST, Patenti del Controllo Generale delle Finanze. Can be consulted online, contains the patents of appointment issued from 1717 to 1801. <https://archiviodistatotorino.cultura.gov.it/patn_detl/?id=4445&den=2&char=b>

Books

Ales, Stefano, *Le Regie Truppe Sarde (1773–1814)* (Roma: Ufficio Storico dello Stato Maggiore Esercito, 1989)
Amoretti, Guido (ed.), *Cosseria 1796* (Torino: Omega, 1996)
Bianchi, Paola. *La guerra franco-piemontese e le valli valdesi (1792–1799)* (Torino: Claudiana, 2001)
Brancaccio, Nicola, *L'Esercito del vecchio Piemonte dal 1540 al 1861. Gli Ordinamenti* (Roma: Ufficio Storico dello Stato Maggiore Esercito, 1922)
Brancaccio, Nicola, *L'Esercito del vecchio Piemonte dal 1540 al 1861. Sunti storici dei principali Corpi* (Roma: Ufficio Storico dello Stato Maggiore Esercito, 1923)
Cais di Pierlas, Eugenio, *Storia del Reggimento di Susa e suo ingresso a Nizza in avanguardia austriaca* (Torino: Gerbone, 1900)

Carutti, Domenico, *Storia della Corte dei Savoia durante la rivoluzione e l'Impero Francese* (Torino: Roux, 1892)
Cerino Badone, Giovanni, *You have to die in Piedmont! The Battle of Assietta, 19 July 1747* (Warwick: Helion & Company, 2023)
Costa de Beauregard, Charles Albert, *Un homme d'autrefois* (Paris: Plon, 1878)
De Geney, Louis Michel, *Le Partisan ou l'art de faire la petite-guerre avec succès* (La Haye: Costapel, 1759)
Fenoil, F., *La Terreur sur les Alpes, avec l'histoire des deux premiers Règiments des Soques* (Aosta: Duc, 1887)
Guichonnet, Paul, *Le Monts en feu. La guerre en Faucigny, 1793* (Annency: Academie Salésienne, 1995)
Ilari, Virgilio, Crociani, Piero, & Paoletti, Ciro, *La Guerra delle Alpi (1792–1796)* (Roma: Stato Maggiore dell'Esercito, Ufficio Storico, 2000)
Ireland, Bernard, *The Fall of Toulon. The last opportunity to defeat the French Revolution* (London: Orion, 2005)
Lefebvre, G., & Mathiez, A., *La Rivoluzione Francese* (Torino: Einaudi, 1960)
Lo Faso di Serradifalco, Alberico, *La difesa di un regno. Il sacrificio dell'esercito del Regno di Sardegna nella guerra contro la Francia (1792-1796)* (Udine: Gaspari, 2009)
Lupo, Maurizio, *Le lame del Re. Sabri e spade dell'Armata Sabauda dal 1560 al 1831* (Torino: Centro Studi Piemontesi, 2007)
Merla, Giovanni, *O bravi guerrieri! L'arrivo di Napoleone in Italia e la guerra delle Alpi* (Tirrenia: Edizioni del Cerro, 1988)
Pinelli, Ferdinando, *Storia militare del Piemonte dalla pace di Acquisgrana al 1850* (Torino: De Giorgis, 1854)
Puletti, Rodolfo, *Caricat! tre secoli di Storia dell'Arma di Cavalleria* (Bologna: Capitol, 1973)
Ricchiardi, Enrico, *Bandiere e stendardi dell'Esercito Sardo (1713–1802)* (Torino: Centro Studi Piemontesi, 2006)
Ricchiardi, Enrico, *Da milizia scelta a reggimenti provinciali: il potenziamento dell'esercito sabaudo dopo l'acquisizione della Sicilia (1713–1737)* (Torino: In Utrecht 1713, Centro Studi Piemontesi, 2014)
Ricchiardi, Enrico, *Musicisti in uniforme. L'arte dei suoni nell'esercito sabaudo* (Lucca: Lim, 2019)
Ricchiardi Enrico, 'Iconografia militare sabauda. L'Esercito Sardo attraverso la figurinistica militare' in *1416, Savoye Bonne Nouvelle*, vol.II, pp.1059–1172
Ricuperati, Giuseppe, *Lo stato sabaudo nel Settecento. Dal trionfo delle burocrazie alla crisi d'antico regime* (Torino: UTET, 2001)
Scharfroth M. F. Les troupes suisses au service du Royaume de Sardaigne. *Armi Antiche* (Torino, 1968: 133-147)
Sterrantino, Francesco, *Le armi da fuoco del vecchio Piemonte (1683–1799)* (Torino: Lorenzo, 2002)
Thaon di Revel de St. André e Pratolungo, Ignazio, *Mémoires sur la guerre des Alpes et les événements en Piémont pendant la Révolution Française* (Torino: Bocca, 1871)

Journal Articles

Antonicelli, Aldo, 'From galleys to square riggers: The modernization of the Navy of the Kingdom of Sardinia', *The Mariner's Mirror*, 102:2, 2016, pp.153–173

De Antonio, Carlo, 'Authion', *Memorie Storico Militari*, 1911, pp.367–526

Del Monte, Dario, & Toso, Dario, 'Le truppe leggere imperiali durante la Guerra delle Alpi. Frei Corps, Grenzen, Jäger', *Acta*, 2007, pp.155–164

De Rossi, Eugenio, 'La cavalleria nella giornata di Mondovì, 21 aprile 1796', *Memorie Storico Militari*, 1909, pp.35–46

Fiora, Paolo Edoardo, 'Origini dell'artiglieria da montagna. Secoli XVII e XVIII', *Armi Antiche*, 1974, pp.99–118

Maltese, Enrico, 'Cosseria (13 aprile 1796)', *Memorie Storico Militari*, 1909, pp.282–319

Pauvert, Bruno, 'L'incursione del cavalier de Bonaud a Saint Martin Vésuble il 1° settembre 1795', *Acta*, 2007, pp.71–99

Ricchiardi, Enrico, 'Uniformi della Guardia Svizzera (1740–1831)', *Armi Antiche*, 1985, pp.107–128.

Ricchiardi, Enrico, 'Uniformi delle truppe leggere dell'esercito del Regno di Sardegna. *Acta*, 2009, pp.107–124

Ruello, Gianfranco, 'La fanteria leggera francese nella Guerra delle Alpi', *Acta*, 2007, pp.127–154

Sconfienza, Roberto, 'I tricenramenti sabaudi del Piccolo San Bernardo nel XVIII secolo. Note preliminari', *Annales Sabaudiae*, 1, 2005, pp.49–58

Further Reading

Books

Bruckner, A. & B., *Schweizer fahnenbuch* (St Gallen: Zollikofer, 1942)

Crowdy, T., *French Light Infantry 1784-1815. From the chasseurs of Louis XVI to Napoleon's Grande Armée* (Warwick: Helion & Company, 2021)

Forczyc, Robert, *Toulon 1793: Napoleon's First Great Victory* (Oxford: Osprey Publishing, 2005)

Gasparinetti, Alessandro, *Uniformi della Marina* (Roma: Edizioni Universali, 1964)

Gautier de Brécy, *Révolution de Toulon en 1793 pour le rètabblisement de la monarchie* (Paris, Touvé, 1828)

Giovara Rotta, Elisabetta, & Romeo, Domenico, *Vive le Roy de Sardaigne. Règiment d'ordonnance national Piémont (1793–1800)* (Venaria Reale: Graf Art, 2011)

Montù, Carlo, *Storia dell'artiglieria italiana, dalle origini al 1815* (Roma: Rivista d'Artiglieria e Genio, 1938)

Journal Articles

Anon., 'Le Chevalier de Saint Amour dernier governeir de Saorge', *Nice Historique*, 7ᵉ année, n°2, 1976, pp.73–76

Cerino Badone, Giovanni, 'Le compagnie cacciatori nell'esercito del Regno di Sardegna. Reclutamento, equipaggiamento, tattica', *Acta*, 2007, pp.15–70

Schafroth, Max F., 'Les troupes Suisses au service du Royaume de Sardaigne', *Armi Antiche*, (1968), pp.133–147

Petitmermet, Roland, 'Quelques notes sur les uniformes des Suisses au service du Royaume de Sardaigne', *Armi Antiche*, 1968, pp.157–199

Sconfienza, Roberto, 'La fortificazione campale nella seconda metà del XVIII secolo. Esperienze e studi fino alla Guerra delle Alpi', *Acta*, 2007, pp.165–205

From Reason to Revolution – Warfare 1721-1815

http://www.helion.co.uk/series/from-reason-to-revolution-1721-1815.php

The 'From Reason to Revolution' series covers the period of military history 1721–1815, an era in which fortress-based strategy and linear battles gave way to the nation-in-arms and the beginnings of total war.

This era saw the evolution and growth of light troops of all arms, and of increasingly flexible command systems to cope with the growing armies fielded by nations able to mobilise far greater proportions of their manpower than ever before. Many of these developments were fired by the great political upheavals of the era, with revolutions in America and France bringing about social change which in turn fed back into the military sphere as whole nations readied themselves for war. Only in the closing years of the period, as the reactionary powers began to regain the upper hand, did a military synthesis of the best of the old and the new become possible.

The series examines the military and naval history of the period in a greater degree of detail than has hitherto been attempted, and has a very wide brief, with the intention of covering all aspects from the battles, campaigns, logistics, and tactics, to the personalities, armies, uniforms, and equipment.

Submissions

The publishers would be pleased to receive submissions for this series. Please email reasontorevolution@helion.co.uk, or write to Helion & Company Limited, Unit 8 Amherst Business Centre, Budbrooke Road, Warwick, CV34 5WE

You may also be interested in:

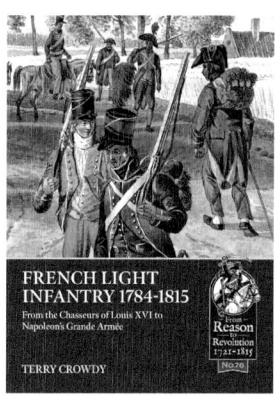
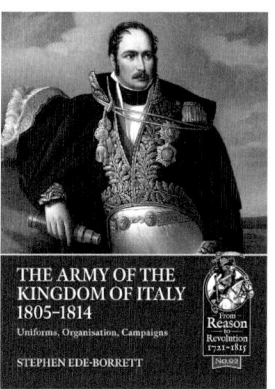
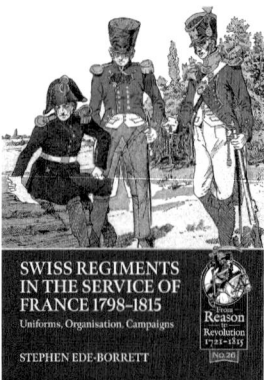